Pryor

Alton City Directory

Pryor

Alton City Directory

ISBN/EAN: 9783337146290

Printed in Europe, USA, Canada, Australia, Japan

Cover: Foto ©Andreas Hilbeck / pixelio.de

More available books at **www.hansebooks.com**

ALTON CITY DIRECTORY,

1876-7,

COMPRISING

AN ALPHABETICAL LIST OF CITIZENS, A CLASSIFIED
BUSINESS DIRECTORY, LISTS OF CITY AND
COUNTY OFFICERS, CHURCHES, SCHOOLS,
SOCIETIES, STREETS AND WARDS.

PRICE $3.00.

ALTON, ILL.

PRYOR & CO. PUBLISHERS.

1876.

PREFACE.

In presenting to the public this work, as the revision of the City Directory of the City for 1876–7, its object and value in its preparation have been constantly held in view. Every effort was made in the canvass to procure the correct location of all citizens, while in connection with their business they become recognized in each and all branches conducted by them; also containing much other matter of utility and interest to the citizens of Alton and to strangers, rendering it a fit representation of the business and enterprise of the City.

The General Directory shows 3,571 names—an increase of 500 over 1873, and which multiplied by $3\frac{1}{2}$ gives Alton a population of 12,500.

For any imperfections or omissions that may occur—notwithstanding the diligence used in gathering the promiscuous matter requisite to complete a work of this kind, especially the large number of names, which is believed to include all that would claim recognition within its pages—the publishers ask the indulgence of the public, trusting that the work will meet with that satisfaction and approval which it has been their earnest endeavor to achieve.

PRYOR & CO.

GENERAL INDEX.

INDEX TO ADVERTISERS.

PRYOR & CO.'S
ALTON CITY DIRECTORY,
1876-7.

MISCELLANEOUS DEPARTMENT.

City Officers.

Mayor—Alexander W. Hope.
Register—James McNulty.
Treasurer—Chas. Holden, Jr.
Assessor—James W. Templeton.
Collector—John Fischbach.
Attorney—John F. McGinnis.
Marshall—John Dawson.
Harbor Master—Rescarrie A. Hoaglan.
Street Commissioner—Benjamin Allen.
Clerk—Frank H. Ferguson.
Engineer—Wm. D. Hodge.
Auditor—Francis H. Ulrich.
Gauger and Inspector—Julius H. Raible.
Inspector of Salted Provisions--Geo. Quigley.
    "   " Petroleum Oils—Geo. Quigley.
    "   " Weights and Measures—Chas. Holden, Sr.
Counselor—Chas. P. Wise.

City Council.

First Ward—T. Biggins, J. Bannon, J. E. Coppinger.
Second Ward--J. W. Ash, B. Runzi, R. G. Perley.
Third Ward—J. Whitehead, G. H. Weigler, F. W. Joesting.
Fourth Ward—R. B. Smith, W. Claflin, N. C. Hathaway.

Board of Education.

John L. Blair, President, Frank H. Ferguson, Secretary, Benjamin F. Sargent, Treasurer. E. A. Haight. Superintendent of Schools.

Members—Louis Haagen, D. D. Ryrie, A. R. McKinney, Geo. Quigley.

Fire Department.

Chief Engineer—J. C. Bramhall.
Ass't   "   —C. Henick.
Fire Warden—C. Ryan.
Engine House Market, bet. Second and Third.
Altona Engine Co. No. 1—Geo. Carhart, President, J. B. Kerwin, foreman.
Lafayette Hook and Ladder Co.—L. Stillwell, foreman.
Hope Hose Co. No. 3—J. Loer, President, J. Elble, Vice President, Frank Schaub, Treasurer, Fred Hoppe, Secretary, cor. Fifth Ridge.

County Officers.

Judge—M. G. Dale.
Clerk—B. E. Hoffmann.
Circuit Clerk—J. H. Heisel.
Attorney—B. Glass.
Treasurer---H. E. Bayle.
Sheriff—J. T. Cooper.
Supt. of Schools—A. D. Luppiger.
Surveyor—W. Rutledge.
Coronor—W. A. Miller.

Masonic.

Hall corner Second and Market.
Piasa Lodge No. 27—meets every Tuesday on or before full moon, F. H. Ferguson, W. M., Wm. Huskinson. S. W., Thos. Cannell, J. W., I. E. Hardy, S. D., Wm. Hyndman, J. D., A. Woodside, Treasurer, F. S. Detrich, Secretary, A. Ash, Tyler.
Irwin Lodge No. 315—meets every Thursday on or before full moon, N. Seibold, W. M., F. Rudershausen, S. W., W. Sontag, J. W., John Tonsor, Treasurer, F. Pfenninger, Secretary, W. Joesting, S. D, C. A. Herb, I. D.
Alton Royal Arch Chapter No. 8—meets every Friday on or before full moon, I. E. Hardy, H. P., F. H. Ferguson, K., H. E.

Bayle, S., Wm. Huskinson, Treasurer, Fred Detrich, Secretary, C. B. Rohland, C. II., Thos. Cannell, P. S., C. A. Herb, R. A. C. Alton Council R. & S. M.. No. 3,—meets First and Third Mondays in each month, R. B. Smith, T. I. G. M., 1. E. Hardy, D. I. G. M., Geo. D. Hayden, P. Cof, W., Geo Barry. C. of G. S.. F. Connor, Conductor, A. T. Bayle, Steward.

Belvidere Commandery, No. 2,—(Knights Templars,) meets every Fourth Monday in each month, G. Barry, E. C., R. C., R. B. Smith, G.. F. H. Furguson, C. G., G. D. Hayden, P., C. B. Rohland, S. W., W. Huskinson, J. W., I. E. Hardy, W., J. H. Koehne, Treasurer, Thos. Cannell, Recorder.

Constantine Counclave. No. 10,—meets first Monday in each month, R. B. Smith, M. P. S., G. Barry, V., S. F. Connor, S. G., C. B. Rohland, J. G., M. M. Dutro, H. P., J. H. Koehne, Treasurer, F. H. Ferguson. Recorder, G. D. Hayden, P., H. Watson, S. B.. I. E. Hardy, H., J. M. Pierson, S.

I. O. of O. F.

Hall south side of Third.

Alton Lodge, No. 2,—meets every Wednesday, J. M. Bryant. N. G., J. Dow, V. G.. F. H. Gifford, Secretary, T. Hyndman. Treasurer.

Germania Lodge. No. 299.—meets every Monday, J. Dietche. N. G.. Wm. Schmoeller. V. G., J. H. Altman. Secretary, J. M. Tonsor. Treasurer.

Pestalozzi Lodge, No. 367,—meets every Thursday. J. Bile. N. G.. Anton Ehrhardt, V. G., S. Lehman, Treasurer, Wm. Betz, Secretary.

Wildy Encampment. No. 1,—meets second and fourth Fridays in each month, W. B. Rowe, C. P., S. Perks. H. P., F. H. Gifford, S. W.. A. T. Ash, J. W , W. H. Temple, Secretary, J. Kellenberger, Treasurer.

Concordia Encampment, No. 99,—meets twice a month. F. Pielott, C. P., H. Titian, H. P., F. Brandeweide, S. W.. R. Rosch. J. W.. L. H. Brueggemann, Secretary, J. M. Tonsor, Treasurer.

Knights of Pythias.

Hall (Castle Hall) Third.

Constantine Lodge. No. 55.—meets every Thursday, W. F. Everts, P. C., J. T. Cooper, C. C., W. A. Haskell, V. C., J. N. Shoemaker, P , H. M. Schweppe, M. of Ex., S. L., Breckenridge. M. of F., J. A. Beach. M. at A., C. Rodemeyer. I. G., A. Ash, O. G., H. E. Bayle, D. G. C.

Miscellaneous Societies.

Alton Turn Verein, Hall cor. Third and Ridge,—meets once a month, A. Neerman, 1st Speaker. A. Vogel, 2d Speaker, H. Behrens, Secretary. F. Rudershausen. Treasurer, P. Paul, 1st Turn Ward.

Ancient Order of Hibernians. Hall Third.—meets once a month. P. Gilmartin, President, P. Mitchell. Vice .President. H. Molloy. Treasurer. P. Sullivan, Marshal.

Hibernian Society----meets in Cathedral School House once a month, D. Hogan. President.

Catholic Total Abstinence Society---meets monthly at Cathedral. Wm. Flynn, President.

Alton Public Library Association. Hall in City Building, Miss Blanche Dolbee, Librarian.

Church Directory.

Church of the Redeemer. (Congregational.) Rev. Robt. West. Pastor, services 10:45 A. M., 7:30 P. M., Sunday school 2 P. M., cor. Henry and Sixth.

Colored Baptist Church. Rev. J. P. Johnson, Pastor, services, 11 A. M. and 7:30 P. M., Sunday school 2 P. M., cor. Seventh and George.

Cumberland Presbyterian Church, Rev. J. Hendricks. Pastor, services 11 A. M., 7:45 P. M., nr. cor. Twelfth and Henry.

First Baptist Church, Rev. T. G. Field, Pastor, services 10:45 A. M., 8 P. M., Sunday school 9:20 A. M., cor. Fifth and Market.

First Presbyterian Church. Rev. C. Armstrong, Pastor, services 10:30 A. M., 7:30 P. M., Sunday school 9 A. M., Second, cor. Market.

German Methodist Church, Rev. M. Schnierle, Pastor, services 10:30 A. M., 8 P. M., Sunday school 9 A. M., Union.

Hunterstown Mission Baptist Church. Rev. —— ——, Pastor. Sunday school 2 P. M., services 7:30 P. M., cor. Cherry and Fifth.

Methodist Episcopal Church. Rev. A. P. Morrison, Pastor, services 10:30 A. M., 8 P. M., Sunday school 9 A. M., cor. Sixth and Market.

Methodist Episcopal (colored) Church. Rev. Henry Brown, Pastor, services 10:30 A. M., 7:30 P. M., Sunday school 3 P. M. Fourth, nr. Ridge.

St. Pauls Episcopal Church, Rev. March Chase, Pastor, services 10:45 A. M., 7:30 P. M., Sunday school 9 A. M., cor. Market and Third.

St. Peters and Pauls Church, State, west Seventh, Rev. M. Kane, Pastor, services, 7:30 A. M., 10 A. M., Vespers 7:30 P. M., Sunday school 2:30.

St. Mary's Catholic Church, Rev. P. Peters, Pastor, services 7:45 A. M., High Mass and Sermon 10 A. M., Vespers and Benediction 3 P. M., Sunday school 2 P. M., cor. Fourth and Henry.

Trinity Chapel. Rev. March Chase, Pastor, services 3:30 P. M., Sunday school 2:30 P. M., State.

Unitarian Church, Rev. —— ——, Pastor, services 10:30 A. M., Sunday school 9½ A. M., cor. Alby and Third.

Hospital.

St. Joseph Hospital, in charge of the Sisters of Charity.

Alton Street Directory.

Alby, 1st e of Main, n from river limits.
Alton, 3d e of Market, n from river to 14th.
Apple, 13th e of Market, n from river to 6th.
Arch, n from Union to Pearl.
Beacon, 1st w of William, n from Park to Bond and n e to Eighth.
Belle, 1st w of Piasa, n from 3d to 20th.
Bloomfield, 4th n of Union, w from State road to Wesley.
Bluff, 6th w of Piasa, n from river to State.
Bond 1st n of Park, w from State to Prospect.
Cherry, 11th e of Market, n from river to 6th.
Cliff, 7th w of Piasa, e from State one block.
Common, 1st e of Ridge, n from Suspension to limits.
County Road, 1st n of river, w from Short to limits.
Court, n e from Easton and 4th to 8th.
Diamond, 1st e of Liberty, n from Pearl to Suspension.
Dry, 1st n w of Beacon from State to Narrow.
Easton, 2d e of Market, n from river to 20th.
Eighth, 8th n of river, e from Beacon to Liberty.
Eighteenth, 18th n of river, e from Belle to Easton.
Eleventh, 11th n of river, e from Belle to Henry.
Fifth, 5th n of river, e from Belle to Henry, and e from Liberty to limits.
Fifteenth, 15th n of river, e from Belle to Easton.
Fourth, 4th n of river, e from William to Henry and limits.
Fourteenth, 14th n of river e from Belle to Henry.
Front, 1st n of river e from Market to limits.
Garden, 1st e of North, n from Pearl to Putnam.

George, 4th e of Market, n from river to 14th.
German, 2d n of Union, e from State road two blocks.
Gold. 2d e of North. n from Union to Bloomfield.
Green, 2d n of Union, e from Garden to Gold.
Grove, 2d n of Suspension, w from Common three blocks.
Henry, 6th e of Market. n from river to 14th.
Hamilton, n e from junction of 10th and Main to 12th.
Hamilton, 5th n of Union, w from State road to Wesley.
Harrison, 2d e of Gold, n from Pearl to Van Buren.
Jefferson, n w part of city running e from State.
Langdon, 5th e of Market. n from river to 14th.
Liberty, 1st e of Henry. n from 6th to Grove.
Madison, n w part of city running e from State.
Main, n w from west end 9th to State.
Market, 1st e of Piasa. n from Market to limits.
Marshall, n w from junction Hamilton and 11th two blocks.
Mill, 4th w of Piasa. n from river to Park.
Monroe, running s from Jefferson parallel with State.
Narrow. 1st n of State, n w from Beacon to Spring.
Ninth, 9th n of river, e from Main to Liberty.
Nineteenth, 19th n of river. e from Belle to Easton.
North. n from Walnut and 6th to Suspension.
Oak, 1st w of Prospect, s one block from State.
Oak, 8th e of Market, n from river to 6th.
Park, 3d n of river, w from State to Mill.
Pear, 15th e of Market, n from river to 6th.
Pearl. 1st n of Union, e from Liberty to State road.
Piasa, 1st w of Market, n from river to 20th.
Plank Road, n from the junction of 11th and Belle to limits.
Pleasant, 1st s of Suspension. e from Henry to Liberty.
Pleasant, 1st e of Common. n from Tremont to limits.
Plumb. 14th e of Market. n from river to 6th.
Prospect, 5th w of Piasa, n from river to State.
Putnam. 3d n of Union, e from Garden to Gold.
Ridge, 7th e of Market. n from river to Union.
Salu, 1st n of Washington, w from Pleasant three blocks.
Second, 2d n of river. e from Piasa to limits.
Seventh, 7th n of river, e from Beacon to Liberty.
Seventeenth, 17th n of river, e from Belle to Easton.
Short. 1st n of river, w from 2d to County road.
Silver, 1st e of Gold, n from Union to Bloomfield.
Sixth, 6th n of river, e from Piasa to Liberty and city limits.
Sixteenth, 16th n of river, e from Belle to Easton.

Spring, from n end of Bluff to Narrow
Spring, 8th e of Market, n from river to 6th.
State, 2d w of Piasa, n from river to Bond, thence n w to Wharf.
    thence n to Main, thence n w to limits.
State Road, n e from Cherry and 6th to limits.
Summit, 2d n of river, w from Mill two blocks.
Suspension, e from eastern end of 14th to Common.
Tenth, 10th n of river, e from Main to Henry.
Third, 3d n of river, e from State to Henry and limits.
Thirteenth, 13th n of river, e from Piasa to Henry.
Tremont, 4th n of Suspension, e from Common three blocks.
Twelfth, 12th n of river, e from Piasa to Henry.
Twentieth, 20th n of river, e from Belle to Easton.
Union, s e from junction 11th and Henry to Plumb and 6th.
Van Buren, 5th n of Union, n w from State road to Fletcher.
Vine, 12th e of Market, n from river to 6th.
Walnut, 10th e of Market, n from river to 6th.
Washington, 1st e of Henry, n from Union to Suspension.
Washington, 16th e from Market, n nr limits, then w to pub. square.
Wesley, w end of Bloomfield, n to Hamilton.
Wharf, s end of Cliff, w one block and n to State.
William, 3d w of Piasa, n from river to Bond.

Ward Boundaries.

FIRST WARD—All that part of the city lying west of the center
of Piasa street and between River and Northern boundary.

SECOND WARD—All that part of the city lying between center of
Piasa and the center of Langdon, and from the River to Northern
boundary.

THIRD WARD—All that part of the city lying east of Second
Ward to the Eastern boundary of city, and North to a line in the
center of Eleventh street and the center of Union street to where
the same intersects the line between section thirteen and twelve,
and from thence on said line to the eastern boundary of City.

FOURTH WARD—All that part of the city lying East of Second
and North of the Third Ward.

PRYOR & CO.'S
ALTON CITY DIRECTORY,
1876-7.

ABBREVIATONS.

ab.........................above.
av .. .. avenue.
bet.........................between.
bds.............. ....boards.
bldg.... ....building.
cor.........................corner.
clk.. .... clerk.
lab.... ....laborer.
carp....... ....carpenter.
s s............. . ...south side.

e................. ....east of.
manufg................manufacturer.
n........................north of.
nr.....................near.
opp........ ....opposite.
s.....................south of
w.....................west of.
n s................. .north side.
w s................... west side.
e s..................east side.

ALPHABETICAL LIST OF NAMES.
A

Ab. Planab, M., Tailor, res. n s. 3d, w Walnut.
Achten John, lab., res. Alby, cor. 19th.
Adams, Clinton, works Oil Factory, res. cor. Piasa and 17th.
Adams, Phebe, teacher school, No. 2, res. 17th.
Adams, Mrs., res. Belle, n 11th.
Adams, Mrs. Sarah, res. cor. 17th and Piasa.
Adams. Mrs., res. cor. George and 17th.
Adams, Wm., lab. H. Basse, res. Ridge n. 6th.
Adams, Wm., lab. T Corbit, res. 17th, nr Easton.
Adams, W. J., salesman, A. H. Drury & Co., res. State, e Spring.
Agne, Wm., polisher, res. Union, nr North.
Agne, Wm., book-keeper, Daniels, Bayle & Co., res Union.
Agard, Hiram, glass blower, res Cherry, s 4th.
Ahrens, Theo., general store, n. s. 2d, w Henry, res. same.
Aichelmann, Frank, carpenter, res. n. s. 3d, e Oak.
Albon, Mrs. Sarah, res. e s Henry, s 8th.
Allen, Benjamin, Street commissioner, res. cor. Madison and State.
Allen, Geo., saw mill, bds. A. K. Root.
Allen, James, drayman, res. cor. State and Madison.

Allen, James, Jr., drayman, res cor State and Madison.
Allen, Mrs. Lydia, res n s 5th, e Walnut.
Alfred, Aaron, horse trader, res n s 2d, w Vine.
Alfred, Mrs. L., res n s 3d, e Langdon.
Alogray, Benjamin, res Madison, cor. Monroe.
Alt, A., machinist, Alton Agricultural Works, res s s 3d e Henry.

ALT, CHARLES, Horse shoer and Blacksmith. Special attention given to horse shoeing and all kinds of general blacksmithing, cor. 2d and Henry, res. 3d, e. Henry.

Alt, George, works Alton Agl. Works, res s s 3d, e Henry.
Alt, Paul, res s s 3d, e Henry.
Altena, I. G., saw and knife maker, cor 2d and Easton, res same.
Althoff, Mrs. L., dress maker, Bond, w William, res same.
Althoff, Fred, works Alton Agl. Works, res n s 5th, e Liberty.

ALTON NATIONAL BANK, and designated depository of United States, Capital $100,000, Surplus $67,000. E. Marsh, President. S. Wade, Vice President, C. A. Caldwell, Cashier, E. P. Wade, Assistant Cashier, cor. Belle and 3d.

Aly—farmer, res. Cyrus, nr. Fletcher.

AMERICAN EXPRESS CO., State St., opp. 3d St., Alton, Ill., E. W. Kilbourne, Agent.

AMMANN, Joseph, Manufacturer of wagons, carriages, etc. Repairing of wood work promptly attended to. Horse shoeing made a specialty, and general blacksmithing done to order, n. s. 2d, e. Ridge, res. Spring, n. 2d.

Ammon, Valentine, janitor, res w s Henry, s 14th.
Anderson, Chas., shipping clk., Plow Works, res 2d, nr Spring.
Anderson, P. J., carriage maker, res 9th, s Piasa.
Anderson, P. J., works C. Phinney, bds same.
Anderson, Tobias M., blacksmith, res Langdon, s 3d.
Anderson, C. A., carpenter, res w s Belle, n 6th.
Andy, Mrs. Charlotte, res n s Easton, s 10th.
Angel, Joseph, cooper, T. H. Proctor, res 2d, e Henry.
Anthony, Jonathan, Engineer, res cor 6th and Easton.

Appel, Louis S, Ex Driver U S Ex Co, res Prospect.
Archibald, Mrs Amanda, res s s 5 e Walnut.
Arbuckle, Levi, lab, res w s Market n 3d.
Arlas, Peter, lab, E Feldwisch, bds same.
Arlington, Mrs Belle, res cor 10th and Easton.
Armstrong, Rev Chester, Pastor, Pres't'n Church, res State n Park.
Armstrong, Henry, carp and builder, 4th e Piasa, res 3d e Alton.
Armstrong. John, (Wm. & J. Armstrong,) res Henry, n 12th.
Armstrong. Wm, (Wm & J Armstrong,) res Main nr State.
Armstrong, Wm & Bro, (Wm & John Armstrong,) Prop'rs Bluff
    Lime Kilns, warehouse 6 Short.
Arrington, Louis. Glass Blower, res s s 3d e Walnut.
Ash, A T, plasterer, bds cor 13th and Langdon.
Ash, John W, Notary Public, office City Bldg, res cor 13th and
    Langdon.
Ash, Wm M, bricklayer, res s s 5th, nr Oak.
Aswege. Eilert, saloon. State bet 2d and 3d, res same.
Atkin, Chas E, tailor, M M Dutro, res cor 3d and Henry.
Atkinson, Geo B, clk, W F Everts, bds same.
Atkinson & Patrick, (W Atkinson, J Patrick,) stone quarry, cor
    Main and 8th.
Atkinson, W, (Atkinson & Patrick) res cor 9th and Belle.
Atkinson, Marion. turner. M H Boals. res 2d nr Oak.
Atwood, John, General Insurance, cor 2d and Market, res Liberty, n
    Suspension.
Atwood, Roger W, (Blair & Atwood,) res Belle opp 6th.
Auten, Aaron O, (Milnor, Auten & Co,) bds cor 3d and Market.
Auten. Edgar M, clk, Auten & Holden, res Easton n Front.

Auten, John A, (Auten & Holden,) res Easton, n Front.
Austin, Wm, watchman, res e s Liberty, n 5th.
Axthelm, Louis, barber, 2d e Henry, bds same.

B

Bachman, Mrs. Anna, res cor Gold and Putnam.
Badenestiel, Valentine, drayman, res n s 5th. w Vine.
Bailey, Alfred, harness maker, res cor 7th and Langdon.
Bailey, Geo. T, works Tobacco Factory, res cor 7th and Langdon.
Baird, Mrs Mary, res s s 8th, e Alton.
Baker, Chas., painter, res State road.
Baker, D. W. (Beckley & Baker) res 16th, e Piasa.
Baker, Henry S., City Judge, res Suspension, e Henry.
Baker, R., bds Empire House.
Baldwin, Stephen, carp., res n s 5th, e Market.
Balster, E. H., painter, res Fletcher, cor Cyrus.
Balster, John, tailor, res e s Ridge, s 5th.
Balster, J. M., tinner, H Stanford, res Ridge, n 4th.
Baltes, Rt. Rev. P J Bishop, Alton Diocese, (Catholic) res State
      w 7th.
Bagley, M F, carp., res 9th, e Piasa.
Banks, Benjamin, mason, res cor Garden and Greene.
Bannan, James, Deputy Sheriff, res nr Marshall.
Bantz, Wm., carp res Washington
Barbour, Harvey, dentist, H H Roberts, res Upper Alton.
Bard, Frank, driver, res s s 3d, e Ridge.
Bargman, Wm., cigar maker, C Behens, bds Empire House.
Barnell, Mrs A., dress maker, res cor 9th and Alby.
Barnes, Henry, lab, res Piasa, s 17th.
Barnett, Chas., mason, res cor 10th and Alby.
Barnett, Mrs E. A., res s s State, w 7th.
Barnett, John, basket maker, W Armstrong & Bro., res State.
Barney, V., bds A L Daniels.
Barrett, James, lab, res w end Russell.
Barry, A. S., insurance, res cor State and Bluff.
Barry, Geo, Commercial traveler, res cor State and Bluff.
Bartlett, M. S., works transfer cor of St L., res cor 8th and Easton.
Bartlett, Mrs. res e s Piasa, s 10th.
Bartling, Henry, lab, E Feldwisch, bds same.
Barton, Mrs Elvira, res Alton, n 6th.
Basse & Gray, (H Basse, G Gray) wholesale liquors, e s State, s 3d.
Basse, H., (Basse & Gray) res Mill, cor 4th.
Bassett, Sylvester, farmer, res cor 14th and Langdon.
Bassett, S Wesley, engineer, res 14th w Langdon.
Bastam, Chas., weaver, res w s Belle, n 18th.
Bates, Z., (Maupin & Bates) res State nr Spring.

Bauer, Mrs Christina, res 7th, w George.
Bauer & Hoffmann, (J Bauer, J Hoffmann) furniture and undertaking, 2d opp City Hall.
Bauer, John, lab, E Feldwisch, bds same.
Bauer, John, (Bauer & Hoffmann) res 3d, e Spring.
Bauer, Wm., printer, Alton Banner, res 7th, nr cor Alton.
Bayle, Geo A.. (Daniels, Bayle & Co) bds same.
Bayle, Hugh E., res 7th, e State.
BAYLIES, MRS. S. T., manager W U Telegraph Co., res Easton cor 4th.
Beach, J A, carpenter, res n s 7th, e Belle.
Beall, C B., (Millen & Beall) res cor Union and Spring.
Beall, Edward, pressman Alton Telegraph, res 13th, w Langdon.
Beam, Miss Anna, teacher school No 2, res 3d.
Beazley, Mrs Elizabeth, res Washington, e Pleasant.
Beck, Leonard, lab, res cor Ridge and 6th.
Becker, Christian, F., shoemaker, bds e s Ridge, s 5th.
Beckley & Baker, (E S Beckley, D W Baker) manufacr's of inks, blueing and mucilage, n s 3d, e Piasa.
Beckley, E S (Beckley & Baker) res 5th, e Market.
Beckman, Frank, works Dousman & Drummond, bds Front, nr Alton.
Beckman, George, carp, res North, n Pearl
Beem, Andrew, res n s 3d, w Langdon.
Beem, Nicholas, clk, S A Cotter, res 3d, nr George.
Beese, Chas., tailor, res s s 2d, e Henry.
Beese, H., clk, Joesting & Sachtleben, res 2d, e Henry.
Behm, Louis, res Union, e Oak.
Behrens, Chas., cigars and tobacco, Piasa, n 2d, res Union, w Ridge.
Behrens, H A., dry goods, res Bozza, e Washington.
Beil, Jos., saloon. s s 2d, e Spring, res same.
Beiser, L., stone mason, res s s 6th, e Ridge.
Bell. Chas, lab, res Easton, s 10th.
Bell, J R., (J R Bell & Co) res Upper Alton.
Bell, J R & Co (J R Bell, G Sauerwein) butchers, n s 3d, e Belle.
Bellas, T R., carp, res Common.
Benedict, Alfred, Marble Works, s s 4th, w Belle, res cor Bond and William.
Bennett, Alex., bds State, w Jefferson.
Benton, Mrs Ursula, res Common.
Berge, Henry, teamster, res s s 6th, w Walnut.
Berge, Mrs Kate, res s s 6th, w Walnut.
Berger, Henry, teamster, E Feldwisch, cor 6th, nr Walnut.

Bernard, Peter, works Glass Works, bds Washington, e Pleasant.
Berner & Gaiser, (Louis Berner, John Gaiser) boot and shoe makers.
   w s Belle. n 3d
Berner, Louis. (Berner & Gaiser) res cor 6th and Easton.
Berner, John, blacksmith, D Miller, res 3d nr Spring.
Berner, Mrs Theresa, res s s 3d, w Spring.
Bernreider. John, cooper. Armstrong Bros., res s s 4th, e Plumb.
Berry, C.. ferryman. bds St Charles Hotel.
Berry. John, ferryman, bds Union Depot Hotel
Berry, R C.. ferryman, bds St Charles Hotel.
Best. W. (D R Sparks & Co) res Litchfield
Betz, Augustus F.. salesman, Blair & Atwood, res cor 6th and
   Liberty.
Betz. Carl, confectionery and restaurant. w s Belle, s 4th. res same.
Betzler. Louis, baker, res w s Ridge. s 5th.
Bigwood, L G. clerk, R Flagg. res Upper Alton.
Biggens. Thomas. boarding Piasa, n 2d, res same.
Bibb, Allen. lab, res Washington. e Pleasant.
Bibb, John, lab, res Washington. e Pleasant
Bibb, Mrs C., res Washington. e Pleasant.
Bicker. Louis, ice dealer. res e s Liberty. n 5th.
Bierbaum. R. (Paul & Bierbaum) res same.
Bieser. August, carp, res n s 5th, w Ridge.
Bilderbeck, B., carp, res n end Diamond.
Bilderbeck, R. wood worker Alton Ag. Works, res Fletcher.
Bilderbeck, Justus, clk. H W Jutting, res Walnut.
Billings, Mrs Elizabeth, res Liberty, s Suspension.
Billings. Henry O., lawyer, res Liberty, s Suspension.
Billue. Wm., clk, W R Parker, bds same.
Bird, John C. clk. Quigley, Hopkins & Co., res cor 11th and Alby.
Birdsall, Jas.. dry goods, n s 3d, w Piasa, res cor 4th and George.
Birdsall, John, clk. J Birdsall, res same.
Bishop, Andrew. grocer, bds cor George and 6th.
Bishop, Wm., glass blower, res cor 11th and Easton.
Bisinger, L., grocer, cor 3d and Cherry, res same.
Biszer, J., scissors grinder, res s s Union, e Ridge.
Black. Alex, lab, res Common.
Blackburn. Wm., painter, res 9th, e Belle.

**BLAIR & ATWOOD, (John L. Blair, Roger W.
Atwood,) wholesale grocers, cor. 2d and Piasa.**

Blair, John L., (Blair & Atwood) res north end of Henry.

BLAIR, MRS. N. C., Proprietor Child House, cor. 3d and Market, res. same.

Blaisdell, E B, book-keeper, res cor Maple and Grove.
Blake, Chas R., (Wise, Blake & Johnston) res Quincy.
Blake, Elias, lab, bds John Whitbeck.
Boals, C., wood worker, Alton Agricultural Works.
Boals, J L., mill hand, M H Boals, res 6th, nr Langdon.

BOALS, M. H., dealer in Lumber, Lath, Shingles, etc., and Manufacturer of Sash, Doors, Blinds, Frames, Moulding, Brackets, etc., office cor. 2d and Oak, res. cor. 6th and Langdon.

Bock, Henry, shoe-maker, res s s 3d, e Henry.

BOEHNING, WM. F., Agent Singer Machine Co., Belle, bds. 7th, nr. George.

Boercker, Wm., baker, 2d, w Ridge, res same.
Bolduke, laborer, res Bloomfield, w Harrison.
Bolden, Harry, (Steward & Bolden) res Henry, nr 3d
Boog, John, res State road.
Bookout, Benjamin, blacksmith, res s s 3d, e Oak.
Boone, Thomas, pilot, res cor North and Pearl.
Booth, John, jeweler, J W Cary, bds cor 3d and Market
Borckman, Chas, furniture and undertaking, 2d, w Ridge, res same.
Borckman, Chas, Jr, cigar maker, res 2d, nr Ridge.
Bordeau, Edward, cooper, Armstrong Bros, res Upper Alton.
Bork, Lorenz, res cor Gold and Putnam.
Boschert, Edward, works Alton Ag Works, res n s 5th, e Ridge.
Boschert, Martin, works Alton Ag Works, res nr Hampton.
Boswell, Eugene A, pressman, Perrin & Smith, res 7th, w Alby.
Boswell, R J, book-keeper, A H Drury & Co, res 7th, w Alby.
Boswell, Mrs S, res 7th, w Alby.
Bostwick, John, clk, R Flagg, res Upper Alton.
Bow, John, lab, res e s George, s 7th.
Bowman, E M, lawyer, res cor 12th and Langdon.
Bowman, Geo, res 15th, w Alby.
Bowman, H B, dry goods, n s 3d, w Piasa, res cor 12th and Langdon
Bowman, J W, barber, cor 3d and Piasa, res Easton, n 5th.
Boyd, Mrs Alice, res s s 8th, e Henry.

Boyd, Dennis, tinner, S. & W. Pitts.
Boyd, Dennis, teamster, res Green.
Boyd, Thos, splitter, Dousman & Drummond, res 8th, nr Henry.
Boyle, Cornelius, res cor 10th and Easton.
Boyle, Mrs Julia, res s s 3d, e Henry.
Boyle, Wm., lab, bds D Ryan.
Bozza, James, Tea dealer, res n s 3d, e Pear.
Bradbury, Mrs Mary, res Marshall, w Belle.
Braddock, Alfred, butcher, res e s Belle, nr 6th.
Bradley, Edward, lab, res State, w Main.
Bradish, D carp, res Spring, n State.
Brady, John, moulder, Alton Ag. Works, bds D Ryan.
Bramhall, Edmund, Jr., brick-layer, res n s 6th, e Market.
Bramhall, Jason, brick-layer, res n s 6th, e Market.
Bramhall, John, driver, Am. Ex. Co., res 6th, e Market
Brandewiede, Francis, saloon, n s 3d, e Belle, res same.
Bratfisch, John, shoe-maker, res n s 3d, e Langdon.
Bratfisch, Julius, clk, F E Hoffmann, res same.
Braun, Mrs Agatha, res n s 3d, e Spring.
Bray, Edward, lab, res Alby, n 10th.
Bray, Jonas, (F K Nichols, Son & Co.) res Bluff, s State.
Brayn, John, carp, res s s 5th, e Liberty.
Brazuell, Daniel, brick-layer, res 8th w Belle.
Breath, Abraham, Real Estate Agt., res cor 12th and Alton.
Breath, E H, Photographer, e s 3d, e State, res cor 12th and Alton.
Breckinridge, Mrs L., res Franklin, w Common.
Breckinridge, S. L., res Franklin, w Common.
Breedlove, Mrs Mary, res Liberty, s Union.
Brenholt, John J., Atty. at Law, over 30, 3d, bds same.
Brennan, Mrs C. L., grocer, cor 2d and Cherry, res same.
Brennan, John, lab, res cor Spring and 5th.
Brennan, J J, (J J & J L Brennan) res cor 2d and Apple.
Brennan, J. J. Bro., (J. J. & J. L. Brennan) Lime kiln, cor 2d and
    Apple.
Brennan, Luke, lime burner, res n s 3d, w Vine.
Brennan, Luke, res cor 2d and Cherry.
Brennan, Martin, lab, res cor 17th and Alby.
Brennan, Stephen, works Tobacco Works, res Alby, cor 17th
Brenner, Geo., clk, T Lehne, res same.
Brenner, John, mason, res State road.
Brenner, Joseph, wagon maker, res cor 3d and Walnut.
Brenner, Martin, mason, res State road.
Brenner, Xaner, lab, s s 3d, w Walnut.

Brewer, Chas, wagon maker, res n s 9th, e Piasa.
Bringaisey, C. Martin, fireman, D R Sparks & Co, res Monroe, e Madison.
Bristol, C. S., tinner, res cor 6th and Alton.
Brittingham. John. machine hand. M II Boals res n s 3d. w Cherry.
Brock, James, works saw mill, res south end Bluff.
Broderick, Mrs Catharine, res n s 3d, e Henry.
Broderick, Mrs Hannah, res w s Belle, n 9th.
Broderick, Wm., saloon, cor 10th and Belle, res same.
Bromleve, John, dyer woolen mills, res Gold.
Bronson, E J, job printing, over 16, 3d. res Market, nr 17th.
Brooks, George, fisherman, res Front, e Easton.
Brooks, Geo., works C B Rohland, res cor 6th and George.
Brooks, Mrs Margaret, res w s Alby, s 6th
Brophy, Pat., glass blower, Glass Works.
Brown, Andrew. res Washington, w Sq.
Brown, Chas., engineer, res n s 3d, e Henry.
Brown, Chas., painter, res cor Ridge and 5th.
Brown, Geo, teamster, res 9th, w Alby.
Brown, Geo T, res cor Alby and 3d.
Brown, Rev Henry, pastor colored M E Church, res e s Easton, s 6th.
Brown, Jacob, mate on Spread Eagle, res s s 2d, e Alton.
Brown, John. lab, res cor 16th and Alton.
Brown, Joseph, bds at Mrs M W Carroll's.
Brown, Julia, clk, II Burton, res same.
Brown, Margaret, prop'r Fifth Av. Hotel, cor 5th and Piasa, res same.
Brown, Robt, glass blower, Glass Works.
Brown, Robert, lab, res Main, w Hamilton.
Browning, lab, res on the Hill, w Cliff, nr River.
Bruch, Mrs A, res s s 3d, w Spring.
Bruch, Frank, cooper, res s s 3d, w Spring.
Bruch, Victor, bar-tender, res s s 3d, w Spring.
Brudon, Mrs S, res n s 2d, e Easton.
Brudon, Wm, undertaker, n s 2d, w Alby, res same.
Brueggeman, A., merchant tailor, n s 3d, e Belle, res cor George and 6th.
Brueggeman, A Jr, clk. A Brueggeman, res same.
Brueggeman, Louis, cigar maker, res n s 3d, e Oak.
Brueggeman, II, cigar maker, 3d, w Piasa, res 3d, cor Apple.
Brueggeman, S II, cigars and tobacco, 2d, w Ridge, res same.
Brueggeman, Wm, works J L Blair's, res same.
Brunner, B, (Brunner & Duncan) res cor 13th and George.

BRUNNER & DUNCAN, (B. Brunner, G. Duncan,) Machinists and Founders, 5th, e Piasa.

Bruner, John, steam-boat Capt., res State, n Jefferson.
Bryant, John, lab, res on the Hill, n Cliff. nr the River.
Buckleman, F F, stone cutter, res cor 19th and Belle.
Buckmaster, J, res Liberty, n Pearl.
Buckmaster, S. A, res Liberty, n Pearl.
Budd, Jas. W., clk. U. S. Ex. Co, bds Knight's restaurant.
Budde, John, grocer. cor Henry and 8th, res same.
Budde, Wm, lab, res cor Pearl and Ridge.
Buff, J, (Buff, Kuhl & Co.) res St Louis.

BUFF, KUHL & CO., (J. Buff, M. Kuhl, T. Knecht, P. Schmiedt,) Soda and Mineral Water Factory. Soda Water, Ginger Ale and Mineral Waters always kept in bottles. Fountains charged. Cor. 2d and Ridge.

Bun, John, works Plow Works, res e s Ridge, s 5th
Bunson, Chas, physician, s s 2d, w Alby, res same.
Burbridge. Geo., machinist G D Hayden, res cor Prospect and State.
Burbridge, J Q, (S W Farber & Co.) res cor State and Prospect.
Burgess, J W, Freight and Ticket Ag't, I. and St Louis, res Henry, cor 5th.
Burgess, Wm, lab, res n s 7th, w Piasa.
Burke, Edward, foreman Castor Oil Factory, res Hamilton, nr Belle.
Burke, Jas, tinner, B Garde, res Hamilton.
Burke, Mrs. res Belle, n 11th.
Burlew, Henry, res s s 2d, e Alton.
Burnett, John R, cooper, res n s 9th, e Piasa.
Burns, James, lab, res n s 3d, e Ridge.
Burns, Mrs Mary, res s s 9th, w Langdon.
Burrie, John, works H Taylor, res same.
Burroughs, Wm H., res cor 6th and Seminary.
Burton, George, (J Burton & Son) res Alby, nr 16th.

BURTON, HANNAH, successor to Mrs. J. Webb, dealer in staple and fancy Dry Goods, Millinery, Ladies' and Childrens' Shoes, n s 3d, e State, res. same.

Burton, John, (J Burton & Son,) res 7th, e Belle.
Burton, J & Son, (J & G Burton,) grocers, Belle, n 7th.
Bushnell, Thos, lab, res cor Easton and 14th.
Bushnell, Robt, lab, res cor Easton and 14th.
Busse, Richard, grinder, Plow Works, res cor 14th and Liberty.
Busse, Richard, works Buff, Kuhl & Co.'s.
Busse, Wm. teamster, bds Farmers' Home.
Butler, Chas, pastry cook, res n s 2d, w Cherry.
· Butler, John, teamster, bds cor 5th and Piasa.
Butler, J K, clk, bds cor 3d and Market.
Butler, ——, lab, res Belle, s 19th.
Butler, Mrs Maria, res w s Market, n 10th.
Butler, S C, printer, Perrin & Smith, res 5th, e Alby.
Butterfield, D C, marble yard, res Common, s Grove.
Butz, Henry, painter, res 6th, e Cherry.
Byrnes, Patrick, lab res Common, nr Railroad.
Byrnes, Peter, helper. res w s Belle, s 18th.

C

Cabrilliac, Alex, book-keeper, res State, cor Jefferson.
Cabrilliac, Mrs Julia, res State, cor Jefferson.
Cahill, James, saloon, w s Belle, s 8th, bds same.
Cahill, Jas, lab, res Cliff, s Elm.
Cahill, Wm, lab, F Shelly.
Cain, Albert, U S Gauger, office cor 3d and Belle, bds St Charles
    Hotel.
Caldwell, C A, Cashier Alton Nat. Bank, res Henry, n 14th.
Caldwell, C D, grocer, cor 4th and State, res Bond, w Beacon.
Caldwell, Mrs Margaret, grocer, cor 9th and Belle, res same.
Caldwell, M P, pork packer and provisions, 85. 4th, res Prospect, s
    State.
Calvey, John, lab, W Armstrong & Co.'s.
Calvey, James, lab, res n s 4th, w Ridge.
Campbell, Thos, logger, res s end Bluff.

CANNELL, THOS., Agent United States Express
Co., State, Opp. 3d, res. Prospect, n. Bond.

Carey, Joseph, lab, res Alley, bet 5th and 6th, e Ridge.
Carhart, Mrs E, res William, n Park.
Carhart, G W, clk, J. Crowe, res State, bet 3d and 4th.
Carhart, Wm N, clk, res William, n Park.
Carpenter, Mrs Annie, res w s Easton, s 6th.

Carpenter, John W, lawyer, res Oak, s State.
Carr, David, lab, res 10th, e Piasa.
Carr, H M. (Flagg, Pierson & Carr) res cor 8th and Langdon.
Carr, Mrs Martha, res s s 2d, e George.
Carroll, John, lab, res Dry, nr Main.
Carroll, John, cooper, Armstrong Bros, res Dry, nr State.
Carroll, John, lab, res 18th, e Alby.
Carroll, Mrs., res cor Main and Hamilton.
Carroll. Mrs M W, res William, n Park.
Carter, Chas, lab, res cor 9th and Piasa.
Carter, Chas. works W C Quigley, bds same.
Carter, David, pressman, Dausman & Drummond, res 8th.
Carter, Edward, hostler, res w s Easton, n 5th
Carter, Mrs Kate, res 8th, e Piasa.
Carter, Richard, waiter, res n s 6th. e Alton.
Cary, J W, watches, clocks and jewelry, s s 3d, e State, res 3d, bet
     Alton and Langdon.
Cashen, Mrs M, res Bluff. s State.
Casey. James. lab, res State nr Main.
Cavenaugh, James. polisher, W Flynn, bds cor 5th and Piasa.
Cavender. Robt S, res Liberty, opp Grove.
Celtman, Louis, butcher, A Crasler. bds same.
Chaffer, Richard, grocer, cor State and Grand Av , res same.
Chaffer. Wm, drayman. res Main, nr State.
Challacombe, Aaron, policeman. res n s State, w Cliff.
Challacombe, Geo E, book-keeper, M H Boals, res 7th, nr Henry.
Challacombe, John, watchman, M H Boals, res 7th, nr Henry.
Chalk, Henry, carp, bds cor 7th and Piasa.

***CHAMBERLAIN, H. W., Wholesale and Retail
   Druggist, Proprietor and Sole Manufacturer
   of Pearline Tooth Powder, Wade's Hair Re-
   storer, and Favorite Cologne, 18, 3d, res. State,
   n. 4th.***

Chamberlain, Thos, clk, H W Chamberlain, bds same.
Champagne. Frank, hostler, res State n 4th.
Chaney, John. furniture, 9, Belle. res Belle. s 9th.
Chase, Rev March, Rector Episcopal Church. res s s 3d, e Alton.
Chaum, Christian. wood worker, Plow Works, res 2d.
Cheney. H A, foreman Railroad Round House. C & A, res Market
     n 9th.
Chouteau. A L. groceries, cor 7th and Belle, res opp cor.

Chouteau, Gus, clk, A L Chouteau, res same.
Claflin, Wm, carp, res Common, n Grove.
Clampitt, James, lab, res n s 7th, w Piasa.
Clampitt, Thos, brakeman, res n s 7th, w Piasa.
Clark, Mrs Catharine, res Vine, n 2d.
Clark, Matthew, lab, res s s 3d, nr Washington.
Clark, N B, conductor, bds Main, w Hamilton.
Clark, Jos, brakeman, bds cor 7th and Piasa.
Clarkson, Mrs Elizabeth, res n s 2d, e Easton.
Claybold, Frank, works Brewery, res 15th, w Langdon.
Clement, Everet, Traveling Agt, res cor 7th and Langdon.
Clement, Miss Laura, Principal School No. 3d, res cor George
  and 5th.

GO WITH THE CROWD TO ANDREW CLIF-
FORD, wholesale and retail Grocer and dealer
in Flour, Feed and Country Produce, Belle,
bet. 5th and 6th, res. same. Established 1836.

Clifford, Mrs C N, res cor 3d and Market.
Coates, Wm, cook, res 7th, e George.
Cobeck, John, tobacco roller, res s s 7th, e Henry.
Cole, Benjamin, lab, Bloomfield, cor Fletcher.
Coley, ——, brick-layer, res s s 4th, e George.
Collet & Ground, (J W Collet, O B Ground) prop's Madison Mills,
  Upper Alton Station
Collet, J W, (Collet & Ground) res Upper Alton.
Collins, Edward, Mill hand, M H Boals, res 3d, nr Cherry.
Collins, John, Agt Spread Eagle, res Dry, n State.
Collins, John, lab, res w s Cherry, n 2d.
Collins, Mrs Mary, res cor 19th and Belle.
Collins, Wm, feather renovator, res n s 6th, w Walnut.
Colmon, E R, roller, Dausman & Drummond, res Front, w Alton.
Colmon, Mrs Jane, res Piasa, n 16th.
Colmon, W J, roller, Dausman & Drummond, res Front, nr Alton.
Comle, Augustus, lab, res Henry, n 3d.
Commons, Dan, lab, bds T Biggins.
Condin, James, lab, res cor Washington and Common.
Condlin, Dennis, lab, res Union, nr Walnut.
Condon, John, lab, res cor Washington and Common.
Conlin, James, lab, res e s Liberty, n Union.
Connolley, Robt, shoemaker, res s s 6th, e Liberty.
Connor, S F, Travelling agent, res 3d, e Alton.

Convery, Patrick, lab, res Liberty, n 8th.
Conway, Mrs Margaret, res n s 3d, w Cherry.
Cook, Chas, butcher, res n s 3d, e Henry.
Cooley, Stephen, lab, res cor 4th and Pear.
Cooper, J T, (Roper & Cooper) res 9th, w Langdon.
Copley, John, engineer, H Basse.
Coppinger & Biggins, (J E Coppinger, T Biggins) Lime kiln and
    building materials, office s s 3d.
Coppinger, J E, (Coppinger & Biggins) res Main.
Coppinger, John W, Att. at Law, s s 3d, res Oak, w State.
Coppinger, Thos H, student, bds J E Coppinger.
Corbit, Thos, brick yard, cor 10th and Market, res same.
Costelo, John, lab, bds T Biggins.
Cotter, David, driver, A Clifford, res cor 16th and Alby.
Cotter, James M, res Spring, n State.
Cotter. L F, druggist, res Prospect, c State.
Cotter, S A, druggist, e s Belle, n 3d, res Prospect, nr State.
Coudy, R, Prop'r St Charles Hotel, w s State, res same.
Coughlin, Jeremiah, lab, res 10th, w Henry
Coupland, George, tailor, res Court, e Alton.
Cousley, James, policeman, res 8th, w Alton.
Cousley, John, printer, res e s Alby, s 6th.
Cousley, Robt, 1st clk, Post Office, bds Alby, s 6th.
Cowell, Wm, lab, res e s Alby, s 9th.
Craig, Jos, clk, R DeBow & Co, res cor 8th and George.
Craig, Joseph, lab, G Meyer, res same.
Craig, Wm, sawyer, res Wharf, s State.
Cramer, Geo, lab, res n s 5th, e Ridge.
Crandall, C M, crockery, 12, 3d, res 2d, e Easton.
Crane, H J, Dept U S Coll'r, office cor 3d and Belle, res State.
Crasler, August, meat market, n s 2d, e Ridge, res same.
Crause, Conrad, salesman, D R Sparks & Co, res Union.
Crawford, N., polisher, Plow Works, res cor 3d and Ridge.
Crawford, Zachariah, works W Smith, res same.
Creals, Thos, works Glass Works, res w s Liberty, s 8th.
Cregan, Edward, assorter, Dausman & Drummond, res 2d, nr George.
Cregan, John, drayman, res s s 2d, e George.
Crisman, Rev E P., Supt. Board of Missions, res cor 11th and
    Langdon.
Crocker, J B, bds H M Schweppe.
Crofton, James, works Glass Works, res cor 19th and Market.
Crofton, John, lab, res 4th, e Piasa.
Cronan, Ben, machinist, Plow Works, res 2d, nr Langdon.

Crossman, C L, Photographer, 2d, e Piasa, bds cor Henry and 8th.
Crossman, W V, Auction and Commission, cor 3d and Piasa, res cor Henry and 8th.
Crowe, Frank, clk, J Crowe, res same.
Crowe, Joseph, grocer, State, bet 3d and 4th, res State, cor Park.
Cruse, John, clk, W V Crossman, res Union.
Crume, Daniel, machinist, res n s 7th, e Henry.
Cue, James, cooper, Armstrong Bros, res Spring.
Culp, Mrs Catharine, res Piasa, s 17th.
Cummings, Mrs B, res cor Park and Mill.
Cummings, James, lab, res Piasa, nr 9th.
Cunningham, Mrs Ann, res Belle, s 19th.
Cunningham, Frank, engineer, res cor 5th and Alby.
Cunningham, John, lab, res cor 19th and Belle.
Curdie, John, saloon, 2d, opp City Hall, res Belle, s 7th.
Curley, Mrs Mary, res Jefferson, e State.
Curtis, Richard, lab, res Bloomfield, w Harrison.
Cutter, George, engineer, res cor 12th and Easton.

D

Dahlgreen, Swante, machinist, Plow Works, res Langdon, n 2d.
Dahlstrom, John, machinist, Plow Works, res cor 4th and George.
Dahlstrom, Oscar, machinist, Plow Works, res cor 4th and George.
Dalabanty, Thos, lab, res Cherry, n 3d.
Dale, Samuel, lab, res cor 16th and Alby.
Daley, James, lab, res cor 14th and Easton.
Daley, Joseph, switchman, C. & A.
Daly, Thomas, glass blower, bds Spring St. House.
Daniel, Bro., teacher Cathedral School, rooms same.
Daniels, A L, (Daniels, Bayle & Co.) res Alby, n 6th.
Daniels, Bayle & Co, (A L Daniels, G A Bayle, Wm B Pierce) manufacturers of crackers and buiscuit, cor Easton and 2d.
Dannenberg, Henry, tailor, res n s 5th, e Ridge
Dausman & Drummond, (Henry Dausman, J T & John M Drummond) manufacturers of Plug Tobacco, cor 2d and Alton.
Dausman, Henry, (Dausman & Drummond) res St Louis.
Davis, Chas, clk, F P Owings, res cor 5th and Alby.
Davis, Chas E, physician, (Reg.) s s 3d, w Piasa, res Belle, s 7th.
Davis, Chas E, works for Hayner, res s s 4th, e Henry.
Davis, Fred, clk, T P Nisbett & Co, res Alby, bet 6th and 7th.
Davis, George, works Oil Factory, res Salu.
Davis, Geo. T, student, bds F Hopkins.
Davis, Jas, clk, res s s 2d, e Market.

Davis, James H H, lab, res s s 4th, c Henry.

DAVIS, LEVI, Att. at Law. s s 3d, w Piasa, res. 2d, c Market.

Dawes, Henry. brick-layer, res Belle, s 17th.
Dawson, Edwin, engineer, res n s 3d, w Langdon.
Dawson, John, saloon, n s 2d, w Vine, res 3d, w Cherry.
Dawson, Richard, teamster, res s s 3d, c Walnut.
Day, Harry, conductor, bds cor 7th and Piasa.
Day, Miss M, dress maker, res cor 3d and Henry.
Dean, John, blacksmith, G Luft, res cor 4th and Spring.
Dean, Mrs R D, laundry, res n s 3d, w Langdon.
DeBow, R, (R DeBow & Co.) res Upper Alton.
DeBow, R., & Co. (R DeBow, W E Schweppe,) wholesale grocers, 14th and 16th, 2d.
Dedman, Wm, engineer, res Plank road, n 20th.
Delancy, Mrs Margaret, res Park, cor Mill.
Delmont, Edward, barber, bds Market, s 3d.
DeLong, John. lab. res n s 5th, c Market.
DeLong, John, lab, res e s Easton, s 11th.
DeLong, Levi, clk, res e s Easton, s 11th.
Degenhardt, Charles, carp, res Spring, nr Main.
Degenhardt, Mrs W, res s s 9th, w Henry.
Degnan, Patrick. lab, res Dry, n State.
DeGrand, A, physician, res n s 8th, c Langdon.
Dennison, George, lab, res Market, n 16th.
Dennison, Peter, gardener, res cor Washington and Sq.
Dennison, Wm, lab, res Market, s 17th.
Dennler, Edward, works Alton Ag Works, res s s Union, c Ridge.
Derrick, James. lab, res Washington, c Pleasant.
Deterding, E F, clk, res 2d, c Walnut.
Deterding. F W. res n s 2d, c Walnut.
Dettmers. Frank. clk, J H Oltmanns, bds same.
Dettmers, Herman, tailor, res n s 6th, w Cherry.
Detrich. J E, book-keeper, F Shelly, bds same.
Devany, Mrs Bridget, res Piasa, nr 9th.
Devine, Thos, stone cutter, res Main, nr State.
Devitt, Richard, lab, bds T Biggins.
Devlin, Patrick, lab, res cor 8th and Liberty.
Dewyer, Mrs, res 2d, w Piasa.
Diamond, Bernard, works Tobacco Works, res cor Spring and 5th.
Diamond, F, painter, res c s Easton, n 10th.

Diamond, Harry, works Topping Bros.. res Marshall.
Diamond, John P. painter. res Salu.
Dick, Mrs. Catharine. res e s Ridge, n 5th.
Dick, George, porter, res e s Ridge, n 5th.
Dick, George. tailor, res Alley. bet 5th and 6th, e Ridge.
Dick, John, painter. C Rodemeyer, res 6th, nr Spring.
Dietchy, Joseph, saloon, cor 3d and Ridge, res 4th, e Henry.
Dietz, Chas, tailor, H C G Moritz, res cor 2d and Spring.
Dietz, Christ, butcher, J R Bell & Co., res Upper Alton.
Dietz, Joseph, lab res cor 3d and Plum.
Dietz. M H. (M H Dietz & Co.) res same.

DIETZ, M H. & Co., Steam Dyers and Cleaners. Velvet, Woolen and half Woolen, goods of every description. beautifully cleaned or dyed, State. bet. 3d and 4th.

Dietz, Philip, lab. res cor 2d and Cherry.
Dietz, T, Lime kiln. nr cor Railroad and 3d, res cor 3d and Plum.
Dietz, Wm. lab. res cor 3d and Plum.
Dillon, Miss Mary, res State, e Bond.
Dimmock. Mrs Chas, res n s 12th, e Alton.
Dimmock, E L. res n s 2d. e Market.
Dittman, Fred, lab, res Apple, n 2d.
Dittman, John, lab, T Dietz, res Plum, n 2d.
Dobson, Robt., res Belle. s 17th.
Dodge, J T., res e s Market, s 3d.
Dodson, John. plasterer, res Bloomfield, w Harrison.
Doebel, Mrs Julia, res cor 4th and George.
Doepke. F., merchant tailor. 2d. Junction 3d, res 3d.
Doerr, Jacob, bricklayer. res n s 3d. w Ridge.
Dolbee, Mrs., res south end of Oak.
Donahoe, Mrs. Ann, res 7th, w Belle.
Donahoe, Michael, lab, res 7th, w Belle.
Dorsett, Mrs Elizabeth, res Henry. n 3d.
Dorsey. B., fisherman, res Frout, e Easton.
Dorsey, John, lab, F. Shelly.
Doty, George, engineer. bds Robt. Reagans.
Doty. Richard, blacksmith. bds Robt. Reagans.
Dougherty, Wm, bricklayer, res s s 5th, nr Vine.
Dow. Alfred, res west end of Franklin.
Dow, John, clk, W V Crossman. res Alby, nr 8th.
Dow, Miss Julia, teacher School No. 2.

DOWNES, P., dealer in Groceries, Provisions and Country Produce, e. s. Belle, bet. 5th and 6th, res. same.

Downes, Patrick, lab, res Common, nr Railroad.
Downes, Thos, lab, res n s 3d, e Henry.
Downes, Thos, lab, res s s 9th, w Henry.
Downey, P H, engineer, C & A, res cor 18th and Market.
Doyle, John, carp, res cor 18th and Belle.
Doyle, John, lab, res s end of Liberty.
Doyle, Michael, stone cutter, res Main, w Hamilton.
Doyle, Timothy, lab, res Union, e North.
Driesoner, Michael, carp, res cor 9th and Liberty.
Drennen, Chas, brakeman, C & A, res Market, s 16th.
Drew, Henry, barber, res n s 3d, w Ridge.
Drew, Wm, cook, res Washington, w Sq.
Driscoll, James, brakeman, bds cor Alby and 19th.
Drury, A H, (A H Drury & Co.) res State, w 7th.

DRURY, A. H., & Co., (A. H. & F. W. Drury,) wholesale dealers in Farm Machinery, Wagons, Buggies, Leather, Saddlery Hardware, Belting, etc., Short, w State.

Drury, F. W, (A H Drury & Co.) res State, e Spring.
Drury, Wm, Traveling Agt., res n s State, e Spring.
Drummond, John H, Tobacco roller, res Bluff, s State.
Drummond, John M, (Dausman & Drummond) res 3d, cor Alton.
Drummond, J T, (Dausman & Drummond) res Mill, n 4th.
Duker, Mrs Effie, res s s Union, w Ridge.
Dulcy, Michael, lab, res Alton, n 2d.
Dunavan, John, watchman, Railroad, res Alby, cor 18th.
Duncan, G. (Brunner & Duncan) res cor 7th and Alton.
Dunlap, Albert, Agt. Howe Machine, res Grove, cor Common.
Dunn, Mrs Helen, res Market, s 17th.
Dunn, James, carp, res Market, s 18th.
Dunn, Pat, machinist, Alton Ag. Works.
Dunn, W A, engineer, res cor 10th and Easton.
Dunnagan, I R, works Glass Works, res n s 3d, nr Plum.
Dunnigan, James, res Russell.
Dunnigan, Lawrence, lab, res Russell.
Dunnigan, Thos, lab, W Armstrong & Co.
Durwin, John, lab, res Belle, s 17th.

Dutro, M M, merchant tailor, w s Belle, s 4th, res Bluff.
Dwyer, John, lab, res State, n Jefferson.
Dye, John, book-keeper, Perley & Woodman, res cor Langdon and
　9th.
Dyson, Bernard, wool sorter Woolen Mill, bds Belle.

E

Eaton, Henry, S, clk, Milnor, Auten & Co, res 12th.
Eaton, N. J.. Sec. Ins. Co., res cor 11th and George.
Eckert. Chas., lab, T. Dietz, res e s North, n 6th.
Eden, Christ, carp, res n s 4th, w Ridge.
Edwards, E L, Traveling Agt, res s s 3d, e George.
Eggs, Benedict, works Empire House, bds same.
Ehret, J B, boot and shoe maker, State, s 4th, res William.
Ehrhardt, Anton, Farmers' Home, s e cor 2d and Spring, res same.
Eichhorn, Egidi, lab, res s s 6th, w Walnut.
Eichhorn, Jos, lab, F. Shelly.
Eikenhorst, Theo. clk, J Kindler, bds same.
Einsele, Jos., cooper, res 2d, e Henry.
Elble, Frank, saloon, 2d, e Junction 3d, res 3d.
Elble, John. clk, G Mihsel, bds same.
Elble, Mrs Louisa, res Washington.
Elert, Chas, temperer Plow Works, res 2d, nr Langdon.
Elfgen, Bertram, grocer, cor 16th and Belle, res same.
Ellen, Chas, works Plow Factory, bds Farmers' Home.
Elliot, R H, Ticket Agt., C & A Depot, res s s 7th, e Alby.
Ellsworth, Hiram, lab, res e s Henry, s 3d.
Ellsworth, Mrs O, res s s 8th, e Henry.
Ellsworth, Wm, res e s Henry, s 3d.
Elmerig, Peter, bds Empire House.
Elsen, Adolph, carp res s s 3d, w Oak.
Elsen, Fritz, hostler, J Miedel, res same.
Emerson, Mrs, res s s 3d. e George.
Emerson, Carey, Traveling Agt. Blair & Atwood, res 3d, e George.
Emery, George, clk, Ins. office, res cor 15th and Langdon.
Ensinger, W F, painter, e s Belle, n 4th, res s s 12th, e Langdon.
Eppenberger, Mrs Barbara, res Walnut, s 5th.
Ernst, Henry, works Dr Guelich, res n s 3d, w Ridge.
Essig, Andrew, tailor. M M Dutro, bds Empire House.
Essling, Henry, wagon maker, bds cor Bond and Beacon.
Estes, Chas, painter, bds Bond, w Beacon.
Estes, C H, paper hanger. s s 4th, e State, res same.
Esterly, Jacob, lab, res Washington, e Pleasant.

Evens, Geo., glass blower, Glass Works.
Evering, John F. lab. res cor Spring and Ridge.

EVERTS, W. F. Wholesale and Retail Druggist, dealer in pure Drugs, Medicines, Chemicals, Fine Soaps, Perfumery, Fancy and Toilet Articles, etc., Prescriptions carefully compounded, n. s. 3d, w. Piasa, res. State, n. 4th.

Ewing, Mrs. Mary A., res Common, n Sq.

F

Fahrig, B, clk, Hartman & Co, res cor 6th and Ridge.
Fahrig, —— lab. res s s 7th, w Ridge.
Fahrig, Jacob, grocer, cor Union and Ridge, res same.
Fahrig, Lorenz. res w s Ridge, n 6th.
Failey, James, works Glass Works.
Failey, Patrick, lab, res e s Alby, n 9th.
Fairbanks, Jas, lab, bds T Biggins
Fairbank, Theo, lab, F Shelly.
Fairley, Peter S, works Tobacco Factory, res Union, e Liberty.
Fallon, Wm, carp, res State road.
Farber, S W, (S W Farber & Co.) res cor 4th and Easton.

FARBER, S. W., & CO., (S. W. Farber, John O. Burbridge,) Propr's of Alton City Mills, 2d, bet. State and Piasa.

Farley, James, drayman, res s s 8th, e George.
Faulstick, Henry, plasterer, res cor Walnut and 3d.
Fecht, Henry, carp, res e s North, n 6th.
Fecht, Herman, works Robt, S Cavender, bds same.
Feger, Louis, carriage maker, D Miller, res 12th.
Feizer, John, cooper, res s s 2d, e George.
Feldwisch, Ernst, brick yard, cor Oak and 4th, res cor Cherry and 4th.
Feldwisch, John, lab, E Feldwisch, bds same.
Feldwisch, Wm, res Washington.
Fels, Fred, saloon, 2d, e Junction 3d, res same.
• Fenton, Robt. butcher, Murphy & Co, bds Jos. Murphy's.
Ferch, Andrew, lab, F Shelly.
Ferguson, Mrs. Eliza, res n s 2d, e Market.
· Ferguson, Mrs. Elizabeth, grocer, cor Ridge and Union, res same.

Ferguson, Frank A, City Clerk, office City build'g, res 2d, e George.
Ferguson, Helen. res cor Beacon and State.
Ferguson. Jane, res cor Beacon and State.
Ferguson. Wm J. carp, res w s Alby, s 9th.
Ferner, Mrs, res 2d. opp. City Hall.
Ferrell, Mrs P, res Salu.
Fesler, Henry, res cor 5th and Liberty.
Fitchtel, Mrs B, res 4th, e Plum.
Field, Rev T G, Pastor 1st Baptist Church. res cor 12th and George.
Filley, Chas A. driver U. S. Ex. Co., res State, nr Prospect.
Filley, H M. clk. res State, bet Prospect and Oak.
Filley. Mrs Martha, res State, w Prospect.
Findlay, Thos, fireman, bds n s 2d, w Langdon.
Finegan, Mrs Margaret, res Railroad, e Henry.
Finlay. P, lab, res w s Belle, n 9th.
Finlay, T J. fireman, res cor 5th and Spring.
Fingleton, James A, tinner, res Alby, s 19th.
Fingleton. John. tinner, res n s 9th, w Alby.
Fischbach, B, clk. J Raible, bds 3d Junction, 2d.
Fischbach, John, (McKinney & Fischbach) res cor 6th and Langdon.
Fischbach. Martin, general store, 3d Junction. 2d, res same.
Fischer. Mrs A., grocer, cor 5th and Ridge. res same.
Fischer, Fred, carp. res cor Ridge and 5th.
Fischer, Lorenz. lab, res w s Cherry, n 2d.
Fish. Henry, (Fish & Walter) res Belle. n 6th.

***FISH & WALTER, (H. Fish, B. Walter,) Distillers,
Rectifiers. and wholesale dealers in Foreign and
Domestic Wines and Liquors, cor. 2d and State.***

Fisher, Mrs C M, Variety Store, cor Pleasant and Henry.
Fisher, John. watch maker, s s 2d. e Langdon, res same.
Fisher, U E, Mail contractor, res s s 2d, e Easton.
Fisland. John. grinder, Plow Works. res cor 5th and Langdon.
Fitz, James, fireman. W Armstrong & Co, res Main.
Fitzgerald, Alex, lab. res 12th, w Alby.
Fitzgerald. James, broom maker, res Common.
Fitzgerald, James, teamster, res Alton, n 2d.
Fitzgerald, John. watchman, res cor Green and Garden.
Fitzgerald. Thos. lab, res Russell.
Fitzgerald. Thos. lab. res Oak, s 3d.
Fitzgibbons, Richard, lab, res cor 14th and Belle.
Fitzmorris, John, blacksmith, Plow Works, res 2d, nr Henry.

Fitzpatrick, James, lab, res Main, w Hamilton.
Fitzpatrick, John, lab, res Wharf. s State.
Fitzpatrick, Michael, pressman, Dausman & Drummond, bds T.
    Biggins.
Fizer, John, cooper, Armstrong Bros, res 2d, nr Easton.
Flach, John, carpet weaver, cor 2d and Alby, res same.
Flagg, M, lab, res cor Spring and Railroad.

---

*FLAGG, RICHARD, Cash dealer in Dry Goods
and Notions. Large stocks good Goods, uniform
Low Prices. 32, 3d, res. 12th, bet. Easton and
Alton.*

Flagg, R H, (Flagg, Pierson & Carr) res cor 5th and George.
Flagg, Pierson & Carr, (R H Flagg. Wm M Pierson, H M Carr)
    Dry Goods and Notions, s w cor 3d and Piasa.
Flanagan, C J, Supt. Planing Mill, M H Boals, res 2d, nr Oak.
Flanagan, Michael, lab, bds T Biggins.
Flanagan, Patrick, lab, bds T Biggins.
Flanagan. Wm E, tool dresser, M H Boals, res 2d, nr Oak.
Fleck. Alexander, res cor 8th and George
Fleming, John, lab. res Belle, s 20th.
Fletcher, Dennis, works Plow Factory, res s s Liberty, n Union.
Fletcher. Mrs. H., res State, n Jefferson.
Floss. Joseph, music teacher, res cor Summit and Prospect.
Flynn, Dennis, lab, res cor 18th and Alby.
Flynn, Michael, clk, P Mitchell, res Belle.
Flynn, Thomas, switchman, C & A yard, res Alby.
Flynn, Wm, stone cutter, res cor 18th and Belle
Flynn, Wm., marble dealer, cor 5th and Belle, res cor 10th and
    Langdon.
Foman, Peter, lab, res Hampton, w Harrison.
Fonke, Herman, weaver, res cor 7th and Belle.
Foraster, Thos, bds Empire House.
Forbes, James H, tea and coffee dealer, res Henry, n 9th.
Ford. Archibald, lab, bds Putnam, w Gold.
Ford, John, engineer, res Belle, n 16th.
Ford, John, works Glass Works.
Formhals, Geo, tailor, H C G Moritz, res cor Jackson and Monroe.
Forrest, James, plasterer, res e s Ridge, n 6th.
Forrester, T N, painter, bds w s State, s 4th.
Fortnier, James, butcher, res s s 3d, e Vine.
Fowler, Mrs Eliza, res cor 7th and Piasa.

Fox, James, lab, res n s 4th, w Ridge.
Fox, John, assorter, Dausman & Drummond, res 4th, nr Ridge.
French, Anthony, res cor 3d and Alby.
French, Mrs S, res cor 9th and Easton.
Frey, George, works for Hayner, res Main, nr State.
Frick, C H, Ins. Agt., res cor Spring and State.
Fries, T., Prop'r Empire House. 3d, e State, res same.
Fritch, Julius, (Fritch & Koch) res same.

FRITCH & KOCH, (Julius Fritch, C. Koch,) Meat Market and dealers in Fresh Salt and Dried Meats, Hams, Lard, Bacon, Sausage, etc. Also dealers in Live Stock, Wool, Hides and Tallow, s. s. 2d, w. Oak.

Fry, Mrs. C., res s s 2d. e George.
Fuchs, Mrs Mary, (Kuhn & Fuchs) res same.
Fuller, Augustus, baker, res n s 8th, w George.
Fuller, Gus, baker, Daniels. Bayle & Co., res 2d
Fuller, O. L, baker, res n s 2d, w George.
Fuller, L H, marble yard, n s 4th, w Belle. res State, w Prospect.
Funger, Frank, lab., F Shelly.
Funk, Ildo A, book-keeper, bds Summit, e Prospect.
Funk, S B, book-keeper, res Summit, e Prospect.
Funke, Herman, warper, Woolen Mill, res cor 7th and Belle.
Funke, Simon, lab, res cor 6th and Cherry.

G

Gafney, James, lab, res Dry, n State.
Gaiser, John, (Berner & Gaiser) res 2d, e Market.
Galbally, Richard, glass blower, res Vine, n 2d.
Gallagher, Andrew, works Glass Works.
Gallagher, Jas, lab., bds T. Biggins.
Gallagher, John, lab, T Deitz, res 3d, cor Vine.
Galvin, James, mason, res s s 3d, e Walnut.
Gambrill, A H, Att. at Law, w s Belle.
Garde, B., stoves and tin-ware, cor State and 4th, res Hamilton, nr Belle.
Garde, Mrs., res Hamilton.
Garde, James, teamster, res Hamilton, nr Main.
Garene, Joseph, R, messenger, W. U. Telegraph, res 4th.
Gareen, John, basket maker, W Armstrong & Bro, bds William.
Garloch, Fred, farmer, res State road.

Garloch, John, farmer, res State road.
Garvin, J P, physician, s s Belle, s 4th, bds cor 3d and Market.
Gaskill, Sydney, box maker, res Monroe, w Madison.
Gaskins, F, machinist, Alton Ag. Works.
Gaskins, Wm S, clk, res Union, e Ridge.
Gates, Wm C. peddler, res Alby, n 10th.
Gaukrodger, Hartley, lab, res cor 19th and Market.
Gault, T J, (Kellenberger & Gault,) res same.
Gavan, Philip, teamster, res Piasa, nr 9th.
Geisel, Henry, stone cutter, res Belle, n 18th.
Gent, Andrew, shoe-maker, res Washington.
Geran, T B., res cor 4th and Henry.
Gerhardt, Wm., porter Blair & Atwood, res 7th, e Henry.
Gessert, George. miller, res e s Alby, s 2d.
Gibbons, Mrs. res e s Easton, s 11th.
Gibbons, James. lab., bds 1st, w Cherry.
Gibbons, Mrs. Mary, res e s Alby, n 9th.
Gibson, Robt, physician, n s 2d, w George, res same.
Gifford, F A, clk, bds Kight's restaurant.
Gihre, Mrs B, res n s 3d, e Ridge.
Giler, John, engineer. res cor 5th and Alby.
Gill, Jas, lab, F Shelly.
Gill, Mrs Jane, res Belle, n 11th
Gillmartin. Patrick. engineer, res s s 2d, e Henry.
Gillispie, Mrs Chas. res cor Park and William.
Gillies. Mrs Ann, res Alby, nr Railroad.
Gilman, I D & Co, (I D Gilman, Mary Wills) millinery, w s Belle.
    s 4th.
Gilman, I D; (I D Gilman & Co.) res same.
Ginter, Geo A. carp, M'II Boals, bds 2d, nr Oak.
Ginter, L, (Wheelock, Ginter & Martin) res cor 4th and Alby.
Ginther, Henry, lab, res s s Union, e Ridge.
Girbig. George. shoe-maker, res cor 4th and Plum.
Glaser, Michael, lab. res Piasa, nr 9th.

GLEN, A. J., Watch maker, all kinds of Watches, Clocks and Jewelry carefully repaired, s. s. 3d, nr. Piasa, res. s. s. 9th, w. Langdon.

Glen, A J, Jr, watch maker, A J, Glen, res same.
Glen, John. clk, Hollister & Co.
Gleich, Louis, machinist, Plow Works. res cor 2d and Spring.
Glynn, Pat. glass blower, bds cor 3d and Vine.

Goegen, Clment, cooper, res s s 3d, w Spring.
Goehringer, J, cigar maker, J A. Neininger, res Alby.
Gocken, Clements cooper, A Gundall, res 3d, e Ridge.
Goetz, Christian, gardener, res Liberty, n Pearl.
Goetz John F, boots and shoes, and notions 3d, Junction 2d, res same.
Goldie, James, moulder, Brunner & Duncan, res Easton, n 8th.
Gollmer, Adam, saddler, res n s 5th, e Spring.
Gollmer, Chas, works Soda Factory, res s s 3d, w Oak.
Gollmer, Mrs D. res n s 2d, e Henry.
Goodman, Andrew, blacksmith, J H Koehne, res Alby.
Goodwald, Emil, shoe-maker, J Ronshausen, res 1st.
Goodwin, Chas, carp, res s s 3d, w Walnut.
Gorman, Daniel, lab, res Hamilton.
Gorman, John, lab, res 1st, w Cherry.
Gormley, Jas, lab, res Elm, w Cliff.
Gosro, ——, mason, res Hampton, w Harrison.
Gossrau, R. books and stationery, 2d, w Ridge, res same.
Gottleb, Albert, cigar maker, J A Neininger, res Union.
Gottlob, Bernard, lab, res cor 6th and North.
Gottlob, Fritz, res n s 2d, e Spring.
Gottlob, Wm, grocer, n s 2d. e Spring, res same.
Gottlob, Wm, cigar maker, J A Neininger, res Union, nr Liberty.
Gottsleben, Lorenz, school teacher, res s s 6th, w Cherry.
Goudie, James, moulder, res cor 9th and Easton.
Gould, Edmund, brick-layer, bds Jason Bramhads.
Gould, J B. Agt. C. & A. Railroad, res cor 7th and Alby.

GOULDING, E. H., Dealer in Watches, Clocks and Jewelry, Silver ware, Spectacles, Fancy Goods, and Domestic Sewing Machines, cor. 3d and Piasa, res. cor. Prospect and Summit. Watches and Jewelry repaired.

Grady, Edward, lab, res s s 9th, w Henry.
Graff, Chas, painter, C Rodemeyer, res 4th, nr Ridge.
Grahling, John, lab, res n s 6th, e Oak.
Grassle, Henry, res William, n Park.
Gratian, Joseph, Organ builder, res cor 6th and Easton.
Graves, Mrs C, res Marshall.
Graves, Wm, res Washington, e Sq.
Gray, G, (Basse & Gray) res 7th, e State.
Gray, James, brick layer, res Mecnanic, s 8th.

Greding, Gustave, res s s 2d, e Henry.
Green, James, lab, res Alby, s 18th.
Green, Warren, lab, res e s Henry, s 4th.
Greenwood, F B, commission clk, res w s Henry, s 12th.
Greenwood, Mrs, res w s Belle, n 9th.
Gregory, James, brick moulder, T Corbit, bds same.
Grenceback, Henry, foreman Armstrong Bro.. res North Alton.
Griffin, Joseph, cooper, res Henry, n 3d.
Grigsby, B G. engineer, M. H. Boals. res Upper Alton.
Grimm, Michael. lab. res cor Hampton and Harrison.
Grisom, Wm, res s s 3d, e Langdon.
Grobber, Edward, lab, F. Shelly, res State.
Groblinghoff, Wm., res Bond. w William.
Grody, Mrs.. res 14th, w Langdon.
Groff, Philip, cooper. T & J Jun, res 6th. e Ridge.
Grossheim, George. lab, res n s 5th. e Ridge
Grossheim. J.. lab, Sweetser & Priest res cor 6th and Oak.
Grosheimer. ——, painter, Alton Ag. Works.
Ground, O B. (Collet & Ground) res Upper Alton.
Gruhn. Chas. shoe-maker. res Ridge. n 4th.
Grundee, Mrs Lizzie, res e s Alby, s 9th.
Guelich, Emil, physician. cor 3d and Henry, res same.
Guertler. Peter, clk. Fish & Walter. res cor Alby and 16th.
Gudell H. E.. grocer, cor 7th and Henry, res same.
Guiler. John, engineer. C. & A., res cor 5th and Alby.
Gundall, Adam, cooper. 2d, e Walnut res same.
Guy, Mrs. E., res s s 3d, w Ridge.

H

Haagen, Louis. general store, 30, 3d res cor State and 7th.
Haagen, L J., clk. L. Haagen. res same.
Haagen. Paul. clk., L Haagan, res same
Haars. Conrad, lab, res n s 5th, e Ridge.
Haas. Jacob, carp, res cor 5th and Cherry.
Habersberger, Frank, brush maker. res s s 5th, w Ridge.
Hack, Fred, harness maker, n s, 2d, e Spring, res same.
Hack, Peter, shoe maker, n s 2d, e Spring, res cor 3d and Oak.
Hack. Wm. (Wilhelms & Co,) res cor 3d and Oak.
Hackett, Patrick, lab. res 2d, w Spring.
Haff. John, carp, res cor Piasa and 7th.
Hagan, John, brick-layer, res Plank road, cor 20th.
Hagee, Wm P, clk, H W Chamberlain. bds St Charles Hotel.
Haight, E A. Principal District School No. 2, res Langdon, cor 11th.

Haight, Robt. Teacher School No. 2, res 5th, e Alby.
Hajek, Vincent, tailor, res n s 2d, e Vine.
Hale, Anthony, sawyer, res n s State, w Main.
Hale. John, sawyer, res Main, cor Jefferson.
Hale, Leo. works for Hayner, res n s State, e Madison.
Haley, John. brick-layer. res s s 3d, e Walnut.
Hall, Mrs Ann, res cor Easton and 4th.
Hall, Mrs Hester A, res cor Spring and 5th.
Hall, Theo, cooper, res s s 2d, e Henry.
Hall, Thos, carp, res s s 6th, nr Alby.
Halverson, John, lab, Plow Works, bds 4th, e George.
Hamill, Joseph, works for Topping Bros, res Maple, n Grove.
Hanahan, Mrs. Bridget, res Dry.
Hancock, H, shipping clk, Daniels, Bayle & Co., res 3d.
Hancock, Leonard, lab, res w s George, s 2d.
Hanemann. John, cigar maker, res cor 6th and Spring.
Hanker, Henry, packer Cracker Factory, res n s 3d, w Langdon.
Hanley, John res State, n 4th.
Hanley, John, lab, res Godfrey, w Cliff.
Hanley, John J, clk, J Curdie, res State.
Hanley, Mrs Mary, res State, n 4th.
Hanolt, August, painter, res n s 3d, w Ridge.
Hanson, Andrew, blacksmith, res 3d, w Market.
Hanson, Mrs M E, res cor 3d and George.
Hapgood, Chas. H, (Hapgood & Co.) res Prospect, s State.
Hapgood & Co., Plow manufacturers, Front.
Hapgood, Hutchins, foreman, Hapgood & Co, res 2d nr Langdon.
Hardgrove, John, lab, bds T Biggins.
Hardin, Morris, waiter, Thos. Knight, bds same.
Hardin, Mrs. Rebecca, res s s Union, w Ridge.
Harding, Robt H., plow maker, res s s 2d, w Langdon.
Harding, James H., blacksmith, res s s 2d, w Langdon.
Harding, John H., blacksmith, Plow Works, res 2d, nr Langdon.
Hardy, A. W., engineer. res Market. s 16th.
Hardy, Mrs. E., Teacher School No. 2d, res 9th.
Hardy, Miss Ida, Teacher School No. 3, res Alby.
Hardy, Isham, constable, res Spring, n State.
Hardy, I. E., physician, (Reg.) e s Belle, s 4th, res Alby, n 5th.
Hardy, I. J., engineer. res cor Meenanie and 8th.
Hardy, L., engineer, Daniels, Bayle & Co., res Market, n 14th.
Hardy, Miss Laura, Teacher School No. 2, res Alby.
Hardy, Wallace, confectioner, res cor 9th and Market.
Harms, Fred, tailor, A Brueggeman, bds State, s 3d.

Harms, Henry, tailor, bds State. bet 2d and 3d.
Harnatt, Morris, lab. res on the Hill. s Elm.
Harrington, Lewis, lab, bds n s 3d, w Market.
Harris, Benjamin B, foreman, Bridge Repairs, res 11th, nr Langdon.
Harris, B. W., engineer, res n s 5th, e Alby.
Harris, Mrs. Helen, res s s 5th, e Walnut.
Harris, Lewis, carp, res n s 10th, w Langdon.
Harris, Jas. L., book-keeper, Howe Machine Co., bds 6th, e Market
Harris, Wm., lab, res n s 3d, w Langdon.
Harrison, Miss Belle, Teacher School No. 5½, res Upper Alton.
Harrison, George, Insurance Agt., res Maple, s Franklin.
Hart, H. W., (Platt & Hart) res 7th, nr State.
Hart, H. W., Jr., Asst. book-keeper, A. H. Drury & Co., res cor
      7th and State.
Hart, John W., res n s 9th, w Market.
Hart, Joseph, works Mrs. E. C. Billings, bds same.
Hart, Saml., teamster, res n s 2d, e Vine.
Hart, Martin, lab. res s s 5th, e Spring.
Harting, ——, machinist, Alton Ag. Works.
Hartinett, Morris, fireman, F. Shelly.
Hartman, & Co., (Jacob Hartman, Conrad Kruse) groceries and
      feed, n s 2d, w Henry.
Hartman, Jacob, (Hartman & Co.) res same.
Hartman, Peter, Tobacco worker, res s s 3d, w Henry.
Hartman, Mrs. Matilda, res s s 3d, w Henry.
Hartmann, J. J., hardware, n s 2d, e Ridge, res same.
Harville, Lewis, grocer, res n s 5th, w Alby.
Harville, Mrs. S., grocer, s s 5th, e Market, res n s 5th, e Market.
Haskell, A. S. & W. A., physicians, n s 2d, e Market.
Haskell, A. S., (A. S. & W. A. Haskell) res Henry, cor Pleasant.
Haskell, W. A., (A. S. & W. A. Haskell) bds same.
Hastings, Jas. W., res Railroad, e Henry.
Hasting, Joseph H., saloon, cor 2d and Apple. res 3d, nr Plum.
Hastings, Thos., lab, res cor 8th and Alton.
Hathaway, Noel, res cor Henry and 12th.
Hauk, Fred, lab, res State.
Haven, Lawrence, lab, res cor State and Main.
Hawkins, Mrs., res 14th, w Langdon.
Hawkins, Mrs. R. W., res State, w 7th.
Hawkswell, Mary, res e s Market, s 2d.
Hawley, Andrew, Ag. Agt., res Bluff, s State.
Hawley, G. E., hardware, res cor 3d and Alton.
Hawver, James E., clk, res n s 2d, e Market.

HAYDEN, GEO. D., Machine Shop and Brass Foundry, w. s. Belle, bet. 4th and 5th, res. cor. Alby and 5th.

Hayden, Wm., res cor 10th and Alton.
Hayden, Thos., lab. bds T Biggins.
Hayes, James N., marble cutter. W. Flynn, bds Union Depot.
Hayes, John B., mason, res cor Union and Liberty.
Hayes, Samuel, butcher, res cor Union and Liberty.
Hayke, W., tailor, A. Brueggeman, res 2d.
Hayner, J. E., saw mill, County Road, res State.
Haywood, Jesse watchman, res cor Pearl and Diamond.
Haywood, Robt., painter, rooms n s 2d. e Henry.
Hazard, E. M., Traveling Agt., res cor 17th and Market.
Hazard, E. M., machinist, res cor 17th and Market.
Heckler, Adam, boot and shoe maker, 2d, w Piasa.
Heffernan, Jas., lab, res Wharf, s State.
Hefner, Jos., painter, res w s Ridge. n 6th.
Hellrung, Henry, brick yard, res e s Oak, s 6th.
Held, Mrs. res s s 3d, w Ridge.
Hellrung, Mrs. M., res s s 6th. w Cherry.
Hellrung, Peter, peddler, res w s Ridge n 6th.
Heide, Henry, res n s 2d, e George.

HEMKEN, GERHARD, Saloon, keeps the choicest brands of Liquors, Wines and Cigars, the best and coolest Lager Beer, always on draught. Free lunch every morning. Call in and see him, cor, 2d and Langdon, res. same.

Henckell, Theo., dry house foreman, Dausman & Drummond, res 2d, nr George.
Hendrich, John, lab, res Oak, n 2d.
Hendrich, Joseph, works F. Shelly, res n s 6th, e Oak.
Hendrich, Mrs. Mary, res Oak, n 2d.
Hendrick, Rev. John, Pastor Cumberland Presbyterian Church, res 14th, w Langdon.
Heneck, Chas., printer, Alton Banner, res cor 6th and Walnut.
Hendy, James, policeman, res w s Ridge, n 6th.
Henry, Chas., baker, G. Kaeser, bds Empire.
Henry, James, mason, res Belle, n 20th.
Henry, John, lab, F. Shelly.
Henry, Jos., lab, F. Shelly.

Henry, Mrs. S., res Washington, e Pleasant.
Herb, ——, Pastor Baptist Church, res Easton, n 6th.
Herb, C. A., general store, cor Washington and 3d, res same.
Herb, Jacob, clk, C. A. Herb, res same.
Herb & Meyers, (Wm. Herb, H Meyers) res same.
Herb, Wm., (Herb & Meyers) res same.
Herman, Joseph. saloon, Junction 2d and 3d, res 3d, nr Junction 2d.
Hermann, G., blacksmith. res n s 4th, e George.
Herring, Moses, teamster, M. H. Boals, res Alley, bet 2d and 3d.
     e Cherry.
Herrmann, B., plasterer, res cor 7th and Henry.
Herrmann, J. P., general store. cor Ridge and 2d, res 3d, w Ridge.
Heslinger, J., cooper, res n s 3d, e Henry.
Hetzinger, John, lab, res Alley, bet 2d and 3d, e Cherry.
Heupel, Anthony, pressman, Perrin & Smith, res 3d, e State.
Heupel. A., bds Empire House.
Hewett, H. L., with Hapgood & Co., res cor 5th and Henry.
Hewit. F., Loan Broker, s s 3d, res Upper Alton.
Hibbard, Geo. H., works J. Crowe. bds same.
Hibbard, Mrs. M. E., res Prospect, n Summit.
Hickey, Michael, lab, res Dry, nr Main.
Hickey. John, lab, res e s Liberty, s 5th.
Hickey, Joseph, lab, res e s Liberty, s 5th.
Higgins Edward, lab, res s s 2d, e Langdon.
Higgins, E. J., lab, saw mill, res Cliff, s Elm.
Higgins, ——. moulder, Alton Ag. Works.
High, Saml. Y., carp, M. H. Boals, res 2d, nr Oak.
Highland, Mrs., res Alley, bet 2d and 3d, e Cherry.
Highwardon, LeRoy, waiter, Thos., Knight, bds same.
Hilary, Bro., Teacher Cathedral School, rooms same.
Hilker Henry, shoemaker, 2d, w Piasa, res George, n 6th.
Hill, Geo., cigar maker. C. Behrens, res 3d, nr Ridge.
Hill, Henry, lab, res e s Ridge, n 5th.
Hill, Wm., fisherman, res 10th w Henry.
Hill, W. H., salesman, A. H. Drury & Co., res State.
Hilt, Louis, trimmer, D. Miller, res Main, nr State.
Hinckell, Mrs, F., res s s 2d, w Langdon.
Hinckell, Theo., works, tobacco works, res s s 2d, w Langdon.
Hinderhahn, John, fireman, res n s 9th e Piasa.
Hindle, Edward, painter, res n end of North.
Hinterthir, August, carp, res Bloomfield, e Gold.
Hitchcock, Mrs, Sarah, res e s Henry, s 8th.
Hitt, James, H., lab, res State Junction, Main.

Hoaglan, D. S., clothing, s s 3d, res State.
Hoaglan, James, engine wiper, I. & St L. res R. R., e Spring.
Hoaglan, R. A., clk, St Charles Hotel, bds same.
Hoban, James, lab, res R. R. w Spring.
Hobart, S. S., carp M. H. Boals, res 2d, nr Oak.
Hobson, Wm., 2d, Miller, D. R. Sparks & Co., res Bluff s State.
Hodge, W. D., city engineer, res s s 3d, e George.
Hoefert, Fred, saloon, w s State, res same.
Hoefert, Fred, jr. clk, F. Hoefert, res same
Hoff, Michael, plasterer, res cor. Liberty and 6th.
Hoffman, Frank E., restaurant, Piasa s 3d, res Market.
Hoffman, Geo., blacksmith, res cor 7th, and Piasa.
Hoffmann, John, (Bauer & Hoffmann,) res 9th, e Henry.
Hoffmeister, F. W., (Seeley & Hoffmeister,) res 3d, nr Easton.
Hoffmeister,—— restaurant, res cor 3d, and Market.
Hoffmeyer, Mrs. Elizabeth, res cor Spring and 5th.
Hogan, Daniel, weigh master, res Belle, n 11th.
Hohen, Ed, painter, bds cor 4th and William.
Holden, Chas., jr., (Holden & Norton) res 4th, e George.
Holden, Chas., weigh master, res n s 6th w Langdon.
Holden, Geo. printer, Alton Telegraph, res 6th nr Langdon.
Holden, John, (Oldham & Holden) res n s 6th w Langdon.
Holden, Maurice, lab, res Wharf, s State.

HOLDEN & NORTON, (Chas. Holden, Jr., W. T. Norton) publishers, Alton Daily & Weekly Telegraph 4th.

Holden, Richard, (Auten & Holden) res cor 6th and Mechanic.
Holecker, Conrad, lab. res 2d e Junct. 3d.
Holl, George, cooper, res s s 2d. w Oak.
Holl, John, res s s 4th e Henry.
Holland, John, cooper, T H Proctor, res 3d, nr Cherry.
Holland, Wm. cooper, T. H. Proctor, res 3d. nr Cherry.
Holliday, C. W., Ass't P. M. cor res 17th and Market.
Hollster, E.,(Hollister & Co.) res cor 12th and Henry.
Hollster, & Co., wholesale dealers in Fruits &c., 4th e Bell.
Holt, John, engineer, Madison Mills, res 4th e Plum.
Homann, Nicholas, mason, res Hampton, w Harrison.
Hope, Alex. W., lawyer, res cor 4th and Easton.
Hope, Thos., physician, bds St Charles hotel.
Hope, Wm., brick-layer, res State, w Main.

Hopkins, Frank P., clk, Quigley, Hopkins & Co., res cor Alby and 5th.
Hopkins, Geo. K., (Quigley, Hopkins & Co.) cor 12th and Alby.
Hopkins, J. W., night operator, freight office C. & A. Railroad, res cor 7th and Piasa.
Hoppe, F. W., clk. H. B. Bowman, res cor 2d and Oak.
Hoppe, W. C., teamster, res cor 2d and Oak.
Hoppe, Mrs. W., res s s 5th, e Spring.
Hopson, Horace, works Wm. Smith, res same.
Horat, C., (Horat & Miessner) res State, n 4th
Horat, Clem, machinist, Plow Works, res State.
Horat & Miessner, (C. Horat, P. Miessner,) saloon, cor 2d and Piasa.
Horn, Patrick, lab, res 15th, w Alby.
Horneyer, Albert, painter, D. Miller, res North Alton.
Hosford, Miles, lab, C. & A. Round house.
Houghton, L. E., painter, res w s Easton, n 10th.
Houston, Adam, machinist, res 9th, e Belle.
Howard, Mrs. Ann, res w s Belle, s 18th.
Howard, A. F., engineer, res Main, nr State.
Howard, Mrs. Catharine, res n s 7th, e George.
Howard, Frank, blacksmith, C. Rodemeyer, bds Empire house.
Howard, Mrs. Jane, res Washington, e Pleasant.
Howard, John, lab, res Elm, w Cliff.
Howard, Mrs. Julia Ann, res State, nr Main.
Howard, Mrs. L., res e s Market, s 6th.
Howard, Solomon, works Wm. Smith, bds same.
Howard, Thos., sawyer, res Elm, w Cliff.
Howard, Wm., gardner, res cor 9th and Alby.

HOWE MACHINE CO., R. B. Shackelford, Manager, 4th, bet. Piasa and Belle.

Huddleston, Miss Alice, Teacher School No. 3, res Alby.
Huddleston, John, engineer, S. W. Farber & Co., res cor Market and 11th.
Hudgens, Jas. B., clk, res Bluff, w State.
Hudgins, John, drayman, res cor Pleasant and Washington.
Hudson, J. H., carp, res cor Pleasant and Washington.
Hudson, Miss Sarah, Teacher School No. 4, res Washington.
Hufker, Wm., clk. J. Wagner, bds same.
Hughes, Mrs. Mira, res s s 3d, e Ridge.
Hughes, Patrick, lab, res Market, n 10th.

Hugo. E. D., carp. and builder. w s Piasa, s 5th, res Henry, nr 3d.
Hull, James, farmer, res s s 6th, e Ridge.
Humphrey, Joseph, drayman, bds n s 2d, w Walnut.
Humphrey, Thos., sash maker. M. H. Boals. res 2d, nr Cherry.
Humpidge, W. H., clk, H. B. Bowman, bds cor 7th and Belle.
Hungerford, A. L., res cor 9th and Langdon.
Hunter, Henry, fireman. res cor Gold and Bloomfield.
Hunter, John, fireman, res w s Langdon, n 6th.
Hunter, Mrs. Rebecca, res Common.
Hunter. Smith, lab, res cor Gold and Bloomfield.
Hurtgen, John, blacksmith, C. Rodemeyer, bds Empire House.
Husemann, Gotlieb, upholsterer. res cor 4th and William.
Huskinson, Wm., Director C. & A. Railroad, res cor 9th and Piasa.
Hutchison, Mrs. Phebe, res Common.
Hutchison, Robt, works Glass Works, bds cor 3d and Vine.
Hutton, ——, lab, res cor Washington and Pleasant.
Hyndman, Robt., engineer, Woolen Mill, res 7th, w Piasa.
Hyndman. Thos., blacksmith, res Alby, n 16th.
Hyndman. Wm., carp, res Belle, n 14th.

I

Ingham, Mrs. Sina, sewing, res n s 5th, w Vine.
Inveen, A., carp. res w s Henry, s 8th.
Inveen, Miss Emma, Teacher School No. 2. res Henry.
Isach, E., wood worker, Alton Ag. Works.
Issak, Joseph, works Hanson & Co., bds Spring St. House.
Isenor. Chas., fireman. bds cor 7th and Piasa.
Ivy, Mrs. Catharine. res w s Belle, s 18th.

J

Jackel, George, clk, Wise, Blake & Johnston, res State Road.
Jackel, Mrs., res State Road
Jackson, Albert, sawyer, res on the Hill, s Elm.
Jackson, Wm., glass blower, res n s 5th, e Walnut.
James, George, hostler, A. Mathers, bds T. Biggins.
Janssen, Rev. J., Vicar General, Alton Diocese, res State, w 7th.
Jarrett, Joseph, Livery and feed stable, cor Easton and Front, res.
    2d, nr. George.
Jenkins, Richard, grocer, res Belle, n 14th.
Jerman, Wm , lab, res Piasa, n 16th.
Jett, Frank, lab. Daniels, Bayle & Co., res Upper Alton.
Job, Z. B., farmer, res cor 9th and Henry.

Joehl. Casper, diaryman, res n s 5th. w Oak.
Joehl, Jos., lab, F. Shelly.
Joesting, Adolph, baker. Mrs. M. Joesting, res same.
Joesting. Chas. L., works Tobacco Works, res cor 7th and Henry.
Joesting, F. W., (Joesting & Sachtleben,) res cor 8th and Henry.
Joesting, Mrs. Mary. confectionery, fruits. etc.. 11, Belle, res same.
Joesting & Sachtleben, (F. W. Joesting, Wm. Sachtleben,) clothing
     and dry goods, 16th, 3d.
Joesting, Wm., res Washington.
Joesting. Gustavus A., book-keeper, 1st Nat. Bank of Alton. res.
     8th, nr Langdon.
Johnisee, Mrs. Matilda. res 4th, e Langdon.
Johnson, Andrew J., grocer, Washington, e Pleasant, res same.
Johnson, Mrs. A., res cor Alby and 5th.
Johnson, Mrs. A.. millinery, s s 3d, e State. res same.
Johnson, Chas., carp, bds cor Grand Av. and State.
Johnson, C. B., clk, E. Pfeiffer. res Upper Alton.
Johnson, Mrs. E., res w s State, s 4th.
Johnson, Frank. works for Hanson & Co., bds cor 4th and George.
Johnson. F. M., brick yard, res Salu. cor Holman.
Johnson, G., lab. res Pearl, e North.
Johnson. George A., Traveling Agt., res e s George, s 5th.
Johnson, Rev. G. J.. Agt. Shurtleff College, res cor Union and
     Henry.
Johnson. Harrison, oil manufacturer, res Main. nr State.
Johnson, J., plumber. Alton Water Works, bds 3d, nr State.
Johnson. John. lab. res cor Beacon and State.
Johnson, John, flour packer. Collet & Ground. res Upper Alton.
Johnson, Rev. J. P.. Pastor Colored Baptist Church, bds I. H.
     Kelley.
Johnson, John S., clk, res e s George. s 5th.
Johnson. Loman, grinder. Plow Works, res cor 9th and Henry.
Johnson, Lewis. lab. res s s 7th, w Ridge.
Johnson, Mrs. Mary. res 7th, w Belle.
Johnson, Peter, wood worker, Plow Works, res cor 3d and Langdon.
Johnson. ——. baker. Wm. H. Keith, bds 2d, e Market.
Johnson, Reuben. miller, Collet & Ground, res Upper Alton.
Johnson, Richard. works Woolen Mill, res 7th, w Belle.
Johnson. Robt., Supt. Gas Works, res e s Belle. n 7th.
Johnson, Thomas, res e s George. s 5th.
Johnson, Wm., driver. Wm. H. Keith, res Henry, n 7th.
Johnston, Geo. A., (Wise, Blake & Johnston,) res George, n 5th.
Johnston. H. K., Sec. Alton Water Works Co.. res 4th. nr George.

Johnston, Stephen, clk, Wisc. Blake & Johnston, res George bet. 4th and 5th.

Johnston, W. H., teamster, res cor 7th and Henry.

Johnston, Wm., mason, res e s Liberty.

Johnstone, John, lab. Sweetser & Priest, res State.

Jones, Chas., works for Hayner, res n s 3d, w Market.

Jones, George, teamster, res n s State, w Main.

Jones, Miss Laura, Teacher School No. 2, res State.

Jones, Mrs. Lucy, res State, w Main.

JONES, WILLIAM, dealer in Staple and Fancy Groceries, Provisions, Dried Fruits, Canned Goods, etc., c. s. Belle, n. 14th, res. same.

Jones, R. C., Traveling Agt., res Bluff, s State.

Jun, Jacob, (T. & J. Jun) res cor 8th and Liberty.

Jun, Thos., (T. & J. Jun) res Cherry, n 2d.

Jun, T. & J. cooper, Bozza, e Washington.

Jungeblut, Henry, general store, n s 2d, e George, res same.

Justi, Andrew, res s s 2d, e Henry.

Juste, Mrs. Anna, millinery, 2d, c Henry, res same.

Jutting, H. W., general store, n s 2d, e Henry, bds Ridge s 5th.

K

Kaher, Gotlieb, lab, F. Shelly.

Kaeser, G., baker and confectioner, 2d, e Piasa, res same.

Kaeshamer, Anton, works Plow Works, bds Farmers' Home.

Kalm, Adam, barber, Piasa, n 2d, res Belle, cor 7th.

Kane, James, lab, res cor 9th and Alby.

Kane, Rev. M., Pastor St. Peter and Paul's Cathedral, res State, w 7th.

Karer, John. trimmer, C. Rodemeyer, res 4th, nr Ridge.

Kartchoff, John. teamster, res n s 5th, w Vine.

Kaschamer, Anton, blacksmith, Plow Works, res cor 3d and Spring.

Kaufel, E., teamster, res s s Union, e Ridge.

Kaylor, Wm., works Tobacco Works, res Langdon, s 3d.

Kearney, John, teamster, bds P. Sullivan.

Keber, Gottlieb, lab, res cor Henry and 6th.

Keefe, Martin, cooper, res Vine, n 2d.

Keefe, Mrs. S. E., dress maker, res e s Henry, n 3d.

Keefe, Timothy, lab. res Union, e Oak.

Keenan, Mrs. Ann, grocer, n s 2d, w Langdon. res same.

Keenan, Wm., tailor, res n s 2d, w Langdon.

Kehoe, Daniel, lab, res Belle, n 9th.
Kehoe, James, Sacristan, Cathedral, res State, w 7th.
Keiser, I. H., carp, res s s 5th, e Walnut.

KEITH, WM. H., *Baker and Confectioner, cor. 2d and Market, res. 8th, nr. Langdon. Fresh Bread, Pies, Cakes and Crackers in all varieties.*

Kellenberger, A. J., (Kellenberger Bros.) res Maple, nr Grove.
Kellenberger Bros., (E. P. & A. J. Kellenberger) crockery, 7, Belle.
Kellenberger, E. P., (Kellenberger Bros.) res cor 4th and Langdon
Kellenberger & Gault, (E. P. Kellenberger, T. J. Gault) Union Depot Hotel.
Kellenberger, H. G., clk, res Grove, w Common.
Kellenberger, Lewis, Ins. Agt., res cor Grove and Maple.
Kellenberger, Mrs. Louisa L., res bet Fletcher and Hampton. s e part of the city.
Keller, John, trimmer, res s s 2d, w Cherry.
Kelley, Henry, barber, w s Belle, n 3d, res Easton, n 5th.
Kelley, James, lab, res Alby, n 18th.
Kelley, John F. engineer, Alton Telegraph, res Hamilton.
Kelley, J. H., barber, res e s Easton, s 6th.
Kellogg, James clk, W Armstrong & Bro., res William, cor Park.
Kelley, Isaac, H., barber, w s State, n 2d, res 6th bet George & Alton.
Kelly, James, lab, res Monroe, nr Madison.
Kelley, Mrs. M., res Cliff, s Elm.
Kelley, W. E., barber, I. H. Kelley, res same.
Kemp, James, lab res s s 8th e Henry,
Kendall. T. S., lab, res Bloomfield, w Harrison.
Kendler, Jas., lab, F. Shelly.
Kennedy, B., grocer, cor 2d, and Cherry, res same.
Kerr, H. J., freight, Agt. C, & A. R. R., res cor Beacon, and Bond.
Kertkemp, Wm., bar-tender, res s s 9th e Henry.
Kervick, James, slate roofer, bds cor Pearl and Diamond.
Kerwin, John, tinner, res e s George, s 7th. .
Kerwin, Michael. lab, res Alby, cor 18th.
Kerwin, Wm., lab, res w s Alby, n 16th.
Kessler, Andrew, cigar maker, C. Behrens. bds Empire House.
Kidwell, Daniel, carp res s s 3d, e Henry.
Kidwell, James, bricklayer, res n s 5th w Vine.

Kienler, Joseph, barber, II. Sien, res cor 6th and Spring.

KILBOURNE, E. W., Agent, American Express Co. State, opp 3d, res Prospect, n Summit.

Kindler, Joseph, soloon, w s Belle, n 3d, res e s Belle, n 3d.
King, James, foreman, Press Room, Dausman & Drummond, res Belle. n 7th.
King, R. L., traveling agt Blair & Atwood, res Belle, s 7th.
Kinley, Ulrich, works, S. Wade, bds same.
Kinney, Lawrence, lab, bds P. Sullivan.
Kinney, Wm., lab, W. Armstrong & Bro.
Kinney, Wm., lab. F. Shelly.
Kirchner, Geo., shoemaker. bds Piasa, n 2d.
Kirwen, Margaret, res cor 9th and Alby.
Kizer, Mrs. Elizabeth, res s s Union, e Ridge.
Klasner, Joseph, lab, res s s 5th nr Oak.
Kleffner, Warner, stone mason, res Union, nr Walnut.
Kleinpeter, Mrs. Mary, res n s 5th w Ridge.
Kleinschnittger, Mrs. M. catholic books, e s Henry s 4th res same.
Klinchenger, John, machinist, Plow Works, res Henry.
Klinger, Fred, lab, res n s 5th w Oak.

KLUNK & WILLS, (W. L. Klunk, Jas. Wills) undertaking and carpentering, w s State, opp 3d.

KLUNK, W. L., (Klunk & Wills) res Prospect, bet Bond and Summit.

Klupfer, Gustavea, works, R. B. Smith, bds same.
Knecht, Theo., (Buff, Kuhl & Co.) res cor 2d, and Oak.
Knesal, J. L., cooper, res s s 3d, w Spring.
Kniesel, John, A. cooper, A. Gundell, res 3d, e Ridge.

KNIGHT, THOS., Pro'p Knights Restaurant, 2d, e Piasa, res same.

Knight, Murray, cook, T. Knight, bds same.
Knight, Mrs. Nellie. res e s Easton, s 7th.

KNIGHTS, RESTAURANT, Thos. Knight, Pro'p on the Hotel plan $2.50 per day. meals at all hours, first class sleeping rooms for Guests. Ales, Wines and cigars furnished on call. Good Sample Rooms,, 2d, opp New Post Office.

Koch, C. (Fritch & Koch) res 2d, nr Henry.
Koehne, Henry. wagon maker, J. H. Koehne, res same.
Koehne, John, H. wagon maker. e s Belle, n 4th res Alby.
Koehne. Louis. helper. J. H. Koehne. res same,
Kolb, George, Plasterer, res s s 8th e Henry.
Kook, —— tobacco presser, bds State, bet 2d, and 3d.
Koop, Jacob. saloon, cor Ridge, and 5th res same.
Kortkamp, Wm., clk, J. Lohr, res nr Henry.
Krabbe, Fred, bds Empire House.
Kramer, John, lab, E. Feldwisch, bds same.
Kranz, Henry. cigar maker, bds Spring St House.
Kreyling, Wm., baker, 2d, n Ridge, res same.
Kruse, Conrad, (Hartman & Co.) res Union.
Kuhl, Max, (Buff Kuhl & Co.) res St Louis.
Kuehn, C. grocer, State, w Prospect, res same.
Kuhn, Mrs. Caroline, res n s 3d, e Henry.
Kuhn, E., (Kuhn & Fuchs) res cor 5th and Walnut. '
Kuhn, Jacob, res cor 5th and Walnut.
Kuhn, John, porter, Dausman & Drummond, res cor Henry.
Kuhn & Fuchs, (E. Kuhn, M. Fuchs)meat market. s s 2d, e Henry.
Kunsch. Albert, porter, res s s 2d, e Alton.

L

Laird, John, res w s Belle, s 7th.
Laird, J. P., jr., clk, E. Marsh, jr, res Belle. n, 6th,
Lake, Jonn, lab, res cor 7th anc Mecnanic,
Lampert, B., cigar maker, res 2d, e Spring,
Lampert, John K. dry goods, res cor Washington, and Bozza.
Lampert, Jos., I. clk, res 4th, bet George and Langdon.
Lampert, Michael, carp res w s Cherry, 2d.
Lanagan, R., lab, bds T. Biggins.
Landergan, John, lab, res 4th e Langdon.
Landre, Henry, lab, res s s 5th w Walnut.
Lane, Gilbert, clk, bds Knights Restaurant.
Lane, Henry. clk, Auten & Holden. res n s 2d, w Langdon.
Lang, James K. Miller, res cor 3d, and Henry.
Langten, J., boarding house, Front, w Alton, res same.
Langton. Mrs. H. res Belle, s 19th.
Lannarth, Henry. machinist, Plow Works, res 6th, e Cherry.
Landt, J. P., carp res e s Belle, s 4th.
Lapelle, Mrs. Louisa, res Market, n 19th.
Lapelle, Zebidee, lab, res Market, n 19th.
Largent, C. T., clk, R. T. Largent, res same.

Largent. Isaac, B, carp res cor 11th and Langdon.
Largent, Richard, res cor 11th and Langdon.
Largent, R. T., agent Keokuk Northern line packet office, 5.
   Levee, res 4th n State.
Larkin, Andrew, lab, res Wharf, s State.
Lathy, J. B., supt Alton, Agricultural Works.
Lau, Chas., weaver, Woolen Mill.
Laughlin, T. B , carp res William n Park.
Laux. Henry. cooper, res n s 3d, e Langdon.
Lavenue, Arche, 2d, foreman, Dausman & Drummond, res 2d, e
   Alton.
Lawless, John, moulder, res s s 2d. e George.
Lawless, Peter, lab, res Piasa, n 16th.
Lea, Chas., see Alton Ag. Works, res State w Bluff.
Leahy, John. lab, res 5th e Langdon.
Leary, Edward, yard master, C. & A. res w s Belle n 18th.
Lee, M. I., (M. I. Lee & Co.) res State, n 4th.
Lee, M. I., & Co., books and stationery, 20 3d.
Lee, Sol, cook, res e s Easton s 6th.
Leech, Chas , S. clk, Auten & Holden, res 9th nr Langdon.
Leffler, Chas., teamster, H. Neermann, res 3d, w Henry.
Legg, D. B., glass blower, res s s 2d, w Oak.
Legler, Fred, lab, F. Shelly.
Legler, Mrs. Mary, res cor 6th and Ridge.
Lehman, S., (B. Runzi & Co.) res same.
Lehmann. Valentine, blacksmith, J. Ammann, bds same.
Lehne, Heinrich, clk, Auten & Holden. res 2d, nr Langdon.
Lehne, Theodore, grocer, 2d, e Piasa, res Bond. nr William.
Lempke, Henry, machinist, Plow Works, res 2d, e Langdon.
Lempke, Herman, plow maker, res n s 2d, e Langdon.
Lempke, John, machinist, Plow Works, res 2d, e Langdon.
Lempke, John, works Plow Works, bds Farmers' Home.
Lenhard, Ernst, clk, F. Bandewiede, bds same.
Lenhardt. Henry, butcher, Herb & Meyer, bds 2d, e Henry.
Lenna, August, machinist, Plow Works, res cor 3d and Langdon.
Lennand, Patrick, glass blower, Glass Works.
Leonard, Henry, machinist, Plow Works, res cor 6th and Cherry.
Leresche, Louis, res n s 4th, e Henry.
Levis, E., Supt. Ill. Glass Co., res State, cor Spring.
Levis, G. M., book keeper, Ill. Glass Co., res cor Spring and State.
Levis, J , shipping clerk, Glass Works.
Lewis, C. W., scroll sawyer, M. H. Boals, res Upper Alton.
Lewis, James, A. W., foreman, Tobacco Works, res n s 2d. e Alton.

Leyhe, Henry, Captain Spread Eagle, res n s 3d, e Alton.
Leyser, Henry, (Leyser & Bro.) res same.
Leyser, John, wholesale confectioner, n s 3d, w Belle, res same.
Links, Jacob, clk. bds n s 2d, w Henry.
Linsig, Geo., (II. G. Vasel & Co.) res cor 3d and Spring.
Linsig, ——, werks for Hayner, res Alley, bet 2d and 3d, e Spring.
Little, James, lab, res cor Oak and 3d.
Ljumbing, August, wood worker, Plow Works, res cor 3d and
    Langdon.
Loarts, George, grocer, 2d, w Ridge, res 5th.
Lock, John, glass blower, bds Spring St. House.
Loer, Emil, lab, F. Shelly.
Loer, George. engineer, res State, nr Cliff.
Loer, John. boot and shoe maker. w s Belle, n 3d, res Narrow.
Logan, John, res n s 10th, w Langdon.
Logan, W. C., printer, Perrin & Smith, bds Pleasant.
Lohr, Joseph, saloon, e s Belle, n 4th, res 5th, nr Cherry.
Long. D. J., cooper, s s 4th, w Henry, res Alley, bet 3d and 4th,
    w Henry.
Long, Geo., works Planing Mill, res n s 3d, e Langdon.
Long, Mrs. Jane, res n s State, e Cliff.
Long. Patrick, lab, res s s 7th, w Henry.
Loos, Adolf. boot and shoe maker, s s 2d, e Henry, res same.
Lorch, Jacob, messenger, Alton Bank, res s s 3d, e George.
Lorge, George. grocer, res s s 5th, e Oak.
Lotee, Saml., carp, res s s 3d, w Oak.
Lovejoy, Alph C., packer, D. R. Sparks & Co., bds Empire House.
Lowe, H., painter, C. Obermueller, res Upper Alton.
Lowe, John. carp, res cor 10th and Langdon.
Lowe, Wai en. Ins. Agt., res cor 10th and Langdon.
Lowe, Sylvester, carp, res cor Langdon and 10th.
Lowry, D., lab, res Washington.
Lucas, Jacob, fireman. res e s Easton, s 6th.
Luce. James, lab. res e s Alby, n 9th.
Lucid, Mrs. Kate, res cor 10th and Belle.
Luethner, Matthew. marble cutter, res n s 5th, w Vine.
Luft, Geo., blacksmith, e s Belle, n 4th, res cor Ridge and 4th.
Luft, Jacob, shoe maker, res w s Ridge, s 5th.
Luly, Henry, harness maker, bds n s 7th, e George.
Luly, John, clk, A. Clifford, res n s 7th, e George.
Lutz, Henry, stair builder. M. H. Boals, res 3d, nr Ridge.
Lynch, Patrick, lab. res Dry, n State.
Lyons, Cornelius, lab, res s s 4th. e Henry.

Lyons, Mrs. Mary, res s e cor 8th and Henry.

Mc

McArdle, James. tailor, res n s 3d, e Henry.
McAvoy, Daniel. lab, res s s 6th, w Ridge.
McAvoy, Mrs. Margaret, res cor 20th and Belle.
McCarty, Mrs. Eliza, res w s Alby, nr 9th.
McCarty, Mrs. Johanna, res Henry, n 3d.
McCarty, John, lab, res Dry, n State.
McCarty, Mrs. Mary, res s s 2d, e Henry.
McCarty, Michael, assorter, Dausman & Drummond, res Dry, nr
    State..
McCarty, Michael. lab, res w s Alby, e 5th.
McCarty, Michael, lab, res Washington, e Pleasant.
McCarty, Thomas, lab. res w s Alby, s 5th.
McCarty, Thos.. machinist, Plow Works, res Liberty.
McClure, Thos., carp. res cor 8th and Langdon.
McClure, Samuel. clk, Perley & Woodman, res cor 8th and Langdon.
McCorkle, Samuel, printer. Alton Telegraph, res 3d, nr Alby.
McGinnis, John, res cor 3d and Market.
McCorkle, Thos., printer, Alton Telegraph, res 3d, nr Alby.
McCollum, Mrs. Ellen, res s s 3d, e Oak.
McCortor, Mrs. H. J., res 7th, w Belle.
McDonaugh, J P., machinist. res cor 8th and Alby.
McDonnell, G. L., mail contractor. res Spring, n State.
McDonnell. Patrick, lab, res s e cor 8th and Henry.
McElligott. Roger, lab, res cor 19th and Alby.
McElroy, Daniel, fireman, Gas Works, res Belle, n 7th.
McElroy, Thos., tailor, H. C. G. Moritz, bds T. Biggins.
McFetridge, James, lab, res Hampton, w Harrison
McGee, Chas., merchant tailor, cor Belle and 8th, res Market, n 10th.
McGee, John, fireman, res w s Market, n 10th.
McGee, Luke, lab. res s s 6th, e Liberty.
McGinnis, John. F., Att. at Law, cor 3d and Piasa, res State.
McGinnis, Patrick. drayman, res cor 3d and Market.
McGinnis, Wm., drayman, res cor Market and 3d.
McGinty, John, lab, res cor 10th and Easton.
McGovern, Patrick, lab. bds cor 5th and Piasa.
McGowan. Hannah, res cor 7th and Piasa.
McGrath, D., saloon, w s Belle, res same.
McInerney, Austin. clk, T. McInerney, res same.
McInerney, Austin, lab res Common, n Sq.
McInerney, Matthew, lab, res s s 6th. e Alby.

McInerncy, Thos.. grocer, e s Belle. nr 6th. res Common.
McInerney, Timothy, (McInerney & Weaver) res Middletown.
McInerncy & Weaver. (T. McInerncy, J. H. Weaver) carpenters and
  builders, s s 4th, w Belle.
McKee, John M.. cooper, res Union. c North.
McKenna, James, moulder, res n s 3d, w Ridge.
McKenna. ——, machinist, Alton Ag. Works.
McKenna, Michael, engineer, res cor Wall and William.
McKenna. Patrick, lab. res w s Easton, n 8th.
McKinncy. A. R., (McKinney & Fischbach) res Grove, bet Common
  and Liberty.
McKinney & Fischbach. (A. R. McKinney, J. Fischbach) Gen'l
  Insurance, s s 3d.
McKissock, John, engineer. res cor 17th and Piasa.
McLain. Lewis, blacksmith, res State. nr Cliff.
McLanghlin. Mrs. Ann, res Liberty, n 8th.   ·
McLaughlin, Mrs. M., res Railroad. w Spring.
McLaughlin, Pat., wrapper, Dausman & Drummond, res Liberty,
  n 9th.
McLaughlin, Thos., lab. res Gold.
McNeil, David, works Oil Factory, res w s Market, n 3d.
McNeil, J., works C. D. Caldwell, bds same.
McNulty, James, Register, office City Hall, res Beacon.
McPike, Henry C., res cor 4th and Easton.
McPike, II. G., Insurance and Real Estate, cor 2d and Market,
  res cor 20th and Alby.
McPike, J. II., Agt. Wheeler & Wilson Sewing machine, cor 2d
  and Market, res cor 20th and Alby.
McQuatters, Henry, lab, res Langdon, s 4th.

M

Machin, Jos., clk, C. M. Crandall, bds 3d, nr Market.
Machin, J. B., fireman, C. & A., res n s 3d, w Alby.
Mack, Edward, carp, bds cor 7th and Piasa.
Mack, Jas., machine feeder, Dausman & Drummond, res 2d nr.
  Henry.
Mack, James, glass blower, Glass Works.
Mack, Walter, lab, res Alley, bet 2d and 3d, c Cherry.
Mackey, Mrs. Jane, res s s 2d, c Langdon.
Mackle, Wm., gardener, res Common, nr Railroad.
Macrdian, Rudolph, barber, w s State, res Oak, nr State.
Maguire Jacob, lab, res c s Market, n 5th.
Maguire, Mrs. Jane, res c s Henry, n 3d.

Maguire, ——, painter, Alton Ag. Works.
Maguire, Mrs., works Mrs. N. C. Blair, bds same.
Maguire, Mrs. Margaret, res w s Belle, n 9th.
Maguire, Mrs. Virginia, res State, e Bond.
Mahan, Peter, baggage master. C. & A., res Henry.
Mahan, Wm. T., carp, bds n s 2d, w Alby.
Mahon, Peter, boots and shoes, e s Henry, n 3d, res same.
Mahoney, M., boots and shoes, e s Belle, n 5th, res same.
Mahony, John, lab, res Monroe, nr Madison.
Maloney, Thos., blacksmith, W. Richardson, bds Empire House.
Mann, Jabez, works C. & A. Railroad, res Alby, n 16th.
Mann, James, foreman of Water Stations, res cor 16th and Alby.
Mann, ——, painter, res e s Easton, s 11th.
Manning, ——, wood worker, Alton Ag. Works.
Marion, Edward, bds Empire House.
Marmon, John L., tinner, res n s 5th, e Spring.
Marnell, James, lab, res 10th e Belle.
Marnell, John, lab, res 10th. e Belle.
Marnell, Michael, porter Dausman & Drummond, res cor 10th and Belle.
Maroney, Timothy, lab, bds T. Biggins.
Marosick, Frank, lab, F. Shelly.
Marsh, E., Prest. Alton Nat. Bank, res Henry, n 14th.
Marsh, E., Jr., druggist, cor 3d and Belle, res Upper Alton.
Marshall, Thos., fireman, res south end Bluff.
Martin, Mrs. Catharine, res Railroad, e Henry.
Martin, Geo., works Glass Works.
Martin, John, peddler, res Oak, s 3d.
Martin, Mrs. Mary, res Oak, s 3d.
Martin, Wm., waiter, Thos. Knight, bds same.
Martin, W. W., (Wheelock, Ginter & Martin) res cor 6th and Henry.
Mason, Edward, lab, res Bloomfield, w Harrison.
Massey, J. C., carp, res cor 4th and Piasa.
Mather, Andrew, Livery, Piasa, n 3d, res Market, n 4th.
Mather, Richard M., painter, res Marshall.
Mathers, Dick, painter, Alton Ag. Works.
Mather, J., wood worker, Alton Ag. Works.
Mathews, H. S., hides, etc., res cor 11th and George.
Martiar, ——, works Wheelock & Ginter, bds Ridge, s 5th.
Matter, John, rooms 2d, opp. City Hall.
Matter, Philip, res n s 3d, w Ridge.
Matter, Rudulph, chair caner, bds cor 2d and Walnut.
Matthews, A. J., printer, Democrat Office, bds Empire House.

Maul, Anton, watchman, res s s 3d, e Ridge.
Maul, Jacob, works I. & St. L. Depot, res n s 3d, w Walnut.
Maul, John, sawyer, M. H. Boals, res 3d, nr Oak.
Maul, Jos., barber, H. Sien, res 3d, nr Spring.
Maul. Paul, works for Hayner, res n s 3d, e Spring.
Maupin & Bates, (J. H. Maupin, Jr., Z. Bates) fruits, etc., n s 3d,
    e Belle.
Maupin, G. H., (J. H. Maupin & Son) res cor 8th and Alton.
Maupin, J. H., Jr., (Maupin & Bates) res Market, n 5th.
Maupin, J. H., Sr., (J. H. Maupin & Son) res cor Alton and 8th.
Maupin, J. H., & Son. (J. H. Maupin, Sr., G. H. Maupin) grocers.
    cor 4th and Belle.
Maurer, Philip, lab, res n s 3d. w Ridge.
Maxfield, Oscar, painter, res cor 8th and Alton.
Maxfield, Ropt. H., works Woolen Mill, res cor 18th and Belle.
Maxwell, Mrs., res s s 3d, e Oak.
Maxwell, Mrs. Mary, bds Market, s 3d.
Mays, Henry, lab, res cor 10th and Market.
Meetroth, John, drayman, res s s 6th, e Cherry.
Meehan, Mrs. Catharine, res w s Belle, n 7th.
Meehan. John. grocer, n s 3d, e State, res Belle.
Meenach, Mitchell, res cor Plum and 3d.
Meirs, H., machinist, Alton Ag. Works.
Meisenheimer, John, lab, T. Corbit, bds same.
Meisenheimer, Philip, lab, Alton Ag. Works, res n s 6th, e Liberty.
Meisner, Adolph, harness maker, T. Mulligan, res Hunterstown.
Melcher, Fred, mason, res s s 3d, w Ridge.
Melcher, John, printer, Alton Banner, res 3d, nr Henry.
Menard. Jos. L., cooper, Armstrong Bros., res Upper Alton.
Menn, Felix, painter, C. Rodmeyer, res Easton, n 10th.
Merkely, Joseph, gardener, res nr Cemetery, n s.
Messerschmitt, Mrs. Elizabeth, grocer, res cor Cherry and 5th.
Metzger, Mrs. R. res n s 3d, w Ridge.
Meyer, Frank, works brewery, res cor 16th and Market.
Meyer, Frederick, stone cutter, res cor 17th and Alby.
Meyer, George works, Tobacco Factory, res Russell.
Meyer. H., publisher Alton Banner, 4th e Belle, res cor 6th and
    Walnut.
Meyer, Henry, machinist res n s 5th e Oak.
Meyer, John, works, A. S. & W. A. Haskell, bds Empire House.
Meyer, John, A. carp res cor Vine and 5th.
Meyers, Henry, works, A. S. Haskell, bds same.
Meyers, Henry, (Herb & Meyers) res s s 2d, e Henry.

Meyers, Joseph, works, Holister, res 7th e State.
Michael, Peter, brakeman, res n s 2d, w Vine
Michael, Peter, brewer, B. Runzi & Co. res 16th nr Easton.
Middleton, T. justice of the peace, Belle, n 3d, res 2d, e Alby.

MIEDEL, JOHN, Prop'r Old Farmer's Home, cor 2d, and Spring, res same,

Miessner, P., (Horat & Miessner) res cor Spring and 3d.
Mihsel, Geo., saloon, n s 3d, e State res same.
Millen & Beall, (Jas. Millen, C. B. Beall) blacksmiths, e s Belle s 6th.
Millen, A. C. clk, A. Ryrie, res 4th bet Langdon and George.
Millen D., (J. & D. Millen) res Oak.
Millen Jas., (Millen & Beall) res Dry, nr State.
Millen, J. & D., plow manufacturers, cor 4th and State.
Millen, John, (J. & D., Millen) res s s 9th, w Langdon.
Millen, J. C., grocer, and pork packer, 4th e Langdon, res 4th e George.
Millen, Robt., plow maker, res n s 9th, e Belle,
Miller, Adam, works, Glass Works, res 19th, w Market.
Miller, Andrew, lab, res Pearl, e North.
Miller, D., carriage manuf'g, cor 5th Belle, res 7th, nr Easton.
Miller, Fred, cooper, res s s 6th w Cherry.
Miller, Gabriel, res cor 9th and Easton.
Miller, George, brakeman, res cor Main and Hamilton.
Miller, Henry, lab, T. Dietz, res Union.
Miller, Herman, I. conductor, res e s Market, s 5th.
Miller, James, blacksmith, res Dry, nr Main.
Miller, Jesse, Glass Works. res 19th w Market.
Miller, Jonathan, carp, res w s Alby, s 9th.
Miller, Jos., foreman, F. Shelly, res n s 6th e Oak.
Miller, Mrs. Margaret, res s s 8th e Alton.
Miller, —— works, Wheelock & Ginter, bds e s Ridge, s 5th.
Millison. Thos., lab, res 1st, cor Cherry.
Milnie, Mrs. Anna E. res Alby, n 18th.
Milnie, Harry, clk, Seely, & Hoffmeister, res Alby, n 18th.
Milnor, Auten & Co. (Geo. C. & C. W. Milnor, Aaron O. Auten, Wm. A. Morrison) Hardware and Ag. Imp., 13 n s 3d.
Milnor, C. W., (Milnor, Auten & Co) bds Knights Restaurant.
Milnor, Geo. C., (Milnor, Auten & Co) res Spring, n State.
Milnor, —— carp Wheelock, Ginter & Martin.
Mischell, John, bds Empire House,

Minick, Elles, works, Glass Works.
Minick, Geo., works Glass Works.
Mitchell, J. C., marble cutter, res Alby, nr 5th.
Mitchell, Leander, res cor Summit and Prospect.
Mitchell, P., grocer, e s Belle, res 7th nr Belle.
Mitchell, Mrs. res w s Belle, n 7th.
Mitchell, W. II., Pres. 1st Nat., Bank of Alton, res Chicago.
Mohr, Andrew, carp, res Green.
Mohr, George, stone cutter, res Meenanie, s 8th.
Mold, George, lab, res n s 3d, w Ridge.
Moloy, Mrs. M., res State, s 7th.
Molt, John, foreman, Alton Banner, res 3d, nr Henry.
Monahan, Jonn, section boss, res Alby, n 20th.
Monks, Andrew, lab, res Belle, n 16th.
Montgomery, Columbus, white washer, res n s 3d, w Ridge.
Montgomery, Mrs. Eliza, res cor 7th and Easton.
Montgomery, Jas. C., printer, Perrin & Smith, res cor 7th and
    Easton.
Montgomery, John, book keeper, Woolen Mill, res cor 7th and
    Easton.
Montgomery, Thos., clk, R. De Bow & Co. res cor 7th and Easton.
Montross, C. A. res cor 9th and Langdon.
Montross, O. W., machinist, G. D. Hayden res cor 9th and Lang-
    don.
Mook, Philip, book keeper, Alton National Bank, res cor 3d, and
    Langdon.
Mooney, Patrick, lab res cor 16th, and Alby.
Mooney, Thos., helper, res cor 17th and Market.
Moore, John, fireman, Glass Works.
Moore, Wm., lab, T. Dietz, bds Spring St House.
Moran, Bernard, lab. res s s 6th e Liberty.
Moran, George, tinner, S. & W. Pitts, res Elm.
Moran, Jas., tinner, S & W. Pitts, res Elm.
Moran, John, lab, res Elm, w Cliff.
Moran, Wm., silver plater, e s State, s 3d, res William.
Morgan, Jas., res State, cor Oak.
Morick, Adam, shoemaker, res cor Ridge and 5th.
Morick, Chas., shoemaker, res cor Ridge and 5th.

*MORITZ, H. C. G., Merchant Tailor, and dealer
in Gents', Youths' and Boys' clothing and furnishing goods. All goods sold by the yard, cut
out free of charge. cor 3d and State, res cor
Madison and Monroe.*

Morrisey, Ed., lab, res Godfrey, w Cliff.
Morrisey, James. drayman. res cor 14th and Belle.
Morrison. Rev. A. P.. Pastor 1st Methodist Church, res s s 6th. w Alby.
Morrison, Mrs. P., res n s 5th. c Spring.
Morrison, Wm. A.. (Milnor. Anten & Co.) res State.
Moses. John, works Plow Works, bds Spring St. House.
Moses, Wm., machinist, Plow Works, res cor 2d and Spring.
Motherway. Edward. teamster. res cor Main and Hamilton.
Motley. Thos.. teamster, res cor 19th and Alby.
Mozer, Chas., messenger, Am. Ex. Co., res cor 8th and Easton.
Mraseck. Frank, stone mason, res n s 2d, c Spring.
Mueller. Jacob. cooper, res cor 2d and Oak.
Mullen, Patrick, lab, res e s Liberty. s Union.
Mullen. Patrick, teamster, res s s 8th, w Henry.
Mulligan, T., harness and saddles, 2d, e State, res same.
Mulshanock, Thos. cooper. res s e cor Seminary Sq. and 6th.
Munger. Mrs. A. G., res State. c Beacon.
Munson, M. D.. cooper. T. H. Proctor, res Upper Alton.
Munson. James. brakeman, res s s 3d. c Ridge.
Munson, T., res cor 4th and Langdon.
Murphy, Mrs. Anna. res Bluff, s State.
Murphy, U. S., res cor 14th and Henry.
Murphy. W. A., reporter. Alton Telegraph, res cor 13th and Langdon.
Murphy, Mrs. Bridget, res s s 4th, c Henry.
Murphy & Co.(Jos. Murphy.C. Schreiber) meat market e s Belle, n 4th.
Murphy, Daniel, lab, res Russell.
Murphy, Dennis. clk, bds cor 7th and Piasa.
Murphy, D. J.. clk, H. B. Bowman, res cor 7th and Piasa.
Murphy, Jos., (Murphy & Co.) res 3d, e Washington.
Murphy, Leonard, teamster, res Alby. s 18th.
Murphy, M., glass blower, Glass Works.
Murphy, Michael, lab, res 19th, e Alby.
Murray, Chas., A., Real Estate, and Insurance, cor 2d and Market,
    res cor 2d and Easton.
Muwnex, Mrs. Mary, res e s Alby, n 9th.
Myers, Mrs. Mary, res w s Alby, s 6th.

N

Nagle, Adam, lab, res Jefferson, w State.
Nagle, F., saloon, cor Bozza and Washington, res n s 3d, e Henry.
Nagle, Richard, engineer, res 16th, cor Market.
Nathan. Barnett. res e s George, nr 8th.
Nantge, ——. lab, res s s 3d, w Ridge.
Neary, Roger, pressman, Dansman & Drummond, res Piasa, n 2d.

NEERMANN, A.. Upholsterer, and Dealer in Carpets, Oil Cloths, Wall Paper and Window Shades, also Manufacturer of Mattresses, s. s. 3d, res. same.

Neerman, Henry, bakery, n s 2d, w Henry, res same.
Neff, Alfred, painter, res Washington, c Sq.
Neff, Mrs., res Washington, c Sq.
Neininger, John, bds Empire House.
Neininger, J. A.. cigars and tobacco, Piasa, n 3d, res cor Union and Liberty.
Nelson, Mrs. Mary, res Hampton, nr Cyrus.
Nemier, Henry, res s s 5th, c Cherry.
Nett, Peter, moulder. Brunner & Duncan. res cor 7th and Alton.
Nevins, Mrs. Kate, res Wharf, s State.
Nevins, John, lab, res Wharf, s State.
Newman, Barney, lab, res c s Henry, s 4th.
Newman, Chas., res w s Easton, s 12th.

NEWMAN, JAMES, Prop'r Centennial '76 Saloon, cor. Front and Market, opp. Union Depot, res. 2d, nr. George.

Newman, James, Sec. Ins. Co.. res w s Easton, s 12th.
Newman, Mrs. Minerva, res 7th, w Belle.
Newton, Chas., works Glass Works.
Newton, Chas., student, res Common.
Newton, Chas. W., carp., res Common.
Nichols, C. H., (F. K. Nichols, Son & Co.) res 12th.
Nichols, F. K., & Co. (F. K. H. L. & C. H. Nichols, Jonas Bray.) Woolen Mill, cor 7th and Belle.
Nichols, F. K., (F K. Nichols, Son & Co.) res 12th, cor Alton.
Nichols, Henry C.. (F. K. Nichols, Son & Co.) res 12th.
Nichols, Robt. L.. fireman, bds cor 12th and Alby.
Nichols, Stephen H., Traveling Agt., res c s Market, n 4th.
Nichols, William, traveling agt. Woolen Mill, bds cor 5th and George.
Nienhaus, Henry, carp., res cor 8th and Henry.
Nienhaus. H. D.. machine hand, M. H. Boals, res 3d, nr Oak.
Nisbett, J. P.. (T. P. Nisbett & Co.) res Court, c Alton.
Nisbett. T. P., (T. P. Nisbett & Co.) res Court, e Alton.
Nisbett. T. P., & Co., (T. P. & J. P. Nisbett) grocers, cor 2d and Market.
Noll, Wm.. wagon maker, res s s 5th, c Liberty.

NOONAN, ED., Justice of the Peace and General Insurance Agt., n. s. 3d, over C. B. Rhoads' Shoe Store.

Noonan, Dennis, coal dealer, res cor 3th and Market.
Noonan, John, res cor 7th and Liberty.
Noonan, John, teamster, res cor 8th and Market.
Noonan, M. J., Peddler, res 7th, w Belle.
Norton, Rev. A. T., res cor 10th and George.
Norton, Miss Belle, Teacher School No. 2, res George.
Norton, W. T., (Holden & Norton) res cor 10th and George.
Norris O. G., clk. and operator, C. & A. Freight office, bds cor 3d and Market.
Nott, Joseph, carp, res Diamond, n Pearl.
Nott, J. W., carp, res Diamond, n Pearl.
Nuss, Henry, grocer, cor 3d and Ridge, res same.
Nutt, Levi, miller, res cor 12th and Langdon.

O

O'Brien, Christ, lab, res Railroad, e Henry.
O'Brien, John, pressman, Dausman & Drummond, res Piasa, n 2d.
O'Brien, Thos., lab, res w s Alby, n 16th.
O'Connell, Philip, lab, bds T. Biggins.
O'Connor, James lab, res Belle, s 19th.
O'Connor, Michael, lab, res Railroad, w Spring.
O'Donnell, John, fireman, Glass Works, res n s State, e Madison.
O'Hare, Owen, engineer, C. & A., res Main.
O'Leary, Edward, yard master, C. & A.
O'Leary, Thos., policeman, C. & A. Railroad, res cor 18th and Belle.
O'Melia, Andrew, teamster, res e s Walnut, n 2d.
O'Neil, Edward, works Tobacco Factory, res cor 4th and Easton.
O'Neil, James, teamster, res e s Henry, n 3d.
O'Neil, James, pressman, Dausman & Drummond, res Front, w Alton.
O'Neil, Michael, lab, res Marshall.
O'Neil, Patrick, lab, res n s 3d, e Oak.
O'Rourke, Thos., lab, res cor 10th and Alton.
Oben, M. teamster, res n s 5th, w Oak.
Oben, M. F., saloon and billiard hall, corner 2d and Piasa, res cor 5th and Oak.
Oberbeck Fred, carp, res cor Langdon and 3d.
Oberlatz, John, shoe maker, res cor 3d and Langdon.
Obermueller, Ch., painter, cor 2d and Piasa, res 3d.
Ohly, Henry, cooper, Ridge, s 3d, res 4th, nr Ridge.

Ohley, Henry, cooper, Armstrong Bros., res Cherry, n 2d.
Obley, Wm., cooper, Armstrong Bros., res cor 5th and Henry.
Oklass, Mrs. Jane, res Liberty, s Suspension.
Oldham, Charles, res n s Union, e North.
Oldham, George, (Oldham & Holden) res Union.
Oldham, George, Jr., clk, Oldham & Holden, res Union.
Ottmanns, J. H., general store, 2d, w Ridge, res same.
Organ, James, carp. res Alby, cor 18th.
Organ, John, lab, res Dry, nr Main.
Organ, Mrs. Mary, grocer, cor 9th and Alby, res same.
Ortman, Andrew, works Brewery, res Belle, n 16th.
Osborne, Albert, works Glass Works.
Oswegen, David, lab, res s s 6th, w Cherry.
Ott, Andrew, works Alton Ag. Works, res s s 6th, w Vine.
Owings, D. F., clk, res, State e Spring.
Owings, F. P., fancy groceries and seeds 15, Belle, res State.

P

Pack, J., machinist, Alton Ag. Works.
Paddock, Gay, hardware, res cor 4th and Alton.
Palm, Adam, barber, res n w cor 7th and Belle.
Palmer, Morgan, lab, res cor Vine and 5th.
Palmer, Noel, engineer, res Union, w Ridge.
Pape, Conrad, fireman, res s s 5th, e Liberty.
Parker, Alex, lab, res Washington.
Parker, Geo., basket maker, W. Armstrong & Bros., res State.
Parker, Newton, lab, res Monroe, nr Madison.
Parker, Wm., basket maker, W. Armstrong & Bro., res State.
Parker, W. R., grocer, cor 9th and Belle, res same.
Parks, John, lab, res 6th, w Spring.
Parks, Mrs. Margaret, res 7th, e State.
Pates, Thos., foreman, Hapgood & Co., res 2d, nr Langdon.
Patrick, J., (Atkinson & Patrick) res cor 5th and Seminary Sq.
Pattison, W. E., book-keeper, Quigley, Hopkins & Co., res cor 11th
    and Langdon.
Paul & Bierbaum, (C. Paul, R. Bierbaum,) general store, 2d, e
    Langdon.
Paul, C., (Paul & Bierbaum) res 2d, w Henry.
Paul, Philip, clk, Quigley, Hopkins & Co., res 2d, w Henry.
Paul, Philip W., fireman, Tobacco Works, res n s 3d, e Langdon.
Peale, Chas., painter, res s s 6th, e Liberty.
Peffer, B., cooper, State road, res same.
Pelott, C., wood worker, Alton Ag. Works.

Pelott. F., wood wooker, Alton Ag. Works.
Percival, Peter, blacksmith, C. & A., res State, cor Main.
Percival, Mrs. M., grocer, cor State and Main, res same.
Perkins, Mrs. Clara, res Common.
Perkins, James, lab, res s s 9th, w Henry.
Perks, Samuel. sexton, res s s 5th, e Walnut.
Perley, R. G., (Perley & Woodman,) lumber, cor Henry and 2d. res cor 4th and Alton.
Perley & Woodman. (R. G. Perley, D. Woodman) lumber yard, cor 2d. and Henry.
Perrin, Mrs. Isabella, res s s Pleasant, e Henry.
Perrin & Smith, (T. H. Perrin, E. A. Smith) book and job printers. State, opp. 3d.
Perrin, T. H., (Perrin & Smith) and publisher of "Our Faith," monthly, res Pleasant.
Perrot, Abraham, mason, res cor 5th and Liberty.
Perry, John, teamster, res Belle, s 19th.
Peters, Mrs. Ellen, res cor 19th and Belle.
Peters, Rev. P., Pastor St Mary's Catholic Church, res cor 4th and Henry.
Peterson. John, tailor, H. C. G. Moritz, res State.
Pfaff, John, carp, res n s 3d. e Oak.
Pfaff, Valentine. stoves and tin-ware, n s 2d, e Ridge. res same.
Pfeffer, Benjamin, tailor, res Langdon, s 2d.
Pfeffer, B., tailor, res 3d, Junction 2d.
Pfeffer, Adolph, tailor, H. C. G. Moritz, bds St. Charles Hotel.
Pfeiffenberger, Lucas, Architect, n s 3d, w Piasa, res State.
Pfeiffer, E., boots and shoes, 3d, w Piasa, res Belle, n 6th.
Pfenninger, J., druggist, cor 2d and Henry, res 2d, w Henry.
Phare, W. H., Real Estate and Loan, res Oak, s State.
Phelan, A. E., glass blower, res s s 2d, e Henry.
Phelan, Geo., glass blower. Glass Works.
Phelan, John, works Glass Works, res e s Alby, n 9th.
Phelan, Mrs. Phebe, res e s Alby, n 9th.
Philan, Mrs. Mary. res cor 16th and Market.
Philips, J. M., steam-boat mate, res William, n Park.
Phinney, C. L.. grocer, res cor 3d and Easton.
Phinney, Chas , wholesale grocer, Short, res cor 12th and Langdon.
Phinney. Henry, wholesale grocer, res cor 12th and Alton.
Phipps, Mrs. L., res 4th, e Langdon.
Pickard, George, clk, res cor Mecnanie and 8th.
Pickard, P. weigh master, res cor 4th and Langdon.
Piclot, Frank, carp, works Alton Ag. Works, res 3d, w Spring.

Pierce, Thos., res e s Alby, n 6th.
Pierce, W. C., physician. (Reg.) cor 3d and Belle, res 2d, nr Alby.
Pierce, Wm. B., (Daniels, Bayle & Co.) bds 2d.
Pierson, Norton, works Sweetser & Priest. res n s 7th, e George.
Pierson, N. R., clk, Sweetser & Priest, res 7th. nr George.
Pierson, Wm M., (Flagg, Pierson & Carr) res cor 5th and George.
Pile, Chas., works W. Armstrong & Bro., res Main, nr Belle.
Pile, Geo., harness maker. res State, nr Cliff.
Pile, Jas., lab, res State, nr Cliff.
Pile, Samuel, lab, res State, nr Cliff.
Pilgrim, Fritz, lab, Sweetser & Priest, res 3d, e Spring.
Pinckard. Wm. G., clk, Milnor, Auten & Co., res Henry.
Pinkstone, Samuel, carp, res Alby, cor 17th.
Pitts, George, works for Wm. Smith, res Washington.
Pitts, Samuel, (S. & W. Pitts,) res State. cor 7th.
Pitts, Samuel. Sr., clk, S. & W. Pitts, bds State, cor 7th.
Pitts, S. & W.. stoves and tin-ware, w s State.
Platt, Miss A., res State, w Oak.
Platt, Mrs. A. B., res n s State, w Bluff.
Platt, Chas., book-keeper, T. Knight, bds same.
Platt & Hart, livery and sale stable, w s State, n 3d.
Platt, Wm. H., brakeman, res cor Park and William.
Poattgen, Mrs. Sophia. res 10th. w Langdon.
Podgen, Joseph, painter, res Bond, w Beacon.
Poindexter, Edward. works Glass Works, res cor 6th and Liberty.
Pope, James, works Woolen Mill, res n s Belle.
Pope, James, carder, res Prospect, nr Bond.
Porter, F. A., collector. res cor 20th and Alby.
Porter, Wm., lab, res Alby, n 19th.
Powers, Wm., lab, bds D. Ryan.
Price, Isaac, lab. res cor Walnut and 5th.
Price, Manning F., cooper, res 8th, w Belle.
Priest, H. C. (Sweetser & Priest) bds St. Charles Hotel.
Proctor, Millard, cooper, T. H. Proctor, res same.
Proctor, T. H., cooper. Front, w Henry, res cor Henry and 2d.
Pump, Peter, lab. res 19th, w Market.
Putze, Louis, baker. res n s 5th, e Ridge.
Pyle, O. Z., painter, Ch. Obermueller, res cor 6th and Easton.
Pyle, Samuel, lab. Oil Factory. res State, n Cliff.

Q

Quarton, J., Feed, w s State, n 2d, res 7th, bet Belle and State.
Quigley, C. E.. clk, Quigley, Hopkins & Co., res cor 12th and George.

Quigley, Frank T.. scroll, sawyer, M. H. Boals, res cor North and Union.
Quigley, Geo., res cor Union and North.

QUIGLEY, HOPKINS & CO., (W. C. Quigley, Geo. K. Hopkins,) Wholesale Druggists, 1 and 3, 2d.

Quigley, John, sawyer, M. H. Boals, res cor North and Union.
Quigley, Jos. T. clk, Quigley, Hopkins & Co., res cor 12th and George.
Quigley, W. C., (Quigley, Hopkins & Co.) res cor 12th and George.
Quigley. Thos., fireman, res Dry, s Main.
Quirk, Mrs. Kate, res cor Market and 8th.

R

Radcliffe, T. W., Cash. Ex. Co., bds Prospect, n Bond.
Rader, Chas., machinist, res 13th, e George.
Raible, Julius, H., wholesale liquors, cor 4th and Belle, res same.
Randall. Chas , book-keeper, Dausman & Drummond. res Mill, head of 4th.
Raps, Mrs. Catharine, res south end Bluff.
Rayburn, John, teamster, res s s 3d, c Oak.
Reagan, Mrs. Kate. res n s 3d, nr Plum.
Reagan, Robt.. skiff builder, res n s 2d, e George.
Real, ——, lab, res Washington, c Pleasant.
Reardon, Thos., lab, res cor 10th and Alby.
Redmond, David, lab res Common, nr Railroad.
Redmond, James, fireman, Glass Works.
Redmond, James, lab, res cor 20th and Piasa.
Redmond, John, works Glass Works, res cor 20th and Piasa.
Redmond, Martin. lab, res w s Belle, n 18th.
Redmond, Mrs. Mary, res Marshall.
Redmond, Patrick, lab, res cor 20th and Piasa.
Redmond, Wm., lab, res cor 20th and Piasa.
Redmond, Wm.. lab. res Common, nr Railroad.
Reed, Andrew, blacksmith, res cor 6th and Easton.
Rehm, Geo., cooper, Armstrong Bros., bds cor Spring and 2d.
Reilly. Mrs. Catharine, res Belle, n 16th.
Reilly, Bernard bar-tender for T. Biggins. res w s Easton. s 11th.
Reinwald, Christ. blacksmith, res Belle, n 14th.
Reis, Mrs. Victoria, res n s 4th, w Ridge.
Rempee, John, lab, res n s 4th, w Ridge.
Reuter, Gus, works Woolen Mill. res s s 8th, c Henry.

Reuter, R., weaver, Woolen Mill.
Reyman, Andrew, carp, res cor 3d and Walnut.
Reynolds, Geo., Genl. Agt. McCormick's Reapers and Mowers, cor
2d and Short, bds cor 3d and Market.
Rhoads, Chas. B., boots and shoes, n s 3d, w Piasa, bds St. Charles
Hotel.
Rice, Nichols, baker, bds n s 7th, e George.
Richardson, Wm., white-washer, res Bluff, s State.
Richardson, Wm., blacksmith, w s Belle, cor 5th, res cor 7th, nr.
Langdon.

*RICHMOND, ISAAC J., Post Master, office hours
from 7 to 7, Sunday 8 to 9 A. M., res. cor. 17th
and Market.*

Richmond, Milnor, clk, res 7th, w Alby.
Richter, Henry, lab, res cor 6th and Walnut.
Rickgauer, Wm., carp, res cor 3d and Apple.
Rieg, Nicholas, baker, Wm. Boercker, bds 8th, nr Langdon.
Rilea, Ira, Telegraph repairer, res 8th, e Alby.
Riley, James, teamster, res e s Walnut, s 3d.
Riley, James, lab, res cor 8th and Market.
Riley, John, lab, res Market, s 17th.
Riley, John, baker, Daniels, Bayle & Co., res 2d.
Riley, Philip, policeman, res cor 3d and Oak.
Riley, Mrs. C., res Bluff, s State.
Riley, Wm. S., lab, res n s 3d, e Henry.
Rippe, H. H., foreman C. Behrens, bds St. Charles Hotel.
Rittel, Michael, glass blower, res Cherry, n 3d.
Ritter, Mrs. Amelia, res cor Court and George.
Ritter, Mrs. Catharine, res Bloomfield, w Harrison.
Ritter, H., Photographer, over 14, 3d, res 9th, e Easton.
Ritter, W. J., Photographer, H. Ritter, res George, n 5th.
Roach, Mrs., res Dry.
Roberts, F. L., res northern limits, w Plank road.
Roberts, H. N., Dentist, s s 3d, e State.
Roberts, Wm. A., tanner, R A. Williams, bds same.
Robertson, James, res w s Alby, s 9th.
Robertson, Robt. H., glass packer, res n s 2d, w Cherry.
Robidou, Chas., res 7th, w Belle.
Robidou, David, works Tobacco Works, res w s Belle, n 7th.
Robidou, Joseph, Dentist, w s Belle, n 7th, res same.
Robidou, Lawrence, boot and shoe maker, w s Belle, n 7th, res same.

Robinson, Mrs. Mary, res s s 2d, e George.
Robinson, Wm., machinist, Plow Works, res 2d, nr George.
Rodemeyer, C.. Jr., blacksmith, res Elm, w Cliff.
Rodemeyer, C.. carriage and wagon manufac'g, cor Market and 3d, res Elm, w Cliff.
Roe, John, teamster, res n s 3d, w Alby.
Roenicke, G. F., painter. D. Miller, bds Belle.

ROHLAND, C. B., Dentist, 18, 3d, office hours, 8 to 12 A. M., and 1 to 5 P. M., res. State, at A. S. Barry's.

Rogan, Patrick. grinder. Plow Works, res cor 2d and Langdon.
Rogen, Frank, res Junction 2d and 3d.
Rogert, Pat., works Plow Works, bds cor 2d and Langdon.
Rogge, Dietrich, lab, res s s Union, w Ridge.
Roller, Frank, lab, T. Dietz, res 2d, e Cherry.
Roller, Christian, druggist, res cor 3d and Ridge.
Rolvering, John, tailor, H. C. G. Moritz, bds Empire House.
Ronshausen, John, boot and shoe maker, Piasa, n 2d, res 2d, e Piasa
Root, A. K., hardware, res State, n Jefferson.
Roper, & Cooper, (Geo. S. Roper and Jas. T. Cooper) Real Estate and Insurance, over 30, 3d.
Roper, Geo. S., (Roper & Cooper) res State.
Roper, Geo. D., clk, Roper & Cooper, res State.
Rose, W. B., roller, Dausman & Drummond, res 3d, nr Langdon.
Rose, Wm., assorter, Dausman & Drummond, res 3d, nr George.
Rosenberger, Andrew, farmer, res Washington, e Sq.
Rosenberger, Andrew, Jr., farmer, res Washington, e Sq.
Ross, Isaac, lab, res s s 9th, w Langdon.
Rost, Peter, lab, res Hamilton, w Harrison.
Routledge, Edward, lab, res w s Belle, n 9th.
Rowan, Chas., clk, Hollister. res State. n 4th.
Rowan, Thos., furniture repairer, w s Piasa, s 5th, res cor 6th and Alton.
Rubsam, G., clk, J. Leyser, bds same.
Rudd, James, peddler, res Salu.
Rudershausen, Fred, res s s 9th, w Langdon.
Ruemer, ——, lab, res s s 3d, w Ridge.
Runzi, B., (B. Runzi & Co.) res Alby, n 19th.
Runzi, B., & Co., (B. Runzi, S. Lehman) brewers, cor 16th and Easton.
Rupp, John, carder, res Bluff, s State.
Russell, A. H., clk, res State, nr Cliff.

Russell, Mrs. C. A., res State, nr Cliff.
Russell, C. W., clk, res State, nr Cliff.
Russell, Frank G., printer, Alton Telegraph, res State.
Russell, Geo. S., operator, I. & St. L. Depot, res State.
Rutherford, F., clk, res s s 9th, w Langdon.
Rutherford, Mrs. L., res s s 9th, w Langdon.
Rutledge, Wm., clk, H. C. G. Moritz, bds St. Charles Hotel.
Rutledge, Wm., blacksmith, D. Miller, res Elm.
Ryan, Corniel, res Prospect, n Bond.
Ryan, David, saloon, cor 2d and George, res same.
Ryan, James, lab, res Common, nr Sq.
Ryan, John, lab, res Main, w Hamilton.
Ryan. John, res cor Market and 18th.
Ryan, John, lab, res cor Cliff and Elm.
Ryan, Michael, lab., bds cor 5th and Piasa.
Ryan, Michael, teamster, bds cor 5th and Piasa.
Ryan, Tnomas, lab, res Piasa, nr 9th.
Ryan, Wm., lab, Woolen Mill.
Ryder, S., res s s 2d, e Market.
Rylei, Smith, lab, W. Armstrong & Bro., res 3d.
Ryrie, D. D., Cashier, 1st Nat. Bank of Alton, res 4th, nr George.
Ryrie, J. A., grocer, Short, w State, res 7th, nr Henry.
Ryrie, John A., clk, 1st Nat. Bank of Alton, res 4th, nr Langdon.

S

Sachtleben, Wm., (Joesting & Sachtleben) res cor 7th and Langdon.
Sampson, Mrs Helen, res Langdon, s 4th.
Sargent, B. F., Ass't Cash. 1st Nat. Bank of Alton, res Market, n 2d.
Sauerwein, G., (J. R. Bell & Co.,) res State.
Savage, Anton, policeman, res s s 3d, w Langdon.
Sawyer, B. S., farmer, res cor 9th and Alton.
Sawyer, R. S., (S. T. & R. S. Sawyer) res cor 9th and Alton.
Sawyer, S. T., (S. T. & R. S. Sawyer) res cor 9th and Alton.
Sawyer, S. T. & R. S., Atts. at Law. over 16, 3d.
Scannall, Lawrence, cooper, Armstrong Bros., bds P. Sullivan.
Schaefer, Chas., porter, Blair & Atwood, res s s 5th, e Henry.
Schattel, Andrew, Jr., lab, res Washington. e Pleasant.
Schaub, Frank, cooper, A. Gundell, res 2d, e Ridge.
Schanck. ——, Teacher St. Mary's School, res Henry.
Schaum, Augustus, glass blower, res s s 3d, e Walnut.
Schellenberger, Chas. G., bds Empire House.
Schenk, Henry, grocer, cor 6th and Walnut. res same.
Schlageter, B., turner and umbrella repairer, 2d, e Ridge, res same.

Schlecht, Mrs. Henrietta, res n s 2d, e Spring.
Schlotthauer, H., wood worker, Alton Ag. Works.
Schmidt, Mrs. Caroline, res Langdon. s 2d.
Schmidt. F., tailor, H. C. G. Moritz, bds Empire House.
Schmidt, Mrs. Elizabeth, res n s 5th, e Spring.
Schmidt, Eilert W., teacher. res n s 8th. w Henry.
Schmidt. Otto. works C. Weisman, res 4th. bet Henry and Ridge.
Schmiedt. Philip, (Buff, Kuhl & Co.) res cor 2d and Oak.

SCHMOELLER, JOHN, W., Manufacturer and Dealer in Boots and Shoes. We make a specialty of fine Goods, and sell at Lowest Prices. Repairing neatly done, n. s. 2d, w. Alby, res. same.

Schneider, Christ, works Woolen Mill, res cor 4th and George.
Schneider. Mike, lab, res State road.
Schnierle, Rev. M., Pastor German Methodist Church, res e s North, n 6th.
Schock, Emanuel. painter, D. Miller, res 8th, nr George.
Schoefler, John G. drayman, Quigley. Hopkins & Co., res 4th, w Ridge.
Schoell, Wm., lab, res n s 4th, w Ridge.
Schoppet, Mrs. Caroline, res s s 5th, e Liberty.
Schott, A. H., physician, (Hom.) e s Market, n 2d, res same.
Schreiber, Conrad, stone cutter, res cor 6th and Walnut.
Schreiber, C., (Murphy & Co.) res 3d, e Washington.
Schrempf, Ernest, works Plow Works, res 6th, e Cherry.
Schubert, Frank, butcher, Kuhn & Fuchs, res cor Henry and 3d.
Schubert, Wm., works Woolen Mill, res n s 3d, e Henry.
Schue, Isidor, butcher, Fritch & Koch, bds same.
Schuille, B., carp, res cor 3d and Cherry.
Schulmeier, Joseph, lab, res Alley, bet 5th and 6th, e Ridge.
Schulte, Herman, carp, res cor North and Union.
Schupp, Mrs. C., res s s 3d, w Henry.
Schurtz, Chas., machinist, Alton Ag. Works.
Schwartz, Mrs. Sophia, res s s 9th, e Langdon.
Schwartzbeck, Anton, baker, res cor Bloomfield and Harrison.
Schwartzbeck, Ernest, lab, Plow Works, res cor State Road and Bloomfield.
Schwarze, Wm., lab, res e s Henry, s 4th.
Schweigert, Wm., cooper, A. Gundell, res 3d, w Ridge.
Schweppe, H., (J. W. & H. Schweppe) res Mill. n 4th.

Schweppe, H. M., clk, J. W. & H. Schweppe, res 9th, nr Langdon.
Schweppe, J. W., (J. W. & H. Schweppe) res 2d, e Alby.
Schweppe, J. W. & H., clothing, etc., s s 3d.
Schweppe, W. E.. (R. DeBow & Co.) res Mill, n 4th.
Scoell, Zirach, lab, res cor 6th and Liberty.
Scott, Jacob, engineer, Oil Factory, res Piasa, nr 17th.
Scovill, James F., teamster, res s s 4th, e Plum.
Scullan, Mrs. Eliza, res s s 5th, e Spring.
Scullon, Thos., lab, bds J. Dawson's.
Scully, John, lab, res Wharf. s State.
Scully, Mrs. Mary, res Russell.
Sceger, George, lab, res south end Liberty.
Seeley, Austin, blacksmith, G. D. Hayden, res cor 2d and Alton.
Seely, F. R., (Seely & Hoffmeister) res 2d, cor Easton.
Seely & Hoffmeister. (F. R. Seely, F. W. Hoffmeister,) books and
    stationery, 10, 3d.
Segart, Mrs. M., res e s Henry. n 3d.
Seibert, Chas., cooper, res n s 2d, w Henry. •
Seibold, Chas., teamster, Sweetser & Priest, res s s 7th. e Henry.
Seibold, Nicholas, wagon maker, w s Belle. n 4th, res 7th, nr Henry.
Seigel, Geo., glass blower, Glass Works.
Sery. John, lab, res Green.
Seubert, John, brick-layer, res s s 3d, e Walnut.

---

*SHACKELFORD. R. B.. Manager Howe Machine
Co., bds. cor. 6th, e. Market.*

Shafer, Chas , porter, Blair & Atwood, res 6th, bet Henry and Liberty.
Shanklin, P. G., clk, R. Flagg, res 6th, nr Henry.
Sharkey, John, cooper, Armstrong Bros., res Dry.
Sharps, Geo., machine hand, rooms n s 2d, e Henry.
Shaum. J. J., engineer, res cor Alton and 7th.
Shaw, Newton, works Glass Works.
Shaw, Wm. A., clk, Railroad Office, res 7th, e State.
Shay, Michael, peddler, res Main, nr State.
Shay, Peter, lab, res cor State and Main.
Shea, Thos., lab, res 7th, e Piasa.
Sheean, John, lab, res n s 2d, w Cherry.
Sheean, John, grocer, cor 2d and Langdon, res same.

---

*SHELLY, F., Lime Burner, wholesale and retail
    dealer in Plaster, Cement, Hair, White Sand,
    &c., office immediately above the National Mills,
    res. State, cor. Dry.*

Shelley, Fred, lab, F. Shelley.
Shelly, Fred, lab, works in Brewery, res cor 6th and Vine.
Shelley, Jas., splitter, Dausman & Drummond, res 2d, nr George.
Shelly, Michael, lab, res s s 2d, e George.
Sherwood, Edwin, drayman, res s s 6th, e Easton.
Shields, Gus, baker, Daniels, Bayle & Co., bds Langten House.
Shields, James, saloon, res Belle, n 16th.
Shooler, John, policeman, res Meenanie, s 7th.
Shields, Mrs., res Spring, n State.
Shields, Mrs. M. C., res Belle, n 16th.
Shipley, Mrs. Sarah, res n s 3d, w Alby.
Shoemaker, J. N., publisher, Alton Democrat, bds St. Charles Hotel.
Shope, Franklin, lab, res Belle, s 19th.
Sidway, G. D., harness and saddles, 2d, e State, res Belle, s 7th.
Siegel, works Perley & Woodman, res south end Liberty.
Siem, Wm., hardware, res w s Belle, nr 6th.
Sien, Alex., clk, A. Neermann, res cor George and 3d.
Sien, Henry, barber, Piasa, n 3d, res cor 3d and George.
Sigman, J. S., watch maker, bds Knight's restaurant.
Sikes, Frank, lab, res 4th, e Langdon.
Sikes, Robt., pressman, Dausman & Drummond, res cor 6th and
    Liberty.
Simms, Judson, works C. Phinney, res e s Market, s 6th.
Simms, Mrs. Ann, res Common.
Simms, Mrs. Sarah, res e s Market, s 6th.
Simon, Matthias, lab, res w s Alby, s 5th.
Simpson, Mrs. J., res State, n Jefferson.
Simpson, Mrs. P., res s s 3d, w Ridge.
Sirler, Mrs. Francis, res Alley, bet 2d and 3d, e Cherry.
Slater, John, mason, res cor 19th and Market.
Sleavin, John, marble cutter, W. Flynn, res Cliff, s Elm.
Slicker, Lewis, turner, res n s Park, e William.
Sloman, Mark, clk, R. Flagg, res cor Easton and 10th.
Sloss, Mrs. Mary, variety store, Alby, nr City Limits, res same.
Slup, Stephen, teamster, res Union, e Oak.
Smith, Mrs., res 9th, e Belle.
Smith, Mrs., res cor 8th and Alton.
Smith, ——, lab, res Alley, bet 5th and 6th, e Ridge.
Smith, Albert, farmer, res cor 6th and Market.
Smith, Alex., clk, Quigley, Hopkins & Co., res cor George and 5th.
Smith, Boston W., book-keeper, Blair & Atwood, res cor 8th and
    Alton.
Smith, C. M., physician, (Reg.) cor Belle and 4th, res same.

Smith, E. A., (Perrin & Smith) res Pleasant, e Henry.
Smith, Geo. A., clothing, 31, 3d, res Union, cor Washington.
Smith, Henry, painter, res s s 7th, w Belle.
Smith, Jas., clk, Seely & Hoffmeister, res Henry.
Smith. John W., lab, res Green.
Smith, Robt., lab, res 9th, e Belle.
Smith, R. B., Real Estate, res cor Suspension and Liberty.
Smith, Mrs. Sarah, res n s 6th, e Henry.
Smith, Samuel C., cooper, res Bloomfield, w Harrison.
Smith, Thos., drayman, res cor 8th and Alton.
Smith. Wm., hostler. Platt & Hart, bds Empire House.
Smith, Wm. Elliot, Prop'r Illinois Glass Co., nr Railroad, e Plum.
    res Washington.
Smith, Wm Ellis, clk, Milnor, Auten & Co., res Spring, n State.
Smiley Bros., (W. E. & Geo. H. Smiley,) City shoe store, 14, 3d.
Smiley, Geo. H., (Smiley Bros.) bds 2d.
Smiley, W. E., (Smiley Bros.), bds Belle, cor 7th.
Sneeringer, Mrs. Mary, res n s State, e Spring.
Sneeringer, S. N. grain dealer, res State, s 7th.
Snyder, Mrs. Jane B., res State, e Bond.
Somers, Jos., tailor, H. C. G. Moritz, res cor 4th and Easton.
Somers, Peter, tailor, H. C. G. Moritz, res cor 4th and Easton.
Sonntag. F. L., carpet weaver, res Belle. s 17th.
Sontag, Wm, boss Weaver Woolen Mill.
Sotier, C., saloon, n s 2d, e Henry, res same.
Southworth, Mrs. H., res Wharf, s State.
Southworth, Samuel, lab., res Wharf, s State.
Southworth, Sylvester, sawyer, res Wharf, s State.
Southworth, Thos., lab Oil Mill, res Wharf, s State.
Spaet, Joseph, saloon, res cor Oak and 3d.
Spaet, Joseph, Jr., works M. H. Boals, res cor 3d and Oak.
Spain, Mrs. Bridget, res R. R., n Spring.
Spangenberger, Conrad, lab., res cor 8th and Liberty.
Sparks, D. R. & Co., (D. R. Sparks, W. Best), props. National
    Mill. Short, w William.
Sparks. D. R., (D. R. Sparks & Co.), res Prospect, s State.
Sparks H. B., assistant book-keeper D. R. Sparks & Co., res Pros-
    pect, s State.
Sparks, W. D., book-keeper, D. R. Sparks & Co., res Prospect, s
    State.
Spencer, Jas., blacksmith, Plow Works, res 1st, nr Langdon.
Spinner, Frank, lab., res n s 2d, w Cherry.
Spreen, George, machinist, Plow Works, res cor Alby, s 12th.

Spreen, Wm., carpenter, res w s Alby, s 12th.
Spreen, Wm., dispatcher. C. & A. Round House, res Alby, n 11th.
Squire, ——, res cor Pearl and North.
Stafford, Henry E., wool sorter, res Piasa, s 9th.
Stamps, Henry, engineer, res s s 5th, e Walnut.
Stamps, John, traveling agent, res s s 5th, e Walnut.
Stanford, Homer, stoves and tinware, n s 2d, w Langdon, res cor
    Alby and 3d.
Stanford, H., bds St. Charles Hotel.
Stanford, Mrs. M., res cor 3d and Alby.
Stanton, C., painter, Plow Works, res 2d, nr Langdon.
Stanton, Mrs. Mary, res Washington, e Pleasant.
Stanton, Thomas, railroad man, res Salu.
Stanton, Wm. J., plumber, C. E. Turner & Co., res Godfrey.
Starr, H. B., mate ferry boat, res Washington, e Square.
Starr, Mrs. Thos., res 7th, w Belle.
Stauff, Chas., saloon, n s 3d, w Washington, res same.
Steele, David D., carpenter, M. H. Boals, bds with S. S. Hobart.
Stein, August, grocer, 2d, junction 3d. res same.
Steinberg, Ferd, tailor, H. C. G. Moritz, bds St. Charles Hotel.
Steiner, Charles, teamster, D. R. Sparks & Co.
Steiner, John, wheat buyer, D. R. Sparks & Co., res State.
Steiner, M., saloon, n s 2d, e Langdon, res 8th, e Henry.
Steinheimer, B., saloon, 2d, w Market, res cor Ridge and 6th.
Steinmeiel, Wm., lab., res cor 7th and Belle.
Stell, O. B., traveling agent, res Summit, e Prospect.
Stell, Miss Sarah, teacher, school No. 2, res Upper Alton.
Stenbrun, John, lab., res cor 3d and Cherry.
Stephenson, Sanford E., glass blower. bds cor 3d and Vine.
Stetson, Chas., clerk, res cor 8th and Alby.
Stevens, Richard, clerk, res cor Court and George.
Steward, ——, lab., res Piasa, s 17th.
Steward & Bolden (E. Steward, H. Bolden), barbers, cor Belle
    and 4th.
Steward, Edward, (Steward & Bolden), res George, cor 6th.
Steward, Stephen, barber, res cor 7th and George.
Steward, Mrs. B. W., res cor 9th and Market.
Stewart, Jas. J., printer, Democrat, res Alby, n 4th.
Stewart, Mrs. S., res Alby, s 5th.
Stierle, Daniel, lab., res s s 4th, e Henry.
Still, J., boot and shoe maker, w s State.
Stillwell, John, yard master, bds Union Depot Hotel.
Stillwell, L. M., clerk, J. Chaney, res cor 12th and Alby.

Stiltse, Conrad, plasterer, res n s 3d, e Spring.
Stiner, Mrs. H., res. n s State, w Main.
Stiritz, Andrew, clerk, C. D. Caldwell, res Mill.
Stiritz, Mrs. C., res Summit, e Prospect.
Stites, Thomas, works Tobacco Factory, res cor 5th and Liberty.
Stocker, A. S., cooper, Armstrong Bros., res Upper Alton.
Stone, Mrs. Elizabeth, res cor 9th and Alby.
Store, Lorenz, blacksmith, res cor Bond and Beacon.
Storey, W., physician, (homopathic), n s 2d, w Langdon, res s w
     cor George and 2d.
Storms, George, res s s 2d, e Henry.
Stowell, O. S., book-keeper, Woolen Mill, bds Piasa, s 9th.
Straube, Herman, wagon maker, Henry, s 2d, res Upper Town.
Strauber, Otto, clerk. J. Leyser, bds same.
Strahle, Casper, brewer. B. Runzi & Co., bds same.
Stretmatter, Wm., res State, w Main.
Stringer, Nevin, lab., res Belle, n 16th.
Strabel, Jacob, lab., Sweetser & Priest, res n s 7th, w Liberty.
Strotman, Wm., lab., res Alley bet 5th and 7th, e Spring.
Stutz, John, policeman, res n s 3d, nr Washington.
Stutz, J. L., grocer, n s 2d, e Ridge, res same.
Stutz, Mrs. L., res cor 3d and Washington.
Sudbrook, H., cigar maker, J. A. Neininger, res 4th.
Sullivan, Daniel, engineer, res Park, w State.
Sullivan, Jeremiah, teamster, Plow Works, res cor 2d and Langdon.
Sullivan, John, lab., res Piasa, s 17th.
Sullivan, John, flour packer, res Park, w State.
Sullivan, Mrs. J. C., dressmaker, e s Market, s 2d, res same.
Sullivan, Michael, blacksmith, res s s 2d, w Henry.
Sullivan, Michael, switchman, C. & A. yard.
Sullivan, Patrick, res w s Belle, s 8th.
Sullivan, Sylvester, works Woolen Mill, bds P. Sullivan.
Sullivan, Wm., painter, bds P. Sullivan.
Sullivan, Wm. T., sheet iron worker, res Park, w State.
Sullivan, ——, switchman, C & A.
Sumers, Frank, cooper, Armstrong Bros., bds Empire House.
Sutbrook, Henry, cigar maker, res s s 5th, w Ridge.

SUTTER, JOHN, manufacturer of and dealer in Fine and Common Furniture, also Furnishing Undertaker. Repairing promptly attended to. 2d, bet. Henry and Langdon, res. George, n. 4th,

Sweeney, John, lab, res n s 7th, e Henry.

Sweeney, Thos., wrapper, Dausman & Drummond, res 7th, nr Henry.
Sweeney, Wm., sugar room foreman, Dausman & Drummond, res. 7th, nr Henry.
Sweetser, H. C., (Sweetser & Priest,) res Belle. n 6th.

SWEETSER & PRIEST, (H. C. Sweetser, H. C. Priest,) wholesale and retail dealers in Lumber, Lath, Shingles, &c., 2d, w. Ridge.

Swettenham, Orenzo, hostler, J. Jarrett, bds Front.
Sworts, Henry, fireman, Gas Works, res 8th, w Belle.

T

Tansey, Mrs. Mary, res William, s State.
Taplin, Frank, lab, C. & A. Round House, res Alton, n 12th.
Tatum, Henry, clk, res n s 3d, e George.
Tauton, Mrs. K., res Salu.
Taylor, Fred, lab, bds Spring St. House.
Taylor, Harry, Eng. and Supt. Alton Water Works Co., res. cor. Maple and Grove.
Taylor, Joseph, cooper, res s s 2d, e George.
Taylor, Thos., lab, res Belle, s 19th.
Teasdale, Ben., book binder, over 31, 3d, bds 2d. w Alby.
Temple & Blackburn, painters, s s Belle.
Temple, Chas., carp, res n s 5th, e Market.
Temple, George, carp, res cor 5th and George.
Temple, Wm., painter, res cor Vine and 3d.
Templeton, Mrs. J. W., (Mrs. J. W. Templeton & Co.) res Easton, n 5th.
Templeton, Mrs. J. W. & Co., (J. W. Templeton, Geo. F. Wendt.) dry goods, 36, 3d.
Termahlen, George, tailor, F. Doepke, bds Ridge. s 5th.
Tesson, Frank H., pilot, res n s 2d, w Langdon.
Thayer, Fred, machinist, G. D. Hayden, bds cor 3d and Market.
Theala, Mrs. Jane, res s s Union, e Ridge.
Thinn, John, blacksmith, works for Luft, res cor Oak and 5th.
Thompson, Chas. E., painter, res s s 3d, e Vine.
Thompson, Daniel, lab., res Common.
Thompson, John, liquor, res Common, nr railroad.
Thompson, Samuel, lab., res Piasa, s 17th.
Thompson, Wm., steamboat man. res s s Pleasant, e Henry.
Thornton, James, lab., res Belle, opposite 17th.
Thornton, Philip, grocer, cor Belle and 16th, res same.

Thorpe, Geo., carpenter, bds Thos. Hall.
Thrush, James, teamster, res e s Spring, s 5th.
Tierney, Mrs. Bridget. res cor 17th and Piasa.
Tillin, Ervin. lab.. res n end Alby.
Tillman, Henry. shoemaker, res cor 3d and Langdon.
Tindall Alfred, sewing machine agent. res w s Belle, s 7th.
Tindall. Alfred, cooper, Armstrong Bros.. res Belle, n 6th.
Tindall. D.. wood-worker, Alton Ag. Works.
Tisius, Henry, boot and shoe maker, n s 3d. e Piasa. res 4th nr
     Henry.
Tisius, John, fireman. Glass Works.
Tison, Jacob. lab., res cor Spring and 6th.
Tison, Peter, lab.. res n s 3d. e Piasa.
Tobin. Mrs. Margaret, res Railroad. e Henry.
Tobin, Mrs. Mary, res cor 6th and Oak.
Todd, James A.. stonecutter, res cor Belle and 19th.
Tohey, Mrs. Ann. res Summit. w Prospect.
Tolmon, Miss Clara teacher. school No. 2. bds cor Langdon and
     9th.
Tomlinson, S. C., wagon-maker. res n s Bozza, e Washington.
Tomlinson S., wagon-maker and blacksmith, cor Bozza and Wash-
     ington, res same.
Tonsor, Henry, clk, J. M. Tonsor. bds Spring, cor 2d.
Tonsor, John M., Wholesale and Retail Liquors, 2d, e Junct 3d.
     res, Greenwood.
Toohey. Mrs. Mary. res 4th, w Henry.
Tooncy, Thos., lab.. res Spring, nr Main.
Topping Bros.. (M. H. and J. S. Topping). hardware, 2d, w Piasa.
Topping. J. S. (Topping Bros.). res 11th, cor Alton.
Topping. Lucas. traveling agt.. bds cor George and 6th.
Topping. M. H.. (Topping Bros.), res 8 Market.
Townsend, Chas., lab, A. K. Root. bds same.
Tracy, Samuel, engineer, res cor Belle and 18th.
Tracey, S. S. blacksmith, W. W. Webb, res Belle.
Trapp, Theo.. spinner. res 9th. e Belle.
Tremmel, Jacob, lab, res cor 6th and Vine.
Trendall. Jos.. works M. H. Boals, res cor 7th and Liberty.
Tribble, Frank A., clk. Quigley, Hopkins & Co., bds-cor Market
     and 3d.
Triggs. John, lab. res cor Holman and Salu.
Tuetken. Henry carp, res Bloomfield, e Gold.
Turk, Mrs. Elizabeth. res Belle. n 18th.
Turner, Chas. E., (C. E. Turher & Co..) res Godfrey.

TURNER, CHAS. E., & CO., (Chas. E. & J. B. Turner,) Plumbers, Gas and Steam Pipe Fitters, w. s. State, one door from 2d.

Turner, J. B., (C. E. Turner & Co.) res Godfrey.

TWEDDLE, JOHN, New and Second-hand Furniture, 40, State, res. Bluff, s. State.

U

Uebelhack, John, cooper, res cor 3d and Langdon.
Uhrman, Edward, lab, res nr Godfrey, w Cliff.
Ullrich, F. H., druggist, cor 2d and Langdon, res same.
Ulrich, Christ, clk. J. Miedel, res 2d, e Spring.
Unger, Louis, blacksmith, J. Ammann, res Ridge, n 6th.
Untherbrink, Casper, teamster, res 3d, cor Spring.

UNITED STATES EXPRESS COMPANY, Thomas Cannell, Agent, w. s. State, opp. 3d.

Ursch, Andrew, lab, res e s Cherry, n 2d.

V

Valier, John, lab, res e s Piasa, s 10th.
Van Buskirk, Oscar, engineer, bds cor 7th and Piasa.
Vasel, H. G., (H. G. Vasel & Co.,) res same.

VASEL, H. G., & CO., successors to Linsig & Hoefert, Rectifiers and Wholesale Liquor Dealers and Importers of Wines, Brandies, Gin, &c., 4, 2d.

Vatterott, Henry, grocer, cor 2d and Walnut, res same.
Veech, Harvey, brick-layer, res Marshall, w Belle.
Vincent, Joseph, drayman, res, w s Cherry, s 3d.
Voelkel, Mrs. Catharine, res n s 5th, e Ridge.
Voiles, Chas. works Alton Ag. Works, res n s 4th, w Ridge.
Voiles, Wm., cooper, res Belle, n 11th.
Voiles, Wm., S., cooper, res Belle, n 10th.
Volz, Leonard, drayman, res n s 2d, w Cherry.
Vonstein, John, yard man, M. H. Boals, res 2d, nr Cherry.

W

Wade, Albert, res s s Belle. n 6th.
Wade. E. P., Ass't Cash. Alton Nat. Bank, res Henry, n 10th.
Wade, R. C., tobacco roller, res cor 3d and Ridge.
Wade, Samuel, Vice Prest. Alton Nat. Bank, res e s Henry, n 14th.
Wagner, Alex., stone cutter, res s s 5th, w Oak.
Wagner, Andrew, stone mason, res s s Union, w Ridge.
Wagner, John, saloon, e s Belle. n 4th, res 5th, e Liberty.
Wahl, Joseph, glass blower, res n s 2d, w Cherry.
Walbridge. L. H., box maker, res Elm, w Cliff.
Waldron, Geo. W.. gardener, res west end Summit.
Waldron, Henry, brakeman, res Summit, w Prospect.
Waldron, Mrs. T., res Summit, w Prospect.
Waligura, Frank. weaver, bds Empire House.
Walker, Wm., lab, res Easton, s 10th.
Wall, James. engineer, res n s 2d, w Walnut.
Wallace, Mrs. P. D.. res Market, s 3d.
Walter, B., (Fish & Walter,) res North Alton.
Walter, Geo., clk, res n s 7th, e Belle.
Walter, L., carp, res s s 3d, e Henry.
Walter, Otto, clk, V. Walter, res same.

WALTER, V., dealer in Pianos. Organs and Musical Merchandise, Mathusick, Vose & Son's Pianos, Mason & Hamlin and Estey Organs. Pianos, sold on installments and to rent, cor. 3d and Piasa, res. State.

Walton, C. H.. carp, Dansman & Drummond, res 2d, nr Alton.
Walton, Henry. teamster, res Bluff. s 8th.
Walton. Isaac, barber, cor Piasa and 4th. res same.
Walton, Silas, lab. res Adams' Add.
Waples. Mrs. Adaline, res n s 5th, e George.
Waples. Walter, clk. Kellenberger Bros., res 5th, cor George.
Ward, Fred W., clk, W. F. Everts, bds same.
Ward, Mrs. Margaret, res s s 9th, w Henry.
Ward, Patrick, Clk. City Court, Office City Build'g, res 16th, nr Belle.
Warner. George. lab. res n end of North.
Warren, James. glass blower, Glass Works.
Washington, Carter, lab. res Putnam, w Gold.
Waterman, Mrs. Avis, res n s 6th, w Alby.
Waterman, Ernest, box maker, D. Williams, res 6th, nr Alby.
Watkins, J. L., farmer, res Prospect, n Bond.

Watkins, Perry, baker, Wm., H. Keith, res 2d, nr Langdon.
Watson, Henry, Prest. Alton Water Works Co., res cor Piasa and 9th.
Watts, Roger, lab, Brunner & Duncan, res cor 12th and Langdon.
Weaver, Alex., harness maker, G. D. Sidway, res State.
Weaver, Chas. H., carriage maker, res cor Liberty and 5th.
Weaver, Ed., flour packer, res State, n 4th.
Weaver, Henry, miller, res State, n 4th.
Weaver, Frank, tinner, res State, n 4th.
Weaver, Joseph, carp, res w s Belle, n 17th.
Weaver, J. H., (McInerney & Weaver,) res Belle, n 9th.
Webb, Alex., lab, res Washington, c Pleasant.
Webb, Grundy, works Saw Mill, res south end Bluff.
Webb, John, driver, P. Mitchell, res 3d.
Webb, W. W., Iron works, 2d, c State, res Belle, s 18th.
Webster, James, teamster, res cor 5th and Piasa.
Wedel, Adam, Jr., clk, res 6th, bet Walnut and Oak.
Weerts, Wesley, shoe maker, res n s 2d, w Walnut.
Wehmier, August, blacksmith, bds C. C. Paul.
Wehrli, F., tailor, A. Brueggeman, bds same.
Weicht, Wm., brick-layer, res s s Union, c Ridge.
Weigler, G. H., dry goods, n s 2d, c Henry, res same.
Weinrich, Valentine, lab, res Alley, bet 5th and 6th, w Oak.
Weis, Frank, stone cutter, res cor Ridge and Union.
Weisbach, C., soda water manuf'g., cor 2d and Walnut, res same.
Weishar, R., works Hanson & Co., bds Farmers' Home.
Weishar, J., works Hanson & Co., bds Farmers' Home.
Welch, Mrs., res Bluff, s State.
Welch, James, lab., res Russell.
Welch, John, lab., bds cor 5th and Piasa.
Welch, Mrs. Mary, res 7th, w Belle.
Welch, Michael, lab., res State, n Park.
Welch, Michael, lab, depot, res cor 17th and Alby.
Welch, Patrick, lab., res 1st, w Cherry.
Wempen, John, saloon, Washington, n 3d, res same.
Wendt F., Ag. Imp., cor 2d and Short, res Prospect, s State.
Wendt, F., Jr., clk, F. Wendt, res same.
Wendt, George, carp, res w s Easton, s 6th.
Wendt, Geo. F., (Mrs. J. W. Templeton & Co.) res Easton, n 5th.
Wenzel, Philip, shoemaker, res cor 5th and Liberty.
Werk, Ignotz, peddler, res s s 5th, nr Oak.
West, C., bds cor 4th and Henry.
West, Rev. Robt., Pastor Congregational Church, res cor 4th and
Henry.

WESTERN UNION TELEGRAPH CO., Mrs. S. T. Baylies. Manager, cor. 3d and Belle.

Weston, Wm., clk., res State. nr Cliff.
Wheelock, Ginter & Martin (H. T. Wheelock, L. Ginter, W. W. Martin). Planing Mill. 1st. nr Langdon.
Wheelock. H. T., (Wheelock, Ginter and Martin). res n s 6th, e Henry.
Whitbeck, John, lab., res s s 3d, e Langdon.
Whipple, P. B.. (Whipple & Smiley) res cor 12th and George.
Whipple & Smiley. Insurance, cor 3d and State.
White, D. C., dentist, 2d, e Piasa, res Oak.
White, Gabriel. blacksmith. res cor 5th and Cherry.
White, Geo.. engineer, res e s Henry. n 7th.
White. John, lab.. res e s Cherry, s 5th. .
White, J. C.. works Glass Works.
White, Patrick. lab. res n s Union, w Oak.
White. R. L., barber, 1. H. Kelly. bds Khight's Restaurant.
Whitehead, James. res Union. e Spring.
Widel. Adam, mason, res s s 6th, w Walnut.
Weinrich, Valentine, lab., F. Shelly.
Wilhelms & Co. (J. Willhelms. W. Hack). potters, ne 2d. w Oak.
Wilhelms, Julius (Wilhelms & Co.) res 3d. nr Oak.
Wilhelms. Henry. potter. res n s 2d, e Spring.
Wilhelms. Henry. res s s 3d, e Oak.
Wilkins. Eilert, polisher. Plow Works, res 2d, cor Oak.
Wilkinson, Jas., engineer, M. Wilkinson, res same.
Wilkinson. M., propr. Empire Mills. 2d, bet Piasa and State, res William. cor Park.
Willcox. James, cooper. res 1st. cor Cherry.
Williams. Albert, glass blower. Glass Works.   •
Williams. Allen, lab, res w s Easton, s 10th.
Williams, D.. commission. cor 4th and Piasa, res George, n 2d.
Williams, Louis, works Glass Works.
Williams. Geo.. lab., res Salu.
Williams, Gilbert. lab., res w s Easton, s 10th.
Williams, Henry. works Glass Works.
Williams, Mrs. M. E., res Madison, cor Monroe.
Williams, Richard A.. tannery. Belle, n 12th, res Alby. n 17th.
Williams. Samuel. steward, res n s 6th, e Easton.
Williams, Mrs. Sarah, res e s Henry, s 4th.
Williamson, Albert, glass blower, res n s 3d, w Walnut.

WILLS, JOSEPH, (Klunk & Wills), res Prospect, s. State.

Wills, Mary, (I. D. Gilman & Co.) res Prospect.
Wilson, Mrs. Emma, res s s Union, e Ridge.
Wilson, Huston, conductor, I. & T. H. R. R., res s s 6th,·e Alby.
Wilson, James, clk. res cor 5th and George.
Wilson, Jas., clk, Wise, Blake & Johnston, res George, n 4th.
Wilson, John, clk. M. I Lee & Co.
Wilson, Mrs. Susan, res Common.
Wilson, S. M., res Main, nr State.
Wilt, John, watchman, Alton Ag. Works, res s s 7th, n Ridge.
Winscott, Benjamin, res State, nr Cliff.
Winter, Mrs. E., res s s 3d, e Henry.
Winters, Henry, assorter, Dausman & Drummond, res 3d, nr Henry.
Winters, John, carp, res cor 6th and Ridge.
Wise, Blake & Johnston (Geo. S. Wise, Chas. R. Blake, Geo. A. Johnston), wholesale hardware, 2d and William.
Wise, Chas. P., Att-at-Law, cor 2d and State, res State, nr William.
Wise, Edward, clk. Wise, Blake & Johnston.
Wise, Felix, traveling agt., res Prospect, s State.
Wise, Geo. S. (Wise, Blake & Johnston) res State.
Wise, J. W. book-keeper, S. W. Farber & Co., res Bond, cor Beacon.
Wise, Peter, res State, n Bluff.
Wise, Sebastian, clk, Auton & Holden, res Bond, nr Beacon.
Wizering, E. P. C., insurance agt, res cor North and Union.
Wolf, Bernhard, weaver, res Market, n 16th.
Wolf, Ernst, works Sweetser & Priest, res w s Walnut, s 6th.
Wolf, Henry, lab, res w s Belle, n 9th.
Wolford, A. J., painter res Easton, s 10th.
Wonderle, Stephen, boilermaker, res cor Alby and 12th.
Woodhead, C., works Woolen Mill, res Belle, n 18th.
Woodman, D. (Perley & Woodman), res Litchfield.
Woodroof, John, res cor Alton and 6th.
Woods, Almon, works Glass Works.
Woods, Jas., carp, bds cor Grand av. and State.
Woods, James A., carp, res Main nr State.
Woods, Thos., glass blower, res cor 3d and Apple.
Woodside, A , foreman car repairs, C. & A. R. R., res 14th, cor Alton.
Woodside, Wm., carp, res cor 14th and Alton.

Woodside, ——, machinist, Alton Ag. Works.
Wooldridge, Mrs. E. II., res cor William and State.
Wortman, Benjamin, music teacher, bds cor 7th and Piasa.
Wray, John W., engineer, res 4th, nr Langdon.
Wright. Mrs. Elizabeth, res n s 3d, w Walnut.
Wright, Chas. L., book-keeper, Alton Nat. Bank, res Belle.
Wright, David, clk. P. Downes.
Wright, James, painter, bds cor 5th and Ridge.
Wright, Wm., cooper, T. II. Proctor, res Upper Alton.
Wuerker, C., harness and saddles, 12 State, res Prospect.
Wuerker, F., gunsmith, w s State, n 3d, res 2d, nr Langdon.
Wunderle, Stephen, boilermaker, res cor 12th and Alby.
Wunderlich, Ignotz, carp, res n s 3d, e Langdon.
Wurtzler, Adolph, baker, II. Neermann.
Wutzler, August, mason, res n s 4th, w Ridge.
Wutzler, Louis E., lab, res Belle, s 19th.
Wyss, Saml., Spring St. House, cor 2d and Spring, res same.
Wyss, Wm., clk, S. Wyss, res same.

Y

Yackel, Casper, cooper, res n s 3d, e Ridge.
Yackel, George, works Perley & Woodman, res n s 5th, e Ridge.
Yaeger, Wm., lab., C. & A. Round House.
Yager, John II., Att-at-Law, cor 3d and Piasa, res cor 9th and
　　Langdon.
Yale, Joseph, res Cyrus, nr Fletcher.
Yerger, Mrs. C., res w s Ridge, n 6th.
Yocum, Henry, hostler, A. Mather, res 4th and William.
Yocum, Henry, glass blower, bds Spring St. House.
Yokum, Edward, lab, res cor 9th and Alby.
Yokum, Elijah, machinist, res cor Alby and 7th.
Yokum, George, bookbinder, res Spring, n State.
Yokum, J., glass blower, Glass Works.
Yokum, F. W., printer, Democrat, res cor 9th and Alby.
Young, Julius, butcher, Fritch & Koch, bds same.
Young, Wm., jailer, res Belle, nr 14th.
Yunk, John, saloon, cor Alby and Front, res same.

Z

Zelt, John, lab., bds e s Ridge, s 5th.
Zeltmann, Fred, grocer, n s 3d, w Washington, res same.
Ziegenfuss, Wm., peddler, res State Rd.

PRYOR & CO.'S
ALTON CITY DIRECTORY,
1876-7.

CLASSIFIED BUSINESS DIRECTORY.

AGRICULTURAL IMPLEMENTS.

DRURY, A. H. & CO., Short.
Milnor, Auten & Co., 13, n s 3d.
Reynolds, G., cor 2d and Short.
Wendt. F., cor 2d and Short.

AGRICULTURAL WORKS.

Alton Agricultural Works, Front, 2d and George.

ARCHITECT.

Pfeiffenberger, L., n s 3d, w Piasa.

ATTORNEYS AT LAW.

Brenholt, J. J., over 30 3d.
Coppinger. J. W., s s 3d.
Gambrill. A. H., w s Belle, n 3d.
DAVIS, L., s s 3d, e Piasa.
McGinnis. J. F., cor 3d and Piasa.
Sawyer, S. T. & R. S., over 16 3d.
Wise, C. P., cor 2d and State.
Yager. J. H., cor 3d and Piasa.

AUCTION AND COMMISSION.

Crossman. W. V., cor 3d and Piasa.

BAKERS.

Boercker, W., 2d, w Ridge.
Kaeser, G., 2d, e Piasa.
KEITH, WM. H., cor 2d and Market.
Kreyling, W., 2d, w Ridge.
LEYSER, J. & BRO., n s 3d, w Belle.
Neermann, H., n s 2d, w Henry.

BANKS.

ALTON NATIONAL BANK, cor 3d and Belle.
First National Bank of Alton, cor 3d and State.

BARBERS.

Axthelm, L., 2d, c Henry.
Bowman, J. W., cor 3d and Piasa.
Kahn, A., Piasa, n 2d.
Kelley, H., w s Belle, n 3d.
Kelly, I. H., w s State, n 2d.
Maerdian, R., w s State.
Sien, H., Piasa, n 2d.
Steward & Bolden, cor 4th and Belle.
Walton, Isaac, cor 4th and Piasa.

BATH ROOMS.

Kelly I. H., w s State, n 2d.

BILLIARDS.

Curdie, J., 2d, opp. City Hall.
Oben, M. F., cor 2d and Piasa.

BLACKSMITHS.

ALT, CHAS., cor 2d and Henry.
AMMANN, J., n s 2d, e Ridge.
Luft, G., e s Belle, n 4th.
Millen & Beall, e s Belle, s 6th.
Richardson, W., cor Belle and 5th.
Tomlinson, S., cor Bozza and Washington.

BOOKBINDER.

Teasdale, B., over 31 3d.

BOOKS AND STATIONERY.

Gossran, R., 2d, w Ridge.
Kleinschnittger, Mrs. M., e s Henry, s 4th.

Lee, M. L. & Co., s s 3d.
Seely & Hoffmiester, 10 3d.

BOOTS AND SHOES.

MANUFACTURERS AND DEALERS.

Berner & Gaiser, w s Belle, n 3d.
Ehret, J. B., State, s 4th.
Goetz, J. F., 3d, junc. 2d.
Hack, J., n s 2d, e Spring.
Hechler, A., 2d, w Piasa.
Hilker, H., 2d, w Piasa.
Loer, J., w s Belle, n 3d.
Loos, A., 2d, e Henry.
Mahon, P., e s Henry, n 3d.
Mahoney, M., e s Belle, n 5th.
Oltmanns, J. H., 2d, w Ridge.
Pfeiffer, E., s s 3d, w Piasa.
Rhoads, C. B., n s 3d, w Piasa.
Robidou, L., w s Belle, n 7th.
Ronshausen, J., Piasa, n 2d.
SCHMOELLER, J. W., n s 2d, w Alby.
Smiley Bros., 14, 3d.
Still, J., w s State.
Tisius, H., n s 3d, e Piasa.

BREWERS.

Runzi, B., & Co., cor 16th and Easton.

BRICK YARDS.

Corbit, T., cor 10th and Market.   •
Feldwisch, E., cor Oak and 4th.
Helbrung & Co., cor 6th and Henry.
Johnson, F. M., cor Holman and Salu.

CARPENTERS AND BUILDERS.

Armstrong, H., 4th, e Piasa.
Beach, J. A., w s Piasa, s 5th.
Hugo, E. D., Piasa, s 5th.
Keiser, I. H., Piasa, s 5th.
KLUNK & WILLS, w s State, opp 3d.
McInerney & Weaver, s s 4th, w Belle.
Woods, J. A., e s Belle, n 6th.

CARPETS AND OIL CLOTHS.

NEERMANN, A., s s 3d.

CARRIAGE AND WAGON MAKERS.

AMMANN, J., n s 2d. e Ridge.
Koehne, J. H.. e s Belle, n 4th.
Miller, D., cor Belle and 5th.
Rodemeyer, C., cor Market and 3d.
Seibold, N., w s Belle, n 4th.
Straube, H., Henry, s 2d.
Tomlinson, S., cor Bozza and Washington.

CASTOR OIL FACTORY.

QUIGLEY, HOPKINS & CO., Short, w State.

CIGARS AND TOBACCO.

MANUFACTURERS AND DEALERS.

Behrens, C., Piasa, n 2d.
Brueggemann, H.. 3d. w Piasa.
Brueggemann, S. H., 2d. w Ridge.
KNIGHT, T., 2d, e Piasa.
Neininger, J. A.. Piasa. n 3d.

CLOTHING.

Doepke, F.. 2d, Junction 3d.
Hoaglan, D. S., s s 3d.
JOESTING & SACHTLEBEN, 16. 3d.
MORITZ, H. C. G., cor 3d and State.
Oltmanns, J. H.. 2d, w Ridge.
SCHWEPPE, J. W. & H., s s 3d.
Smith, G. A., 31, 3d.

COMMISSION.

Hollister & Co., 4th, e Belle.
Williams, D., cor 4th and Piasa.

CONFECTIONERY, FRUITS, &C

Joesting, Mrs. M.. 11, Belle.
KEITH, WM. H., cor 2d and Market.
LEYSER, J., & BRO., n s 3d, w Belle.
Maupin & Bates. n s 3d, e Belle.

COOPERS.

Armstrong, W., & Bro., 6, Short.
Gundall, A., 2d, e Walnut.
Jun, T. & J., Bozza.
Long, D. J., s s 4th, w Henry.
Ohley, H., Ridge, s 3d.
Peffer, B., State Road.
Proctor, T. H., Front, w Henry.

CORN MEAL MILL.

Basse, H., Short, w William.

CRACKER BAKERY.

Daniels, Bayle & Co., cor Easton and 2d.

CROCKERY

Crandall, C. M., 12, 3d.
Kellenberger Bros., 7, Belle.

DENTISTS.

Roberts, H. N., s s 3d, e State.
Robidou, J., w s Belle, n 7th.
ROHLAND, C. B., over 18, 3d.
White, D. C., 2d, e Piasa.

DRUGGISTS.

WHOLESALE.

QUIGLEY, HOPKINS & CO, 1 and 3, 2d

RETAIL.

CHAMBERLAIN, H. W., 18, 3d
Cotter, S. A., e s Belle, n 3d.
EVERTS, W. F., n s 3d, w Piasa.
Marsh, E. Jr., cor 3d and Belle.
Pfenninger, J., cor 2d and Henry.
Ullrich, F. H., cor 2d and Langdon.

DRY GOODS.

Ahrens, T., n s 2d, w Henry.
AUTEN & HOLDEN, 26, 3d.
Birdsall, Jas., 35, 3d.

BURTON, H., n s 3d, e State.
Bowman, H. B., n s 3d, w Piasa.
Fishbach, M., 3d, Junction 2d.
FLAGG, R,, 32, 3d.
Flagg, Pierson & Carr, s w cor 3d and Piasa.
Haagen, L., 30, 3d.
Herb, C. A., cor Washington and 3d.
Herrmann, J. P., cor Ridge and 2d.
Joesting & Sachtleben, 16, 3d
·Jungeblut, H., n s 2d, e George.
Jutting, H. W., n s 2d, e Henry.
Oltmanns, J. H., 2d, w Ridge.
Paul & Bierbaum, n s 2d, e Langdon.
Weigler, G. H., n s 2d, e Henry.

EXPRESS COMPANIES.

AMERICAN EXPRESS CO., E. W., Kilbourne,
Agt., w s State, opp 3d.
UNITED STATES EXPRESS CO., T. Cannell,
Agt., w s State, opp 3d.

FLOUR AND FEED.

CLIFFORD, A., Belle bet 5th and 6th.
Quarton, J., w s State, n 2d.

FLOURING MILLS.

CITY MILLS, S. W. Farber & Co., Prop'rs, 2d, bet
State and Piasa.
Empire Mills, M. Wilkinson, Prop'r., 2d, bet. Piasa and State.
National Mills, D. R. Sparks & Co., Prop'rs., Short, w William.
Madison Mills, Collet & Ground, cor Washington and 3d.

FOUNDERS·

BRUNNER & DUNCAN, 5th, e Piasa.
HAYDEN, G. D., Belle, bet 4th and 5th.

FRUIT BASKETS AND CRATE BOXES.

Armstrong, W., & Bro., 6, Short.

FURNITURE.

BAUER & HOFFMAN, 2d, opp. City Hall.
Borckman, C., 2d. w Ridge.
Chaney, J., 9 Belle.
SUTTER, J., 2d, bet Henry and Langdon.
TWEEDLE, J., 40 State.

GENTS' FURNISHING GOODS.

BRUEGGEMAN. A., n s 3d, e Belle.
Hoaglan. D. S., s s 3d.
JOESTING & SACHTLEBEN, 16 3d.
SCHWEPFE. J. W. & H., s s 3d.
MORITZ, H. G. C., cor 3d and State.
Smith, G. A., 31 3d.

GLASS WORKS.

Smith, W. E., Railroad, e Plumb.

GROCERS

WHOLESALE.

BLAIR & ATWOOD. cor 2d and Piasa.
DEBOW, R. & CO., 14 and 16 2d.
Phinney, C., Short, w State.

RETAIL.

Ahrens, T., n s 2d, w Henry.
Bisinger. L., cor 3d and Cherry.
Brennan, Mrs. C. L., cor 2d and Cherry.
Budde, J., cor Henry and 8th.
Burton, J. & Son, e s Belle, n 7th.
CLIFFORD, A., Belle, n 5th.
CROWE. J., State, bet 3d and 4th.
Caldwell, C. D., cor 4th and State.
Caldwell, Mrs. M., cor 9th and Belle.
Chouteau, A L., cor 7th and Belle.
Chaffer, R., cor Grand Av. and State.
DOWNES, P., e s Belle, n 5th.
Eichhorn. E., s s 6th, w Walnut.
Elfgen. B., cor 16th and Belle.
Esterly. Mrs. L., Washington.
Fischbach, M., 3d. junc. 2d.
Ferguson, Mrs. E., cor Union and Ridge.
Fahrig, J. cor Union and Ridge.
Fischer, Mrs. A , cor 5th and Ridge.
Fisher. Mrs. C. M., cor Pleasant and Henry.
Gottlob, Wm., n s 2d, e Spring.
Gudell. H. E., cor 7th and Henry.
Haagen, L., 30 3d.
Hartman & Co., n s 2d, w Henry.
Herrmann, J. P., cor 2d and Ridge.

Harville. Mrs. S.. s s 5th. c Market.
Herb. C. A.. cor 3d and Washington.
JONES. WM., e s Belle. n 14th.
Jungeblut. H.. n s 2d, e George.
Jutting. H. W.. n s 2d. c Henry.
Keenan. Mrs. A.. n s 2d, w Langdon.
Kennedy: B.. cor 2d and Cherry.
Kuehn, C.. State. w Prospect.
Loarts. J.. 2 :. w Ridge.
McInerney, T.. e s Belle. nr 6th.
M IUPIN, J H & SON. cor 4th and Belle.
Meehan. J.. n s 3d. e State.
Messerschmitt. Mrs. E.. cor 5th and Cherry.
Millen. J. C.. 4th. e Langdon.
MITCHELL, P., e s Belle.
NISBETT, T. P. & CO., cor 2d and Market.
Nuss, H.. cor 3d and Ridge.
Oltmanns, J. H.. 2d. w Ridge.
Organ. Mrs. M.. cor 9th and Alby.
Pape, C.. s s 5th. e Liberty.
Parker, W. R.. cor 9th and Belle.
Paul and Bierbaum. n s 2d. e Langdon.
Percival, Mrs. M.. cor State and Main.
RYRIE. A., Short. w State.
Schenck, H.. cor 6th and Walnut.
Sheean. J.. cor 2d and Langdon.
Stein. A.. 2d. w Ridge.
Stutz. J. L.. n s 2d. e Ridge.
Thornton. P.. cor 16th and Belle.
Vatterott. H.. cor 2d and Walnut.
Zeltmann. F.. n s 3d. w Washington.

GUN SMITH

Wuerker. F.. w s State. n 3d.

HARDWARE.

WHOLESALE.

Topping Bros.. 2d. w Piasa.
Wise. Blake & Johnston. 2d and William.

RETAIL.

Hartmann, J. J.. n s 2d. e Ridge.

HARNESS AND SADDLES.

Hack, Fred, n s 2d, o Spring.
Mulligan, T., 2d, e State.
Sidway, G. D., 2d e State.
Wuerker, C., 12, State.

HATS AND CAPS.

Doepke, F., 2d Junction, 3d.
Hoaglin, D. S., s s 3d.
MORITZ, H. C. G., cor 3d and State.
SCHWEPPE, J. W. & H., s s 3d.
Smith, G. A., 31, 3d.

HOTELS

CHILD HOUSE, Mrs. N. C. Blair, cor 3d and Market.
EMPIRE HOUSE, T. Fries, 3d, e State.
Farmers' Home, A. Ehrhardt, cor Spring and 2d.
Fifth Av. Hotel, M. Brown, Prop'r., cor 5th and Piasa.
OLD FARMERS' HOME, J. Miedel, n e cor 2d and Spring.
Spring St. House, S. Wyss, cor 2d and Spring.
ST. CHARLES HOTEL, R. Coudy, w s State.

HOUSE AND SIGN PAINTERS

Ensigner, W. F., e s Belle, n 4th.
Houghton, L. E., 4th, w Piasa.
Obermueller, Ch., cor 2d and Piasa.

INKS, BLUEING AND MUCILAGE MANUFAC-TURERS.

Beckley & Baker, n s 3d, e Piasa.

INSURANCE.

Atwood, J., cor 2d and Market.
McKinney & Fischbach, s s 3d.
McPike, H. G., cor Market and 2d.
Murray, C. A., cor 2d and Market.
NOONAN, E., n s 3d, w Piasa.
Roper & Cooper, over 30, 3d.
Whipple & Smiley, cor 3d and State.

IRON WORKS.

Webb, W. W., 2d, e State.

JOB PRINTERS.

Alton Banner, H. Meyer, 4th, e Belle.
Alton Telegraph, 4th, bet. Piasa and Belle.
Bronson, E. J., over 16, 3d.
Perrin & Smith, State, opp. 3d.

JUSTICES OF THE PEACE.

MIDDLETON, T, w s Belle, n 3d.
NOONAN, E., n s 3d, w Piasa.
Quarton, J., w s State, n 2d.

LEATHER.

DRURY, A. H., & CO., Short.

LIME KILNS

ARMSTRONG, W., & BRO.. ware-house, 6, Short.
Brennan, J. J., & Bro., cor 2d and Apple.
Coppinger & Biggins, County Road, office s s 3d.
Dietz, T., cor Railroad and 3d.
SHELLY, F., County Road.

LIVERY.

Jarrett, J., cor Easton and Front.
Mather, A., Piasa, n 3d.
Platt & Hart, w s State.

LOAN BROKER.

Hewit. F., s s 3d.

LUMBER YARDS.

BOALS, M. H., 2d, bet Spring and Ridge.
PERLEY & WOODMAN, cor 2d and Henry.
SWEETSER & PRIEST, 2d, w Ridge.
SWEETSER & PRIEST, 4th, e Piasa.

MACHINE SHOP AND BRASS FOUNDRY.

HAYDEN, G. D., w s Belle, bet 4th and 5th.

MARBLE YARDS

Benedict, A., s s 4th, bet. Belle and State.

Flynn, Wm., cor 5th and Belle.
Fuller, L. H., n s 4th, w Belle.

MEAT MARKETS.

Bell, J. R., & Co., n s 3d, e Belle.
Crasber, A., n s 2d, e Ridge.
FRITCH & KOCH, s s 2d, w Oak.
Herb & Meyers, n s 2d, e Henry.
Kuhn, & Fuchs, 2d, e Henry.
Murphy & Co., e s Belle, n 4th.

MERCHANT TAILORS.

Docpke, F., 2d, Junction 3d.
Dutro, M. M., w s Belle, s 4th.
BRUEGGEMANN, B. A., n s 3d, c Belle.
McGee, C.. Belle, cor 8th.
MORITZ, H. C. G., cor 3d and State.

MILLINERY.

BURTON, H., n s 3d, e State.
Gilman, I. D., & Co., w s Belle, s 4th.
Johnson, Mrs. A., s s 3d, e State.
Justi, Mrs. A., 2d, w Ridge.
Landt, Mrs. J. P., e s Belle, s 4th.

MUSIC AND MUSICAL INSTRUMENTS.

WALTERS, V., cor 3d and Piasa.

NEWSPAPERS

DAILY.

Alton Daily Telegraph, Holden & Norton, 4th, bet. Piasa and Belle.
Alton Democrat, J. N. Shoemaker, State, opp. 3d.
Morning News, E. J. Bronson & Co., s s 3d.

WEEKLY.

Alton Banner, H. Meyer, 4th, e Belle.
Alton Democrat, I. N. Shoemaker, Prop'r., over 16, 3d.
Alton Telegraph, Holden & Norton, 4th, bet. Piasa and Belle.

MONTHLY.

Our Faith T. H. Perrin, State, opp. Capitol.

NOTIONS.

Mrasek, Mrs. L., n s 2d, e Spring.

Phelan, A. E., s s 2d, e Henry.

ORGAN MANUFACTURER.

Gratian, J., Easton, nr. 6th.

PLUG TOBACCO MANUFACTURERS.

Dausman & Drummond, cor Alton and 2d.

PLUMBERS.

TURNER, CHAS. E., & CO., w s State, n 2d.

PHOTOGRAPHERS.

Breath, E. A., s s 3d, e State.
Crossman, C. L., 2d, e Piasa.
Ritter, H., over 14, 3d.

PHYSICIANS.

Bunsen, C., s s Market. w Alby.
Davis, C., s s 3d. w Piasa.
Garvin, J. P., e s Belle. s 4th.
Gibson, R., n s 2d, w George.
Guelich, E., cor 3d and Henry.
Hardy, I. E., e s Belle, s 4th.
Haskell, A. S. & W. A., n s 2d, e Market.
Pierce, W. C., cor 3d and Belle.
Schott, A. H., e s Market. n 2d.
Smith, C. M., cor 4th and Belle.
Story, W., n s 2d. w Langdon.

PORK PACKERS.

Caldwell, M. P., 85, 4th.
Millen, J. C., 4th. e Langdon.

PLANING MILLS.

BOALS, M. H., cor 2d and Oak.
Wheelock, Ginter & Martin. 1st, nr. Langdon.

PLOW WORKS

Hapgood & Co., Front.
Millen & Bro., State.

POTTERS.

Wilhelms, & Co., n s 2d. w Oak.

RAGS, OLD IRON, &C.

Oldham & Holden, State, n 1st.

REAL ESTATE.

Hewit, F., s s 3d.
McPike, H. G., cor 2d and Market.
Murray, C. A., cor 2d and Market.
Roper & Cooper, over 30, 3d.

RECTIFIERS.

FISH & WALTER, cor 2d and State.
VASEL, H. G., & CO., 4, 2d.

RESTAURANTS.

Betz, C., w s Belle, s 4th.
Hoffmann, F. E., Piasa, s 3d.
LEYSER, J., & BRO., cor 3d and Belle.
KNIGHT, T., 2d, e Piasa.

SADDLERY HARDWARE.

DRURY, A. H., & CO., Short.

SALOONS.

Aswege, E., State, bet. 2d and 3d.
Basse & Gray, State, bet. 2d and 3d.
Beil, J., s s 2d, e Spring.
Biggins, T., Piasa, n 2d.
Brandewiede, F., n s 3d, e Belle.
Broderick, W., cor 18th and Belle.
Cahill, J., w s Belle, s 8th.
Curdie, J., 2d, opp. City Hall.
Dawson, J., n s 2d, w Vine.
Dietchy, J., cor 3d and Ridge.
Ehrhardt, A., cor 2d and Spring.
Elble, F., 2d, e Junction 3d.
Fels, Fred. n s 2d, e Junction 3d.
Fries, T., 3d, e State.
Hastings, J. H., cor 2d and Apple.
HEMKEN, G., cor 2d and Langdon.
Herman, J., Junction 2d and 3d.
Hoefert, F., w s State.
Horat & Miessner, cor 2d and Piasa.
Kindler, J., w s Belle, n 3d.

Koop, J., cor, 5th and Ridge.
Lohr, J., e s Belle, n 4th.
McGrath, D., w s Belle, n 7th.
MIEDEL, J., n e cor 2d and Spring.
Mihsel, G., n s 3d, e State.
Nagle, F., cor Bozza and Washington.
NEWMAN, J., cor Market and Front.
Oben, M. F, cor 2d and Piasa.
Ryan, D., cor 2d and George.
Spite, J., n s 2d, e Ridge.
Sotier, C., n s 2d, e Henry.
Stauff, C., n s 3d, w Washington.
Steiner, M., n s 2d, e Langdon.
Steinheimer, B., 2d, w Market.
Wagner, J., e s Belle, n 4th.
Wempen, J., Washington, n 3d.
Wyss, S., cor 2d and Spring.
Yunk, J., cor Alby and Front.

SASH, DOORS AND BLINDS.

BOALS, M. H., cor 2d and Oak.
Wheelock, Ginter & Martin, Front.

SAW AND KNIFE MAKER.

Altena, I. G., cor Easton and 2d.

SAW MILL.

Hayner, J. E., County Road.

SEWING MACHINE AGENTS.

DOMESTIC, E. H. GOULDING, cor 3d and Piasa.
**HOWE, R. B. SHACKELFORD, Manager, 4th, w
    Piasa.**
SINGER, WM. F. BOEHNING, Belle.
Wheeler & Wilson, J. H. McPike, cor 2d and Market.

SILVER PLATER

Moran, Wm., State, s 3d.

SODA AND MINERAL WATERS.

BUFF, KUHL & CO., cor 2d and Ridge.
Weisbach, C., cor 2d and Walnut.

STEAM DYEING AND CLEANSING.

DIETZ, M. H., & CO., State, bet 3d and 4th.

STONE QUARRIES.

Atkins, & Patrick, cor Main and 8th.
Watson, H., 8-9 and Piasa.

STOVES AND TINWARE.

Garde. B., cor 4th and State.
Pitts, S. W., & Co., w s State.
Plaff, V., n s 2d, e Ridge.
Stanford, H., 2d, e George.

TANNERY.

Williams, R. A., Belle, n 12th.

UMBRELLA REPAIRER.

Schlageter. B., n s 2d, e Ridge.

UNDERTAKING.

BAUER & HOFFMANN, 2d, opp. City Hall.
Borckman, C., 2d, w Ridge.
Brudon, Wm., n s 2d, w Alby.
KLUNK & WILLS, w s State, opp. 3d.
SUTTER, J., 2d, bet. Henry and Langdon.

WALL PAPER.

NEERMANN, A., s s 3d.
Seely & Hoffmeister, 8 and 10, 3d.

WATCHES, CLOCKS AND JEWELRY.

Cary, J. W., s s 3d, e State.
Fisher, J., s s 2d, e Langdon.
GLEN, A. J, 3d, w Piasa.
GOULDING, E. H., cor 3d and Piasa.

WINES AND LIQUORS.

FISH & WALTER, cor 2d and State.
Raible, J., cor 4th and Belle.
Tonsor, J. M., 2d, e Junction 3d.
VASEL, H. G., & CO., 4, 2d.
KNIGHT, T., 2d, e Piasa.

WOOLEN MILL.

Nichols, F. K., Son & Co., cor Belle and 7th.

PRYOR & CO.'S

STILLWATER

CITY DIRECTORY,

1876-7.

COMPRISING

AN ALPHABETICAL LIST OF CITIZENS, A CLASSIFIED BUSINESS DI-
RECTORY, LISTS OF CITY AND COUNTY OFFICERS,
CHURCHES, SCHOOLS, SOCIETIES,
STREETS AND WARDS.

STILLWATER, MINN. :
PRYOR & CO., PUBLISHERS.
1876.

PREFACE.

We present to our patrons a new Directory of the City of Stillwater for 1876–7, its object and value in its preparation have been constantly held in view. Every effort was made in the canvass to procure the correct location of all citizens, while in connection with their business they become recognized in each and all branches conducted by them; also containing much other matter of utility and interest to the citizens of Stillwater and ty strangers, rendering it a fit representation of the business and enterprise of the City.

The General Directory shows 2,400 names, from which an estimate of the number of people living in the City can be made.

For any imperfections or omissions that may occur, notwith. standing the diligence used in gathering the promiscuous matter necessary to complete a work of this kind, especially the large number of names, which is believed to include all that would claim recognition within its pages, the publishers ask the indulgence of the public, trusting that the work will meet with satisfaction and approval which it has been their earnest endeavor to achieve.

PRYOR & CO

GENERAL INDEX.

INDEX TO ADVERTISERS.

THE OLDEST PAPER IN MINNESOTA.

THE

STILLWATER MESSENGER.

Wolf Block, Corner Main and Chestnut Streets.

LARGEST CIRCULATION OF ANY PAPER IN THE ST. CROIX VALLEY.

An Independent Republican Paper.

The FEARLESS FOE of RINGS and RASCALITY in BOTH PARTIES.

Book and Job Printing.

With a fine assortment of TYPE and the best of Presses, our facilities in this respect are unsurpassed.
Terms the most reasonable.

SEWARD & TAYLOR, Publishers.

TAYLOR & CO.,

STEAM

JOB PRINTERS

AND

BOOK BINDERS,

AND PUBLISHERS OF

The Stillwater Lumberman.

Office on Main Street, in Bernheimer Block, Second and Third Floors.

ALL KINDS OF

Printing, Ruling AND Binding

AT EASTERN PRICES.

PRYOR & CO'S.,

STILLWATER CITY DIRECTORY,

1876-7.

MISCELLANEOUS DEPARTMENT.

City Officers.

Mayor—Wm. M. McCluer.
Clerk—E. A. Hopkins.
Treasurer—M. M. Clark.
Attorney—Fayette Marsh.
Surveyor and Engineer—Myron Shepard.
Street Commissioner—John Conklin.
Physcian—C. Carli.

City Council.

First Ward—J. O'Shaughnessy. G. S. Brown, A. Tuor.
Second Ward—P. H. Müller, J. C. Gardner, T. Jassoy.
Third Ward—G. W. Seymour, F. A. Haussner. J. A. Deragisch.

Municipal Court.

Judge—C. P. Gregory.
Ex-Officio Clerk—E. A. Hopkins.
Court Officer—F. L. McKusick.
Chief of Police—M. Shortall.
Policemen—Duncan Chisholm, John Shortall, John Booren,
. Daniel Reardon.

Board of Education.

Ex-Officio President—Wm. M. McCluer.
Clerk—J. C. Rhodes.
Treasurer—R. Lemhicke— A. K. Doe, Joseph Tanner.

Washington County Officers.

Clerk of Court—Harvey Wilson.
Auditor—Geo. Davis.
Register of deeds—A. M. Dodd.
Treasurer—Myron Shepard.
Judge of Probate—E. G. Butts.
Sheriff—J. A. Johnson.
Attorney—Fayette Marsh.
Surveyor—James Stewart.
Sup't of Schools—P. E. Walker.
Coroner—J. C. Rhodes.
Court Commissioner—C. E. Nordgord.

Fire Department.

Chief Engineer—D. Bronson.
First Assistant—King Doe.
Second   "   —Wm. May.
Stillwater, No. 1 (steamer)—F. E. Joy, Foreman, Johnson Lillies,
    Ass.t Foreman. Engine room Commercial Av.
St. Croix Hook and Ladder Co.,—Chas. McMillan, Foreman, P .B.
    Smith, Ass't Foreman. Commercial Av.

Masonic.

Hall Staples Block.

Washington R. A. C. No. 17—W. G. Bronson H. P., E. A. Fol-
son, K., Wm. M. May, S., J. A. Johnson, Sec., Jas. S. An-
derson, treasurer, John W. Dinsmore, Capt. of H., Hugh
Hall, P. S., Leonard Clark, R. A. C., Jas. Mulvey, M. 1st V.,
Wm. Richardson, M. 2d V., Abe Hall, M. 3d V., John M.
Nelson, Sentinel.

St. John's Lodge No. 1—Meets First and Third Mondays in each
month. Hugh Hall, W. M.; R. Lehmicke, S. W., L. Clark,
J. W. E. Capron, Treasurer; ——Chase, Sec., F. E. Joy, S.
D., J. Johnson, J. D.. J. M. Nelson, T.

I. O. of O. F.
Hall, Holcombes New Block.
Stillwater Lodge, No 51,   Meets   every Wednesday evening, Geo.
Low, P. G., L. Grant, N. G., R. Daw, V. G.

Knights of Pythias.
Hall cor Main and Chestnut. Stillwater Lodge, No 7, Meets
every Tuesday evening. R. Lehmicke, P. C., O. A. Rick-
er, C. C., W. W. Hall, V. C., J. Taenhauser, M. of E.,
W. E. Easton, M. of F., T. H. Warren, K. of R. & S., C.
A. Bennett, M. at. A., H. Wheeler, Prel., M. Gillespie, O.
G., J. Larrivie, J. G.

Sons of Herman.
Hall cor Main and Chestnut. Germania Lodge, No 3, meets every
Friday evening, Jos. Taenhauser. Pres't., Emil Wier, Vice
Pres't., D. Jastrom, Sec., H. Steffens, Fin. Sec., F. N.
Schwarz, Treas.

Grand Army of The Republic.
Miller Post No. 14, C. B. Loomis, Com., J. A. Reed, S. V. C..
Myron Shepard, J. V., C. F. Siebold, Quartermaster, C.
A. Bennet, Adj., Jos. Taenhauser, O. of D., Adam Marty.
O. of G., B. G. Merry, Chap.

Miscellaneous Societies.
Stillwater Mannerchor, Meets Wednesdays and Sundays, cor Main
and Chestnut. Emil Krueger, Pres't., Wm. Schermully,
Sec., F. Siebold, Treas., Wm. P. Schilling, Leader.

Stillwater Schutzen Verein, Meets cor Main and Chestnut, F.
Bertchey. Pres't., E. Graff, Sec., E. Krueger, Treas.

Church Directory.
Episcopal Church, Rev. S. J. Brooks pastor, services 10:30 A. M.
7:30 P. M. Sunday School 12 M. 3d.

German Lutheran Church, Rev. Jacob Segrist Pastor; services 10
A. M.. Sunday School 2 P. M. 3d n Oak.

First Presbyterian Church, Rev. I. N. Otis Pastor, services 10:30
A. M. 7:30 P. M.   Sunday School 12 M.   Cor 3d and Myrtle.

Methodist Episcopal Church. 3d, n Myrtle.   Rev. J. H. Macomb
Pastor; services 10:30 A. M. 7:30 P. M.   Sunday School 11:
30 A. M.

Second Presbyterian Church, s s Pine, w Pine.

St. Mary's German Catholic Church, 3d, n Chestnut.   Rev. Mon.
Sigesbert Pastor; services 10 A. M. Vespers 2 P. M.   3d, n
Chestnut.

St. Michael's Catholic Church. Rev. M. E. Murphy Pastor; services 8 and 10:30 A. M. Vespers 7:30 P. M.   Cor Walnut and
3d.

Swedish Lutheran, —— —— Pastor, cor 4th and Oak; services
10:20 A. M.

Universalist Church, Rev. J. Marvin Pastor; services every other
Sunday 10:30.   Sunday School 12 M.   3d.

STREET DIRECTORY.

Abbott, from Holcombe w to Western Row, 1st s Willard.
Alder, from Lake w to 4th, 18th n Chestnut.
Almond, from N. Broadway w to 4th, 10th n Chestnut.
Anderson, from Holcombe w to Western Row, 3d, s Willard.
Aspen, from N. Broadway to Marine, 7th n Churchill.
Balsam, from N. Broadway w to 4th, 14th n Chestnut.
Becher, from Willard s to Hancock, 11th w Lake.
Borup, from St. Cyer to St. Paul Av, 15th w Lake,
Brick, from John n to St. Paul Av, 13th w Lake.
Broadway, from Main s to Goodwood, and from Aspen to Alder
1st w Main.
Burlington, from 2d to 6th, H. and S. add.
Cedar, from Cherry n 1½ blocks.
Center, from Lilly Lake n to Ramsey, 11th w Lake.
Cherry, from Main w to 5th, n Chestnut.
Chestnut, from Lake w to 5th.
Churchill, from 1st to Holcombe, 7th s Chestnut.
Clarke, from 4th w to Marine, 4th n Elm.
Commercial Av, from Main to 2d, n Chestnut.
Cooper, from 4th w to Main, 3d n Elm.
Cornelian, from South Av, to Moore 7th w Lake.
Division, from Sherburne w to limits.

Dubuque, from 3d to 6th H. and S. Add.
Elm, from Lake w to Marine 6th n Chestnut.
Evert, from Ramsey n to Mulberry 9th w Lake.
Fifth, from Hancock n to Wilkin, and from Hudson to Orleans 5th w Lake.
Forward, from South Av. n to Moore, 9th w Lake.
Fourth, from Hancock, n to Alder and from Hudson to Orleans, 4th w Lake.
Goodwood, from Rock, w to Holcombe, 8th n Chestnut.
Greely, from Willard. n to Mulberry, 8th w Lake.
Grove, from Lilly Lake, n to St. Paul Av. 12th w Lake.
Hancock, from 1st, to Holcombe. 8th s Chestnut.
Harriet, from Ramsey, n to Mulberry, 7th w Lake.
Hazel. from Lake w to 4th, 17th, n Chestnut.
Hickory, from 4th, w to Marine, 1st Elm.
Holcombe, from Willard, s to Hancock, 8th n Lake.
Hudson. from 4th, to 6th, H. & L. Add.
Jeannie, from Willard, n to Mulberry, 8th w Lake.
John, from Center. w to Limits.
Juniper, from N. Broadway, w to 4th 12th n Chestnut.
Lake, is the northern extension of Main.
Laurel, from Lake, w to 5th n Chestnut.
Linden, from Lake, w to 5th, 3d n Chestnut
Locust, from Main to 8th, 5th, s Main.
Main, runs north and South. first from Lake.
Magnolia. from N. Broadway, w to 4th, 8th n Chestnut.
Maple, from, 4th, w 2d, s Elm.
Marine, from Maple, n to Moore, 8th w Lake.
Martha, from Ramsey, n to Moore 8th w Lake.
Mary, from Maple. n to Wilkin, 7th w Lake.
Minnesota, from South Av. n to Moore 8th w Lake.
Moore, from 4th w Marine, 6th n Elm.
Mulberry. from Lake w, to City limits, 2d n Chestnut.
Myrtle. from Lake w to Harriet, 1st n Chestnut.
Nelson. from 2d e to Lake, 1st s Chestnut.
Oak, from 3d w. to Sherburne, 2d s Chestnut.
Oakes, from Stlyer n to St Paul Av. 16th w Lake.
Olive, from 2d w. to Owens, 1st s Main.
Orange, from N. Broadway, w to 4th, 8th n Chestnut.
Orleans. from Main. to 6th, at southern City limits.
Owens, from Willard n, to Mulberry 9th w Lake.
Pennock, from w end of Churchill, to Western Row, 2d s Willard.
Pine, from Broadway w, to Sherburne, 3d s Chestnut.

Poplar, from Lake w, ro 4th, 15 n Chestnut.
Putz, from Willard s, to Hancock 10th, w Lake.
Ramsey, from western City limits, e 4th n Willard.
Rice, from Jeannie, w to limits.
Rock, from Locust, to Goodwood, 1st w Main.
School, from 2d w, to 4th, 1st n Laurel.
Second, from Hancock n, to Alder 1st w Main.
Seeley, from Stlyer n, to St. Paul Av. 14th w Lake.
Seventh, from Hancock to Goodwood, and from Prairie to City
    Limits, 7th w Lake.
Sherburne, from Lilly Lake n, to Mulberry, 10th w Lake.
Sixth, from Hancock n, to Chestnut, and from Goodwood to Or-
    leans, 6th w Lake.
Smith, from Oak s, to Hancock, 9th w Lake.
Spring, from w end of Myrtle, to Limits.
Spruce, from N. Broadway, w to 4th, 13th n Chestnut.
Stlyer, from Lily Lake, to limits.
Stimson, from Myrtle, s to Levee bet Main and Lake shore.
St Paul Av. from Owens, w to limits.
St Louis, from Main to 6th, H. & S. Add.
Sycamore, from Lake, w to 4th, 11th, n Chestnut.
Third, from Hancock, n 3d and from Dubuque to Orleans 3d, from
    Lake.
Union, from Myrtle to Chestnut, bet Main and 2d.
Walnut, from Broadway to 5th, s Chestnut.
West, from Stlyer, n to St Paul Av. 17th, w Lake.
Western Row, from Willard, s to Hancock, 12th w Lake.
Wilkin, from 4th, w to Marine, 3d, e Elm.
Willard, from west end of Goodwood, w to Sherburne.
William, from Ramsey, n to Mulberry, 10th w Lake.
Willow, from Lake, w to 4th, 16th, n Chestnut.
Wisconsin, from 4th, w to Marine, 5th n Elm.

WARD BOUNDARIES.

First Ward—Comprises all that portion of the city lying s of a line
west from the Lake through Nelson to 2d, s to Pine,w to Sherburne
and s of John.

Second Ward—All that portion of the city lying n of a line
drawn through Northern Boundry of 1st, and a line drawn
through Linden to 4th, s to Mulberry, w to Limits.

Third Ward—All that portion of the city lying north boundry of
2d.

C. A. BROMLEY'S

NEW

LIVERY

AND

SALE STABLE.

SINGLE AND DOUBLE RIGS,

With or Without Drivers, at any time of the

DAY OR NIGHT.

As Good Turnouts as can be found in the Northwest,

Horses Bought, Stabled and Sold.

PRICE MODERATE.

Stable on Chestnut, between Main and Second.

MANSION HOUSE.

J. DISCH, Prop'r.

In the New Disch Block, Main Street, Stillwater, Minnesota.

BOARD BY THE DAY OR WEEK.

Pleasant and Well Furnished Rooms.   Good Tables.   Try it once and You will Come Again.

Good Stabling in Connection With the House.

RICHARD DAW,

MANUFACTURER OF

CARRIAGES, BUGGIES,

SPRING WAGONS, SLEIGHS, &C.

FIRST CLASS WORK ONLY.

West Side Second, Near SAWYER HOUSE.

PRYOR & CO.'S
STILLWATER CITY DIRECTORY,
1876-7.

ABBREVIATIONS.

ab	above.	e	east of.
av	avenue.	manufg	manufacturer.
bet	between.	n	north of.
bds	boards.	nr	near.
bldg	building.	opp	opposite.
cor	corner.	s	south of.
clk	clerk.	w	west of
lab	laborer.	n s	north side.
carp	carpenter.	w s	west side.
s s	south side.	e s	east side.

ALPHABETICAL LIST OF NAMES.

A

Ashton, Joseph, carp. bds Mansion House.

Ahl, Mrs. Lucy, boarding, res cor William and Mulberry.

Ahn, Nicholas, lab, res cor Smith and Willard.

Akholm, Chas. painter, bds Wexio Hotel.

Albenberg, A. (Albenberg & Conhaim;) res Broadway, cor Walnut.

Albenberg & Conhaim. (A. Albenberg. M. Conhaim.) dealers in cigars and tobacco, Union Blk, Main.

Albenberg, Emanuel, peddler, bds A. Mellin.

Albenberg, Louis, cigar peddler. bds cor Broadway and Walnut.

Alcorn, John, lab, res cor 2d, and Olive.

Allen, Geo. lab, res 7th s Goodwood.

Allen, H. H., real estate & insurance, e s Main. s Myrtle. bds Sawyer House.

Allen, John, teamster, res Main, s Mulberry.

Allen, M. T., sawyer, H. B. & B.

Allen, S. J., lab, H. B. D. & F., res Main.

Allenson, Andrew, carp, bds 2d n Linden.

Allenson, John, patternmaker, D. M. Swain, bds 2d.
Alloyed, Henry, mill hand, H. B. & B.
Alloyed, Joseph, mill hand, H. B. & B.
Almquist, John, mill hand, Seymour, Sabin & Co., bds at Mill.
Almquist, M., lab, bds St. Croix Hotel.
Altwein, Fred, butcher, res Stimson's Alley.
Ambuhl, Tobias, mill hand, H. B. & B., res 5th, n Churchill.
Anderson, Andrew, mill hand, I. Staples, bds at Mill.
Anderson, Anton, tailor, J. A. Ryding, bds Williams House.
Anderson, Christ. lab, bds St. Croix Hotel.
Anderson, Frank, lab. bds Scandinavian House.
Anderson, Frank, res Mulberry, w Main.
Anderson, Godfrey, lab, res Martha, nr Maple.
Anderson, Jacob, mason, res Elm, w Main.
Anderson, James, saw mill, res n s Chestnut, w 4th.
Anderson, John, machinist, res w s 3d, s Mulberry.
Anderson, John, lumberman, bds Mulberry, w Main.
Anderson, Niles, machinist, D. M. Swain, res 2d.
Anderson, Oscar, mill hand, I. Staples, bds at Mill.
Anderson, Ole, mill hand, I. Staples, bds at Mill.
Anez, Winn, mill hand, H. B. & B.
Armstrong, Alex, wall guard at Prison, res 2d, n Chestnut.
Armstrong, C. L., photographer, J. Sinclair, bds same.

ARMSTRONG, D. W., Agt. American Express Co., 2d, n Chestnut, res cor Smith and Willard.

Arnd, August, shoemaker, res e s Holcombe, opp Oak.
Arndt, August, shoemaker, res 6th, s Churchill.
Arndt, Joseph, lab, res 7th, s Churchill.
Arthur, Wm., mill hand, H. B. & B.
Arvien, Frank, lumberman, bds Keystone House.
Aschbach, Gerhard, foreman, brewer, H. Tepass, bds same
Asleson, Ole, mill hand, Seymour, Sabin & Co.
Atterdehl, Alex, carp, res Elm w Main.
Austin, Chas., harness maker, bds Union House.
Austin, E., filer, I. Staples.
Agott, Louis, lumberman, bds Keystone House.

B

Babcock, Adelbert, mill hand, bds John Morgans.
Babcock, Alonzo, mill hand, H. B. & B.
Babcock, Frank, mill hand, H. B. & B. bds at Mill.

Badke, August, lab, res 7th, s Churchill.
Babnholt, Fred, lab, res 7th, n Hancock.
Bakeman, A. F., res w s 2d, n Chestnut.
Baker, —— bds D, Harrigan.
Baker, Fred, teamster, res Stimsons Alley.
Baker, James, lab, res cor Churchill and 6th.
Bank, Fred, watchman, Schulenburg, Bœckeler & Co.
Bansen, Chas., lumberman, res Myrtle, w 3d.
Barclay, Robt., works on lake, bds cor 6th and Churchill.
Barrett, E., moulder, D. M. Swain, res Myrtle.
Barrett, John, engineer, bds P. Barrett.
Barrett, John, lumberman, bds P. Barrett.
Barrett, Patrick, lumberman, res n s Myrtle, w 3d.
Barrett, Thos., lumberman, bds P. Barrett.
Barron, James, lab, res cor Becher and Pennock.
Barron, Patrick, lab, res 4th, n Churchill.
Barron, Richard, lab, res cor Western, Row and Anderson.
Barrons, Michael, mason, bds Pacific House.
Barry, James, lab, res 4th, n Churchill.
Bassett, Alex, lumberman, bds Keystone House.
Bates, Mrs. A., res w s 3d, s Olive.
Battles, G. W., res cor 3d and Pine.
Baumann, Christ, bartender, J. Gieriet, bds same.
Baumann, Fred, lab, Schulenburg, Bœckeler & Co.
Bayer, Anton, shoemaker, N. F. Schwarz, bds Liberty House.
Bean, Chas., (Hersey & Bean) res 3d, s Mulberry.
Bean, Fred C., time keeper, H. B. & B., res 3d.
Bean, Jacob, (Hersey & Bean) res 3d, nr St. Louis.
Beck, John, lab, bds Liberty house.
Beckert, Ernst, lab, res w s 2d, n Olive.
Beedy, Wm., mill hand, Seymour, Sabin & Co.
Beer, John, res 4th, n Goodwood.
Beging, Ed, mill hand, I. Staples, bds at Mill.
Belisle, Moses, mill hand, H. B. & B.
Belkic, Aug., mill hand, H. B. & B.
Bell, Dan W., mill hand, I. Staples, bds at Mill.
Bell, Joseph, teamster, H. B. & B. bds at Mill.
Bell, Joseph, teamster, res e s Broadway, s Walnut.

BELL & LARRIVIE, (Wm. Bell, Jos. Larrivie,) manufacturers of pure Candies, also Fancy Bakers, Fruits of all kinds in their season. Chestnut, w Main.

Bell, Wm., (Bell & Larrivie) res 2nd, s Chestnut.
Bender, Fred, shoemaker, bds Pacific House.
Benedict, David, mill hand, H. B. & B. bds at Mill.
Bengston, M., carp., Seymour Sabin & Co.
Bennett, C. A., Deputy Surveyor Gen'l., res cor Chestnut and 3d.
Benning, Wenzel, rafter, Schulenburg, Boeckeler & Co.
Bensen, J. M., carp., res Main, s Mulberry.
Bensinger, Fred, farmer, res Main, s Chestnut.
Benson, Gilbert, lab., res Holcombe, s Churchill.
Bergen, Ed., mill hand, I. Staples, bds at Mill.
Bergen, John, lab., res cor Putz and Pine.
Bergin, John, lumberman, bds T. Carroll.
Bergin, John, lab., res 6th, s Goodwood.
Bergeron, John, mill hand, S. S. & Co., res Lake.
Bergeron, Louis, contractor, Schulenburg, Boeckeler & Co., res Lake.
Bergin, Patrick, lumberman, bds Greeley, n Spring.
Berglin, Mrs. A., res 2d, s Linden.
Berglund, Elias, lab., bds, Wexio Hotel.
Berglund, Frank, lab., bds Scandinavian House.
Berglund, Wm., clk., Wexio Hotel, bds same.
Bergmeister, H., mill hand, H. B. & B.
Berkle, Joseph, lab., Wolf's Brewery, res Olive, w 2d.
Berkley, Joseph, mill hand, H. B. & B.
Bernhard, Fred, mill hand, Seymour, Sabin & Co.
Berow, Frank, mill hand, Seymour, Sabin & Co., bds at Mill.
Bertchy, Jacob, carp., Schulenburg, Boeckeler & Co.
Besnet, Louis, watchmann, H. B. & B.
Bickford, Marquis L., mill hand, res cor Becher and Abbott.
Biedermann, Fred, lab., res 7th, s Churchill.
Biele, Mrs. Catherine, res Lake.
Bieging, Wm., carp., res Oak, w Martha.
Billig, Moses, lab., H. B. & B., bds 3d, s Churchill.
Billido, Daniel, mill hand, H. B. & B.
Billido, Ed., mill hand, H. B. & B.
Billido, Louis, mill wright, res 3d, nr Dubuque.
Billivou Joseph, carp., res 3d s Churchill.
Billivou, Joseph, mill hand, H. B. & B., bds at Mill.
Binker, Henry, mill hand, H. B. & B., bds at Mill.
Birmingham, John, butcher, bds J. McNall.
Birmingham, —— bricklayer, bds Pine, e 3d.

Blackbird, Peter, lab, res Laurel, e 2d.
Blackbird, Peter, millinery, and American Sewing Machine Agt.,
  cor 2d and Chestnut, res 2d.
Blake, John, lab, res 2d, s Churchill.
Blanchard, R. G., carp, res Owens, s Spring.
Blomberg, Andrew, lab, bds St Croix Hotel.
Blum, Wendelin, harness maker, B. F. Rice, bds Pacific House.
Bodeen, John, works S. S . & Co., res back of Prison.
Bodeen, Jos., mill hand, I. Staples, bds at Mill.
Bodeen, P. P., clk, W. E. Thorne, bds 4tb, n Pine.
Bœckeler, A., (Schulenburg, Bœckeler & Co.) res St. Louis.
Bœttcher, Rev. Chas., Pastor German M. E. Church, res cor Han-
  cock and Holcombe.
Boles, Wm., printer, Stillwater Lumberman, res Main.
Boo, Chas., lab, res w s 2d, s Mulberry.
Boo, Peter, lab, bds Chas. Boo.

*BOOREN, AUG., Propr. St. Croix Hotel, pleasant
and well furnished rooms, good tables, try it once
and you will come again. Good stabling in connection with the house, w s Main s Chestnut, res same.*

Booren, John, policeman, res 2d, n Linden.
Borchordt, Henry, mill hand, res Oak, e Martha.
Bordean, Emmerd, mill hand, H. B. & B. bds at Mill.
Bordwell, Chas. C., shop guard, at Prison, bds same.
Boreen, Andrew, mill hand, I. Staples, bds at Mill.
Born, Albert, machinist, D. M. Swain, bds Pacific House.
Bornet, Aug., mill hand, H. B. & B.
Borscht, Ernst, guard at prison, res 3d, n Olive.
Boss, Joseph, carp, bds Mansion House.
Bossette, Joseph, mill hand, I. Staples, bds at Mill.
Bostrom, Chas., A., lab, res Myrtle, w 6th.
Bostrom, Gus, mill hand, Seymour, Sabin & Co.
Botting, A., shop guard at prison, res same.
Boyle, Dennis, lab, bds Levi Morgan.
Bradley, A. B., teamster, res 6th, n Churchill.
Brady, Hugh, blacksmith, res w s 2d, n Hancock.
Bross, Jos , painter, bds Centennial Restaurant.
Brennan, James, mill hand, H. B. & B.
Brennan, John, lumberman, bds P. Barrett.
Brennan, John, lab, res s part of city.
Brenner, C., (Zurrich & Brenner,) res Oak.

BROMLEY, C. A., Livery & Sale Stable, s s Chestnut w Main, res Broadway n Pine.

Bromley, M. H., foreman C. A. Bromley, res Chestnut w 2d.
Bronson, D. (Hersey Bronson, Doe & Folsom,) res cor 6th and Oak.
Bronson, Frank, clk, res 3d s Linden.
Bronson, W. G., (Stombs & Bronson,) res 2d, cor Laurel.
Bronson, Mrs. S., res 3d, s Linden.
Brooks, Rev. T. J., rector Episcopal Church, res s s Cherry, w 3d.
Brown, Ed. S., (Hersey, Bean & Brown,) res cor 3d and Burlington.
Brown, Elisha, carp, res cor Martha and Spring.
Brown, Geo. S., correspondent, Hersey, Bean & Brown, res cor 4th and Burlington.
Brown, Henry, mill hand, res Broadway s Walnut.
Brown, Jacob, cook, res 2d, s Chestnut.
Brown, John, clk, H. B. D. & F., res 4th, n Pine.
Brown, J. C., bookkeeper, H. B. & B.
Brown, Wm. H., lab, res w s 4th, n Pine.
Bruett, Chas., lumberman, bds P. Barrett.
Bruno, David, teamster, H. B. & B., bds at Mill.
Brunswick, Mrs. M., res Chestnut, w 2d.
Brush, Geo. M., station agent, W. Wis. & St. P. S. & T. F. Rys, lower Main, res Chestnut, w 3d.
Buckingham, Miss H., manufg hair goods, res cor 2d & Chestnut.
Buenger, John, lab, res Schulenburg Add.
Burtzlaff, Albert, sexton, res in Fair View cemetery.
Bulov, F., (Bulov & Thon,) res 2d, cor Mulberry.
Bulov & Thon, (F. Bulov, M. Thon,) merchant tailors, w s 2d, Mulberry.
Buman, John, lab, bds 2d, n Linden.
Buman, Martin, lumberman, bds Mulberry, w Main.
Burlingham, D. L., painter, res cor 3d, e Churchill.
Burman, Alex., lab, bds Spring, w Jeannie.
Burns, B. F., gate keeper at Prison, res Laurel, e 2d.
Burns, Chas., teamster, res cor Greeley and Spring.
Burns, Hugh, mill hand, Seymour, Sabin & Co.
Burns, Luke, lab., res w s 2nd, s Chestnut.
Burns, Peter, mill hand, H. B. & B.
Bursch, Chas., mill hand, I. Staples, bds at Mill.
Bursch, Fred, mill hand, I. Staples, bds at Mill.
Bursch, Chr., sawyer, Schulenburg, Boeckeler & Co.

Bursch, John, saw filer, Schulenburg, Boeckeler & Co.
Bursch, Jul., rafter, Schulenburg, Boeckeler & Co.
Burth, Theo., car repairer, res Lower Main.
Busch, Herman, lab, bds Liberty House.
Buske, Wm., mill hand, I. Staples, bds at Mill.
Buth, August, boots and shoes, e s Main, s Chestnut, res Pine cor 4th.
Butterhausen, Ole, mill hand, H. B. & B., bds at Mill.

BUTLER & McKUSICK, (C. J. Butler, I. E. Mc-Kusick,) Commission, Lower Main.

Butler, C. J., Butler & McKusick, res 3rd, cor Olive.
Butler, Robt., clk, Butler & McKusick, res 3rd.
Butts, E. G., Attorney at Law, and Judge of Probate, cor 2nd and Chestnut, res 2nd, cor Laurel.

C

Cadonau, Mrs., res w s Main, n Nelson.
Cain, Mrs., res w s 2d, n Olive.
Calkins, Hiram, farmer, res nr Fair Grounds.
Callan, Patrick, yardman, I. Staples, bds at Mill.
Campbell, Jos., lumberman, bds J. Donovan.
CANNON, H. W., Cashier Lumberman's National Bank, bds Sawyer House.
Caplazi, Albert, carp, res 4th, s Goodwood.
Caplazi Joseph, lab, res 4th, n Oak.
Capron, Alonzo, tinner, E. Capron, bds same.
Capron, A. A., book keeper, res 6th, n Pine.

CAPRON, EDWARD, Dealer in and Manufacturer of Stoves, Tin, Copper Ware, Chestnut w Main, res 5th, n Pine.

Capron, W. M., clk, E. Capron, res cor 3d, and Churchill.
Capron, Thos., wheat buyer, bds Pacific House.
Cardinal, Albert, mill hand, Hersey, Bean & Brown.
Carey, Richard, yardman, I. Staples, bds at Mill.
Carlin, J. H., fireman, bds D. Harrigan.

CARLEY & LILLIS, (J. Carley, J. C. Lillis,) dealers in dry goods, groceries, provisions &c. Union Block, Main.

Carley, Ed., teamster, I. Staples, bds at Mill.
Carley, J., (Carley & Lillis.) res cor 6th and Goodwood.
Carlgren, Gust., mason, res Spring, w Jeannie.
Carli, C., physician, (Reg.) cor 2d and Mulberry, res same.

CARLI, C. H. Jr., Photographer, Old pictures re-produced and enlarged, Porcelain pictures a specialty, cor 2d, and Mulberry, res same.

Carli, J. R. lab, res Lake, s Sycamore.
Carlson, Chas, lab, bds Wexio Hotel.
Carlson, John, lab, bds Scandinavian House.
Carlson, Nels., boarding, res Mulberry, w Main.
Carr, Frank, rafter, bds Mansion House.
Carroll, Michael, carp. res 4th, s Churchill.
Carroll, Thos, carp. res Greeley, n Spring.
Carrol, Wm., carp, res back of Prison.
Carson, Wm., painter, bds Mrs. S. Bronson.
Casey, Wm., lumberman, res St Paul Ave. w Sherburne.
Casey, Wm., lab, res cor 3d and Mulberry.
Casey, Thos., teamster, I. Staples, bds at Mill.
Casey, Thos., teamster, res St. Paul Av., w Sherburne.
Castello, Michael J., lab, res Lower Main.
Castle, J. W., student, Castle & Lehmicke, bds Pine, e 3d.
Castle, J. N., (Castle & Lehmicke) bds Pine, e 3d.
Castle & Lehmicke, (J. N. Castle, Rudolph Lehmicke,) Attys. at law, cor Main and Chestnut.
Cates, T. L., teamster, I. Staples, res 6th, n Hancock.
Cates, Wm., teamster, H. B. & B., bds at Mill.
Cattenberg, Henry, res cor Western Row and Anderson.
Cayou, Benjamin, wall guard at Prison, res 4th, cor Elm.
Cedargren, John, lab, bds Wexio Hotel.
Cedarstrand, John, mill hand, I. Staples bds at Mill.
Cedarstrand, —— mill hand, res Hickory, w Martha.
Celine, Otto, lab, res Myrtle, w 4th.
Chambers, Miis Clara, teacher, bds H. J. Chambers.
Chambers, H. J., cashier, Seymour, Sabin & Co., res Aspen e 3d.
Chase, Frank, clk, Wardens office, res Cedar.
Chase, Z. W., Surveyor General, logs and lumber, Myrtle, e Main res Chestnut, e 3d.
Chenne, Julian A., clk, res Pennock, e Smith.
Chicle, Chas., shoemaker, res Holcombe, opp Oak.
Chisolm, Duncan, policeman, res Linden, w 2d.

Cholar. Chas., mill hand, res cor St. Paul Av. and Sherburne..
Christianson, Andrew, lab. res 2d, n Myrtle.
Clark. Geo. E.. mill hand, res Owen. n Pine.
Clark. Leonard, book keeper. l. Staples. res 4th, cor Cooper.
Clark. M. M., supt. I. Staples, Saw Mill, res cor 3d, and Walnut.
Clark. Nicholas. machinest. bds Pacific House.
Clark. S. M.. bds J. H. Illingworth.
Clark, Wm., res cor Willard and Owens.
Clay. W. A., log scaler, res 4th, s Goodwood.
Clegg, Chas.. cook, res Anderson, w Putz.
Clewell, O. L., reporter for Pioneer Press and Tribune office, w s
    Main. res Lindon, w 3d.
Clewell, S. A.. (Taylor & Co) res 2d.
Clymer. Joseph, ass't book keeper, H. B. & B. res 2d, s Goodwood.
Cograff. John, engineer. res 4th. n Burlington.
Coleen. Chas.. lab, bds Leveen & Stone.
Collins, Mrs. P., res Chestnut, w Main.
Collins, Patrick, mason. res 5th, s Goodwood.
Collopy, Mary, res 7th, n Churchill.
Colman, L., blacksmith, Seymour. Sabin & Co.
Colman, Seth, R., blacksmith, res w s 2d, n Walnut.
Coltson, Richard, lumberman, bds P. Barrett,
Comfort, O. H.. att. at law, e s Main. s Chestnut, res cor 3d, and
    School.
Comfort, F. V., student, H. R., Murdock, bds same.
Condell. John, lab. res Broadway opp Walnut.
Cohhaim, M.. (Albenberg, & Conhaim) res 3d, n Myrtle.
Conhaim, M. — No 2, book keeper, Albenberg & Conhaim. bds
    3d.
Conhaim, D.. travelling agt. bds Sawyer House.
Conklin, John, F., street com, res s s 3d, s Goodwood.
Conners, James. blacksmith, I. Staples, res Laurel, e 2d.
Connors, Hugh, mil hand, I. Staples, bds at Mill.
Connick, James, teamster, I. Staples, bds at Mill.
Conrad, & Hospes, (W. S. Conrad, A. C. Hospes) wholsale deal-
    ers in cigars and tobacco, w s Main n Myrtle.
Conrad, W. S., (Conrad & Hospes) res 4th, n Linden.
Corm, Aug., shoemaker, Drews & Kern. res 2d.
Cormichael, Dan, filer, I. Staples, bds at Mill.
Corteau, Eugene, mill hand, H. B. & B., bds at Mill.
Cota, Chas., mill hand, I. Staples, bds at Mill.
Cotreau, A. L., teamster, H. B. & B., bds at Mill.
Covell, John, foreman S. S. & Co., res cor 4th and Aspen.

Cowan Wm., photographer, bds D. Harrigan.

***CRANDALL & HENING, (H. M. Crandall, J.
C. Hening.) Pharmacuctists, and dealers in
Drugs, Paints and Oils Staples Block, w s Main***

Crandall, H. M., (Crandall & Hening) res Myrtle, e 3rd.
Crimmins, Dennis, teamster, H. B. & B.
Crimmins, John, lab, res 4th, s Goodwood.
Cromwell, W. V., teamster, H. B. & B., bds at Mill.
Cronick, James, teamster, bds Keystone House.
Cronin, James, lab, res cor Becher and Anderson.
Cross, J. C., scaler, I. Staples, bds at Mill.
Crossman, O. E., clk, S. Selleck, bds 2d.
Crotty, James, lab, res Burlington, w 4th.
Crotty, John, lab, res cor 4th and Burlington.
Crowley, Patrick, mill hand H. B. & B.
Crowley, Timothy, lab, res 4th, s Churchill.
Crowley, Tim, 2d engineer, I. Staples, bds at Mill.
Crane, S. A., lab, bds Leveen & Stone.
Cummings, E., lab, bds Liberty House.
Currie, ———— lab, res lower Main.
Currie, Miss Emma, teacher, bds H. J. Chambers.
Curtis, G. T., mill hand, H. B. & B.
Curtiss, John, bricklayer, res n s Pennock, w Smith.
Curtiss, Mrs. Mary A., res lower Main.
Cutler, Miss E. O., res cor 3d and Chestnut.
Cutler, F. C., (Hospes, Cutler & Co.,) res 6th, s Pine.
CUTLER, H. D., Post Master, office 2d, open 7 a. m. to 7:30 p.
m., res cor 3rd and Chestnut.

D

Dahl, Jacob, lab, bds Wexio Hotel.
Dahlberg, G. A., wagon maker, W. Muller, res Main n Mulberry.
Dahm, John, clk, J. Dahm, res same.
Dahm, Joseph, grocer, S. Main, s Nelson, res same.
Dailey, L. W., planer, res cor 2d and Goodwood.
Daimont, Geo., fireman, L. S. & M. R. R., res Upper Main.
Dake, Jas., mill hand, Hersey, Bean & Brown.
Dale, John, drayman, res 5th, n Maple.
Daley, P. J., blacksmith, I. Staples.
Damas, Bacil, mill hand, H. B. & B., bds at Mill.
Danforth, W. M., filer, H. B. & B., bds at Mill.

Danforth, Stephen, foreman, yard. II. B. & B., res c s Broadway, s Churchill.
Daniels. Peter. filer. I. Staples, res Elm, w Main.
Danielson. Chas., lab, bds Wexio Hotel.
Danielson. Christ, lab, bds St. Croix Hotel.
Darcy, John. drayman. res Main. Schulenburgs Add.
Dare. Julius, mill hand, Seymour. Sabin & Co.
Darms. John, N.. General store. e s Main. s Chestnut. res 2d. n Pine.
Darrah, John. logger, res Pine, s 3d.
Darrah. John. Jr.. logger. res Pine. e 3d.
Davidson. James, engineer, res cor 4th and Hickory.
Davis, Ben. C., farmer, res cor Center. and St. Paul, Rd.
Davivs, Edward. lab. bds cor 5th and Churchill.
DAVIS. GEO., county auditor. office Court House, res cor Olive and 5th.
Davis. H. W., clk, I. Staples.
Davis. J. B.. works for Staples. res cor 6th and Churchill.
Davis. J. P.. lab. res 6th, n Churchill.
Davis, J. S.. scaler. H. B & B.. res cor 3d and Hudson.
Davis. Robt.. book keeper, res cor 4th and Hudson.
Davis, R. R.. agt. C. B.. Newcomb & Co.. res Main. n Myrtle.
Davis. R. S.. clk. bds Broadway.

DAW, RICHARD, manufacturer of carriages. buggies, spring wagons, sleighs, &c.. w s 2d, nr Sawyer House, res 3d, s Mulberry.

Day, D. F., lab. res 4th. s Churchill.
Day, John. bds D. F., Day.
Day, —— blacksmith, res e s Main. n Chestnut.
Deegan, John, lumberman, bds J. Donovan.
Deegan, John, mill hand, I Staples, bds at Mill.
Deeertins, Joseph. A., carp. res Nelson. e 2d.
Deckeler, Adolph, tinner, bds Centennial Restaurant.
Decker, Peter J.. works I. Staples, res Chestnut, nr Bridge.
Degeler, F. A., clk, O. A.. Ricker. bds Centennial Restaurant.
Deleware, Henry. drayman. res 2d. s Chestnut.
Densmore, John. travelling agt. res Oak, w 5th.
Densmore, J. D.. lumberman, res cor Holcombe and Pine.
Denton, S. S.. livery and sale stable, 2d, s Mulberry, res 3d.
Deragisch, Anton. saloon, bds Mansion House.

Deragisch, J. A., clk, Schulenburg, Boeckeler & Co., res cor Laurel and Main.
Deragisch, Jos., saw filer, Schulenburg. Boeckeler & Co.
Deragisch, John, res Lake, n Elm.
Deragisch, Julius J., filer, Schulenburg, res Lake.
Deragisch, J. J., clk, Torinus & Wilkinson.
Deragisch, L. A., saloon, w s Main, s Chestnut, bds Mansion House.
Deragisch, P. S., saloon and billiard hall, w s Main, n Myrtle, res 4th s Walnut.
De Rosa, Geo., mill hand, I. Staples, bds at Mill.
Dewey, Phil, printer, Stillwater Messenger, bds cor 3d and Pine.
Desautels, H., farmer, res Anderson, w Putz.
Desautels, Henry, lab, res Anderson, w Putz,
Desautels, John, farmer, res s s Anderson, w Putz.
Destaffney Aug., mill hand, Seymour, Sabin & Co.
Desteffany, Mrs. Dominica, res 4th, s Goodwood.
Destaffany, Henry A., clk, Schupp & Tozer, res 4th, s Goodwood.
Desteffany, Wm., lab, res Greeley, s St. Paul Av.
Diethert, John, rafter, Schulenburg, Boeckeler & Co., res Schulenburg's Add.
Dietz, Jacob, Propr. Pacific House, cor Nelson and Main, res same.
Dinenn, John, lumbermann, bds Keystone House.

DISCH, J., Prop'r. Mansion House, Main, s Chestnut, res same.

Doe, A. K., (Hersey, Bronson, Doe & Folsom,) res cor 3d and Linden.
Doehr, Steph, rafter, Schulenburg, Boeckeler & Co., res Schulenburg's Add.
Dolquist, Chas., lab, res Greeley s Pine.
Dolson, John W., teamster, Seymour, Sabin & Co., bds at Mill.
DODD, A. M., Register of Deeds, office Court House, res cor 6th and Goodwood.
Doine, James, lab, res cor Hancock and Holcombe.
Dompke, Aug., mill hand, Hersey, Bean & Brown.
Donahue, John, lab, res w s 2d, n Olive.
Donahue, Peter, lab, bds Pacific House.
Donahue, Peter, mill hand, I. Staples, bds at Mill.
Donaldson, John, mill hand, I. Staples, bds at Mill.
Donaldson, C. L., mill hand, I. Staples, bds at Mill.
Donke, Frank, mill hand, Hersey, Bean & Brown.
Donohoe, Henry, moulder, bds P. Barrett.

Donohue, Dan, quarryman, res lower Main.
Donohue, Timothy. confectioner &c., res cor 4th and Churchill.
Donavan, Tim., mill hand, Seymour. Sabin & Co.
Donovaen, Michael, lab, res cor Putz and Anderson.
Donovan. Ed., lumberman, bds Myrtle, w 3d.
Donovan, Jeremiah, lab, res Myrtle w 3d.
Doody, James, lab. res s part of City.
Dorr. W. A., mill hand, res lower Main.
Dougherty, Michael, lab, res Anderson, w Putz.
Downes, Archibald, S lab. res cor Becher and Abbott.
Downes, A. S., clk, B. H. Pleckner, res Pine.
Downes, Arthur, lab, res cor Pennock and Becher.
Downes. Daniel, lab, res s s Oak, w Martha.
Downes, John, lab, res cor Becher and Abbott.
Downes. Henry. lab, res cor Becher and Abbott.
Downes, Stephen, clk, bds J. McNall.
Downes. Wm., lab, res cor Becher and Abbott.
Doyle, Patrick J., lab, res Anderson w Becher.
Doyle, Stephen, lab. res w s Broadway, s Goodwood.
Drager, Fred, rafter. Schulenburg Boeckeler & Co., res Schulen-
burg's Add.
Drake, Addison A., barber, bds Samuel Hadley.
Drake, Geo. F., machinist, bds 2d n Linden.
Draver, Henry, mill hand, Seymour, Sabin & Co.
Drechsler, Conrad, lab, res back of Prison
Drechsler, Conrad, saloon, cor Union and Chestnut, res same.
Drechsler, Christ, saloon, Main. s Chestnut, res same.
Drechsler, Wm., saloon, Lake, res across the Lake.
Drewer, H. C., foreman, Schulenburg, Bœckeler & Co.
Drewke, Alex, mill hand. I. Staples, bds at Mill.
Drewke, Anthony, mill hand, I. Staples, bds at Mill.
Drews, Albert, miller, Townshend & Proctor, res cor 4th and Mul-
berry.
Drews, Hermann, miller, Townshend & Proctor, res cor 4th and
Mulberry.
Drews, Julius, mill hand, I. Staples, bds at Mill.
Drews & Kern, (Albert Drews, F. W. Kern) boots and shoes,
Chestnut, w Main.
Driscoll, John, lumberman, bds P. Barrett.
Duby, Geo. mill hand, I. Staples, bds at Mill.
Dudy, Mrs. Martha, res back of Prison.
Dumas, Edward, cook, res 2d. n Olive.
Dumpke, August, mill hand, res 7th. n Churchill.

Dumpke. Frank, lab. res 7th, n Churchill.
Duncan. John, res William. nr Rice
Duncan. M. barn boss. I. Staples. bds at Mill.
Duncan, Malcolm, mill hand, res William, nr Rice.
Duncan. Neil. mill hand. I Staples. bds at Mill.
Duncan. W. II., mill hand. I Staples. bds at Mill.
Dunn. Thos., raftsman, bds cor 3d and Churchill.
Dunn. Thos., J., confectionery. S. Main. res Lower Main.
Dunn. Wm.. lab. res lower Main.

DURANT, WHEELER & CO. (E. W. Durant, R. J. Wheeler, A. T. Jenks) logs and lumber bought and sold on Commission, rafts delivered at any point on the Mississipi River, office in Staples Block.

Durant. E. W.. (Durant. Wheeler & Co.) res cor Pine and 2d.
Duras. James, res cor 3d and Laurel.
Durocher. Alexander. carp. res 3d. s Churchill.
Durose. James. shoemaker, A. Buth, res 3d.
Durrell. Geo.. W.. sawyer, bds Pacific house.
Dyson. Chas.. mill hand. H. B. & B. bds at Mill.

E

Easton, A. B.. (A. B. Easton & Son.) res e s 3d. s Pine.
Easton, A. B. & Son, (A. B.. & Wm. Easton) publishers. Stillwater Gazette, cor Main and Chestnut.
Easton. Wm.. (A. B. Easton & Son) res e s 3d. s Pine.
Egan. Mrs. Ellen. res w s Broadway, s Goodwood.
Eggert. George. mill hand. I. Staples. bds at Mill.
Eggert. Carl. foreman, Schulenburg, Boeckeler & Co.. res Schulenburg Add.
Eivison. Peter, supt cars. H. B. & B. bds at Mill.
Elder. Henry. lab. res Lake.
Eldridge. A.. books, stationery and wall paper, w s Main. n Chestnut res same.
Elfstrom, Chas.. mill hand, I Staples. bds at Mill.
Elg. John. mill hand. I. Staples. bds at Mill.
Ellengen. J. P.. mill hand. H. B. & B.. bds at Mill.
Ellis. Wm., machinist. bds Pacific House.
Elliott, Edward. lab. res 4th, s Churchill.
Elliott. Daniel. cook. res cor Anderson and Smith.
Elliott. James. machinist. Stombs & Bronson.

Ellsperman, Chas., painter, bds A. Mellin.
Elmquist, Chas., shoemaker, bds Wexio Hotel.
Elvrum, Peter, carp, res cor Mulberry and Main.
Emered, Napoleon, mill hand, H. B. & B., bds at Mill.
Engquest, Gustaf, lab, bds St. Croix Hotel.
Engquest, Jos., lab, bds St. Croix Hotel.
Engstrom, Gus., mill hand, I. Staples, bds at Mill.
Erickson, A., lab, bds Wexio Hotel. •
Erickson, Mrs. C., res cor 2d and Olive.
Erickson, —— lab, res w s 2d, n Clive.
Erickson, Peter, lab, bds Scandinavian House.
Erkstrom, Daniel, mill hand, Seymour, Sabin & Co., bds at Mill.
Estabrook, Dan, mill hand, Hersey, Bean & Brown.
Estabrook, Chas., boss carp, I. Staples.
Estes, Howard, bar keeper, Sawyer House, bds same.
Etter, Louis, lab, res back of Prison.
Evans, E. L., works L. S. & M. Depot, res cor St. Paul av, and Owens.
Evans, Geo,, baggage master, L. S. & M. Depot, res n s Olive, w Jeannie.
Even, H., lab, res 2d, s Chestnut.
Everman, Christ, mill hand, H. B. & B., res Schulenburg's Add.
Evermann, John, scaler, Schulenburg, Boeckeler & Co., res Schulenburg Add.

F

Fairbairn, J. H., sawfiler, Schulenburg, Boeckeler & Co.
Farall, E. K., (Ryan & Farall,) res 3d, cor Goodwood.
Farmer, E. D., res e s 3d, s Mulberry.
Farmer, H. C., livery and hack stable, 2d, n Chestnut, res 3d.
Fassmann, L., butcher, res Holcombe, n Hancock.
Ferdinand, John, teamster, H. B. & B., bds at Mill.
Feis, C., res cor Olive and 2d.
Ferguson, Christopher, lab, bds 6th, s Churchill.
Ferguson, Frazer, lab, res cor Western Row and Anderson.
Ferguson, Harvey, works on lake, res 6th, s Churchill.
Ferguson, Thos., clk, res cor Western Row and Anderson.
Ferguson, Thos., clk, bds Mrs. S. Bronson.
Ferguson, Michael, res Western Row s Anderson.
Ferrend, Mrs. P., boarding house, Chestnut, w Main, res same.
Fetz, Lorenz, (Wolf & Fetz,) res 3d, s Goodwood.
Fetzendin, Christ, lab, Wolf's Brewery, res 2d.
Fetzenden, Natzi, works in brewery, bds Mansion House.

Fifield, Chas., engineer, res Anderson, w Becher.
Finch, F., mill hand, Seymour, Sabin & Co., bds at Mill.
Fischer, August, tailor, bds C. Drechsler.
Fischer, Wm , tailor, C. Hillmer.
Fister, Martin, lab, res w s Main, n Nelson.
Fitzgerald, Edward, carp, bds D. Harrigan.
Fitzgerald, James, lab, res w s Broadway, s Goodwood.
Fitzgerald, James, Blacksmith, bds D. Harrigan.
Fitzgerald, Mrs. Mary, res w s Broadway, s Goodwood.
Fitzgerald, Patrick, lab, res w s Broadway, s Goodwood.
Fitzgerald, Richard, lab, res w s Broadway, s Goodwood.
Fitzpatrick, John, lumberman, bds J. Donovan.
Flaherty, John, blacksmith, bds Pacific House.
link, John, lab, res Elm, w Main.
lood, Martin, lab, res Schulenburg's Add.
lorythay, John, machinist, bds Pacific House.
Flynn, Daniel, lab, res n s Oak, w Holcombe.
Fochten, Henry, lab, bds Liberty House.
Fohla, Axle, sawyer, H. B. & B. bds at Mill.
Foley, James G., clk, Auditor's office, res Broadway.
Foley, Wm., lab, res Lower Main,
Folsom, E. A., (Hersey Bronson, Doe & Folsom) res cor 4th and
    Cherry.
Folsom, E. H., (Taylor & Co.) res Union Block, Main.
Foran, Michael, lumberman, res Rice, e Martha.
Foran, James, lumberman, res cor 4th and Laurel.
Foram, Wm., raftsman, res cor 3d and Churchill.
Force, Nelson, mill hand, bds John Morgan.
Forcia, Adolph Sr., mill hand, H. B. & B.
Forcia, Adolphus Jr., teamster, H. B. & B. bds at Mill.
Forcia, James, mill hand, H. B. & B. bds at Mill.
Forcia, Thos., mill hand, H. B. & B. bds at Mill.
Fortune, Michael, res w end St. Paul Av.
Fosman, Lewis, butcher, H. B. D. & F.
Foss, Herman, mill hand, bds Oak, e Martha.
Foss, Z. H., blacksmith, res Cherry, e 3d.
Foster, Chas. W., clk, P. O. bds cor 3d. and Chestnut.
Fox, Mrs., res 6th, n Hancock.
Fox, Tim, mill hand, Seymour, Sabin & Co.
Foyle, R. A., foreman, Seymour, Sabin & Co., res School e 3d.
Francis, Thos., confectionery &c., w s Main, s Myrtle, res 2d, s
    Chestnut.
Franke, John, lab, bds, St. Louis House.

Franz, Adam, shoemaker, N. F. Schwarz, bds Liberty House.
Frazier, Angus, lab, bds R. Sutton.
Frazier, James, sawyer, H. B. & B., bds at Mill.
Frederick, A., (Frederick & Jackson,) res Goodwood, w 4th.
Frederick & Jackson, (A. Frederick, Oscar A. Jackson,) music
    dealers, w s Main, s Chestnut.
Frederickson, C., carp, Seymour, Sabin & Co.
Fredrickson, Edward, mill hand, I. Staples, bds at Mill.
Freeman, Benjamin, lab, bds John Freeman.
Freeman, John, lumberman, res s s Oak, w Holcombe.
Freiberg, Ben. F., clk, res Myrtle, w 2d.
Freiheit, Wm., sawyer, bds C. Drechsler.
French, Chas W., (Prince & French,) res Olive, opp Jeannie.
Frid, J., lab, bds St. Croix Hotel.
Fritchie, Rudolph, log scaler, res St. Paul av, w Center.
Fry, Daniel, confectionery, &c., cor Myrtle and Main, res 5th, cor
    Laurel.
Furbisch, Joseph, carp, bds Pacific House.

G

Gabbart, Henry, lab, res Goodwood, e 7th.
Gabbart, Henry Jr., mill hand, Hersey, Bean & Brown.
Gabbart, Robt., mill hand, H. B. & B.
Gahagan, Vincent, blacksmith, bds Williams House.
Gallagher, Wm., mill hand, Hersey, Bean & Brown.
Garbe, Albert, lab, res Holcombe, n Hancock.
Gard, S., confectionery, &c., Chestnut, w 2d, res same.
Gardner, Fred, clk, bds Mrs. S. Bronson.
Gardner, J. C., guard at Prison, res cor Everett and Spring.
Gamer, Wm., works D. H. Hersey, res same.
Garrity, Patrick, lab bds Olive, e 3d.
Gartzke, Carl, setter, Schulenburg, Boeckler & Co., res Schulen-
    burg's Add.
Gasolin, David, lumberman, res cor 3d and School.

GASSMAN, H. U., manufacturer of Carriages, Bug-
gies, Spring Wagons, Sleighs, &c., Blacksmith-
ing and Horseshoeing a specialty, w s 2d, nr
Sawyer House. res 2d n Olive.

Gatchell, Robt., teamster, res cor 2d and Pine.
Gatske, Wm., blacksmith, I. Staples, bds at Mill.
Gearien, Wm., butcher, bds J. McNall.

Genero, Louis, mill hand, I. Staples, bds at Mill.
Genet, Julius, works Staples' Mill, res Nelson, s 2d.
Gerard, Damas, mill hand, Hersey, Bean & Brown.
Gerard, Desire, carp, H. B. & B., bds at Mill.
Gerard, Geo., mill hand. H. B. & B. bds at Mill.
Gerant, Joseph, cook bds Keystone House.
Gesse, Jos., edger, Schulenburg, Boeckeler & Co. res Schulenburg
    Add.
Gicriet, A. J., watch maker. W. J. Stein, res 3d.
Greriet, John, saloon and billiards, cor Main and Chestnut, res 3d,
    s Churchill.
Gilbertson, Nels, mill hand, I. Staples, bds at Mill.
Gillespie, A. L. log dealer, e s Main, s Myrtle, res cor Holcombe
    and Pine.
Gillespie, John, lab, res 4th, s Churchill.
Gillespie, M.. baggage master, Depot, res 80 South Main.
Gillis, James, lumberman, bds P. Barrett.
Gilman, Edward, teamster, O. Mower, bds same.
Gilmore, Mrs. Louisa, dress maker, 2d, n Chestnut, res same.
Giossi, Joseph, carp, res cor 4th and Oak.
Giossi, Wm., workman, Staples Mill, res 5th, s Goodwood.
Girard, Geo., mill hand res e s Broadway, s Walnut.
Girard, Pere, mill hand, I. Staples, bds at Mill.
Glade, John, rafter, Schulenburg, Boeckeler, & Co.
Glarner, John, butcher, res Chestnut, nr Bridge.
Glasberner, Geo., brewer, res Lower Main.
Glaspie, John, lab, res Lower Main.
Glass, Peter, lab, res cor 6th and Goodwood.
Glaser, Christ, foreman, Schulenburg, Boeckeler & Co. res Schulen-
    burgs Add.
Godfrey, Chas., raftsman, bds A. Wilmet.
Goff, E. N., lab. res 6th, s Goodwood.
Goff, John, lab. res 6th, s Goodwood.
Goff, Rufus, E., lab, res, 5th, s Churchill.
Gohagan, Vincent, blacksmith, Seymour, Sabin & Co.
Goodman, Philip, lab, res 4th n Churchill.
Goodrich, Chas, tallyman, res cor 4th and Cherry.
Goodrich, John, deputy Surveyor Gen'l, res cor Cherry and 4th.
Goodrich, Frank, butcher, H. B. D. & F. bds Chestnut w Main.
Goodwin, R. F. physician,(Hom.) Union Block, Main, res same.
Goodsell, J. engineer, S. S. & Co. res upper Main.
Goodsell, Joseph, mill hand, Seymour, Sabin & Co. bds at Mill.
Goodsell, Merritt, mill hand, Seymour, Sabin & Co. bds at Mill.

Gorrie, Wm., supt, pub schools, res cor 4th and Linden.
Gordan, Adam, lumberman, bds P. Barrett.
Gorham, Philip, mill hand, I. Staples, bds at Mill.
Gowan, Wm., lab. bds John Glaspie.
Grady, Con., mill hand, Hersey Bean & Brown.
Graham, Wm., machinist, Stombs & Bronson, res co Olive and 6th.
Granstrom, Oscar, machinist, Seymour, Sabin & Co.
Grant, Byron, lumberman, bds P. Barrett.
Grant,——rafter, bds A. Mellin.
Grant, Geo., lumberman, bds P. Barrett.
Grant, Lewis, steward, Sawyer House, bds same.
Grant, Peter, blacksmith, II. B. & B., bds at Mill.
Grant, Ratchison, lumberman, bds P. Barrett.
Graves, Wm. foreman, I. Staples, res cor Walnut and 6th.
Gray, A. R., machinist, res Chestnut, e 2d.
Gray, Isaac, Steamboat Capt., res 3d, n Olive.
Greader, Mrs. Barbara, res cor Becher and Pennock.
Greeley. Elam, lumberman, res cor Spring and Greeley.
Greeley, Judson, lumberman, res cor Greeley and Spring.
Gregory, C. P., Municipal Judge. office w s Main, n Chestnut, res cor 2d and Laurel.
Green, Henry, stone cutter. bds Pacific House.
Green, John, contractor and builder, res cor Stimson Alley and Chestnut.
Green, R. E., traveling agt, Conrad & Hospes.
Grevinghause, Adolph, mill hand, Seymour, Sabin & Co., res back of Prison.
Griffin, James J., works Seymour, Sabin & Co., res Schulenburg's Add.
Griffin, James H., carp, res e s 2d s Goodwood.
Griswold, Miss M. F., artist, res cor 2d and Chestnut.
Gruber, H., lab, bds St Croix Hotel.

GRUENHAGEN, JOHN A., Maunfacturer and dealer in all kinds of Boots and Shoes. We make a specialty of fine work, and sell at lowest prices, repairing neatly done. Chestnut, nr Bridge, res Stimson's Alley.

Grunke, Herman, tailor, res 5th, n Churchill.
Grusemann, Jacob, cook, res cor Holcombe and Churchill.
Guerest, Wm., butcher, C. Lacomb.
Gueslander, Oscar, mill hand, Hersey, Bean & Brown.

Guilford, John, mill hand, I. Staples, bds at Mill.
Guise, Fred, teamster, Hersey, Bean & Brown.
Guse, Christ, saw filer, Schulenburg, Boeckeler & Co., res Schulenburg's Add.
Guskie, Albert, mill hand, Hersey, Bean & Brown.
Guskie, Gotlieb, mill hand, Hersey, Bean & Brown.

H

Haack, Aug., lab, Schulenburg, Boeckeler & Co., res Schulenburg's Add.
Hadley & Jackson, (S. Hadley, C. Jackson,) barbers, e s Main, n Chestnut.
Hadley, Reuben, res cor Western Row and Willard.
Hadley, Samuel, (Hadley & Jackson,) res cor Willard and Western Row.
Hag, August, lab, bds 2d, n Linden.
Haggerty, Thos., lab, res cor 4th and Burlington.
Haggerty, Tom, mill hand, I. Staples, bds at Mill.
Haines, D. H., clk, P. Potts, bds D. Harrigan.
Halen, John, carp, res Martha, nr Hickory.
Hall, Mrs. A., matron Penitentiary, res same.
HALL, ABE, Deputy Warden, Penitentiary, res same.
Hall, Watson, painter, res cor 2d and Churchill.
Hall, Wm., guard at Prison, res Wilkinson, w 4th.
Hamilton, James, lab, res Elm, w Main.
Hamm, H. J., mill hand, res lower Main.
Hampson, Frank, baggage master, res cor Nelson and Main.
Hand, —— works L. S. & M. R. R., res Laurel, e 2d.
Hanitsch, W., boot and shoemaker, Main, s Chestnut, res 6th, n Olive.
Hanley, Michael, lab, res cor Anderson and Smith.
Hannon, Michael, mill hand, I. Staples, bds at Mill.
Hansen, Chas., lab, bds Leveen & Stone.
Hanson, & Co., (Nels Hanson, L. Torinus, A. Skow,) meat market, Union Block, Main.
Hansen, Hans, lab, res cor 5th, and Churchill.
Hansen, Hans, lab, res w s 2d, s Mulberry.
Hanson, Hogan, mill hand, H. B. & B., bds at Mill.
Hanson, Nels, (Hanson & Co.,) res 5th, cor Churchill.
Hanson, W. E., watchman, I. Staples.
Happner, Edward, saloon, w s Main, s Chestnut, res same.
Hardiman, Bernard, lab, res 5th, s Goodwood.
Hardwick, Leo, mill hand, I. Staples, bds at Mill.

Hardyman, John, teamster, H. B & B., bds at Mill.
Harkins, Mrs. S., res lower Main.
Harner, Joseph, foreman Wolf's Brewery, res same.
Harper, A. A., bookkeeper, Schupp & Tozer, res cor 3d, and Goodwood.
Harper, W. J., clk, J. N. Darms, bds same.
Harrigan, Con., lab, res cor Becher, and Pennock.
Harrigan, Dennis, boarding, Main, n Nelson, res same.
Harrigan, John, lab, res 4th, s Mulberry.
Harris, Geo., mill hand, res Commercial av, c 2d.
Harris, Leonard, lab, bds M. Gillespie.
Harison, Edward, lab, res Everett n Spring.
Hart, Alfred, lab, res 2d, s Mulberry.
Haskell, Geo., O., foreman, Hersey Bronson, Doe, & Folsom, res 2d, cor Laurel.
Hausner, August, carp, res Wilkin, w 4th.
Hausner F. A., carp, Seymour, Sabin & Co.
Hausner, Wm., mill hand, Seymour, Sabin & Co.
Hausner, Wm., clk Conrad & Hospes.
Hatch, Wm., lab, res cor 3d and Pine.

HATHAWAY, C. M. blacksmith and wagon maker, 3d, s Myrtle, res 2d.

Hawkenson, August, (Hawkenson & Johnson) bds Wexio Hotel.
Hawkenson & Johnson, (A. Hawkenson, O. Johnson) boot and shoe makers, 2d, n Myrtle.
Hayes, Dennis, mill hand, I. Staples.
Hebenstreit, John, clk, I. Staples, res Holcombe, bet Pine and Willard.
Hebenstreit, Mrs. M. res cor Holcombe and Willard.
Heffernan, James, carp, res Linden e 4th,
Heffernan, Wm., tinner, Torinus & Wilkinson.
Hefty, David, lab, res 4th s Goodwood.
Hefty, Fred, mill hand, res 2d and olive.
Hefty, Henry, butcher, res 4th, n Walnut.
Helly, Daniel lab bds Pacific House.
Hemphill, H. G., engineer, bds Pacific House.
Hemquist, John, carp, bds Scandinavian House.
Hempstead, Henry, res Myrtle, n Main.
Hendrickson, Hans, tailor, bds Williams House.
Hening, J. C. (Crandall, & Hening,) bds H. M. Caandall.
Hennegan, W. D., night guard, at Prison res same.

Henry, Joseph, lab. bds Liberty House.
Herald, James, teamster, bds Keystone House.
Herald, W. S., blacksmith, M. Moffatt, bds 2d n Chestnut.
Hern, Wm., driver H. C. Farmer, bds same.
Herron, Ben, lab, res Western Row, n Anderson.

HERSEY & BEAN, (Roscoe F, Dudley H. Eugene, M. & Edward L. Hersey, Chas. & Jacob Bean) logs and pine lands, Hersey & Staples Block.

HERSEY BEAN & BROWN, (R. F. & D. H Hersey, C. & J. Bean, Ed. S. Brown) north western saw and planing mills, office cor Main and Myrtle.

Hersey, Bronson, Doe & Folsom, (D. H. Hersey, D. Bronson, A. K. Doe, E. A. Folsom) general merchandise cor Main and Myrtle.
Hersey, Dudley, H., (Hersey & Bean) res 3d, cor Burlington.
Hersey Edward, L. (Hersey & Bean) res Bangor Main,
Hersey, Eugene, M., (Hersey & Bean) res Bangor Main.
Hersey, Roscoe, F., (Hersey & Bean) res Pine, cor 6th.
Hessler, —— butcher, H. B. D. & F. res 2d, s Chestnut.
Highwarden, Mrs. Mary, res 6th, s Olive.
Hildebrandt, J. T., merchant tailor, cor Stimson alley, and Chestnut, res Stimson Alley.
Hillmer, Christ, merchant tailor, Chestnut, w Main, res 7th.
Hills, Goe., lab, res w s Main, s Chestnut.
Hinchey, James, lab, bds D. O'Neill.
Hines, John, lab, res w s 5th, s Chestnut.
Hines Martin, lab, res lower Main.
Hines, Patrick, mill hand, H. B. & B.
Hoesli, John, butcher, res 2d, s Chestnut.
Hoge, ——merchant tailor, res Linden, w 2d.
Holberg, Peter, mill hand, I. Staples, res Elm, w Main.
Holcomb, Chas., Dept. Sheriff, res cor 2d and Churchill.
Holcombe, Edwin W., res Main, s Chestnut.
Holcombe, Gustave, shop guard at Prison, res 4th cor Hickory.
Holcombe, W. W., res Main, s Chestnut.
Holm, Andrew, mill hand, I. Staples, res Elm, w Main.
Holmes, Dan, mill hand, H. B. & B., bds at Mill.
Holmes, Ed., lab, res cor 3d and Pine.
Holmquest, C. M., mill hand, I. Staples.
Holmquest, Peter, lab, bds Wexio Hotel.

Holt, Christ, lab, res Churchill, w 7th.

Holtquest, Frank, lab, res 4th s Olive.

Holtmann, Wm., lab, Schulenburg, Boeckeler & Co., res Schulenburg's Add.

Hopkins, E. A. Jr., City Clerk, and Ex. Officio clk, Municipal Court, office w s Main, n Chestnut, res 4th, s Goodwood.

Hopper, A. A., clk, bds F. E. Joy.

Hospes, A. C., (Conrad & Hospes,) res Mulberry, w 3d.

Hospes, Cutler & Co., (L. Hospes, F. C. Cutler, O. G. Hospes) Merchant Tailors and Clothiers, cor Chestnut and Main.

Hospes, Ernest L., with Schulenburg, Boeckeler & Co.

Hospes, E. L., (E. L. Hospes & Co.)

Hospes, E. L. & Co., (E. L. Hospes, W. W. McPherson, W. K. Wurdeman) hardware, Hospes blk.

Hospes, Louis, (Schulenburg, Boeckeler & Co.,) res cor 1st and Sycamore.

Hospes, O. G., (Hospes, Cutler & Co.)

Howard, Henry, lumberman, bds P. Barrett.

Howard, John, lab, bds C. Drechsler.

Hubbard, F., wagon maker, C. M. Hathaway, bds G. Law.

Huber, Carl, printer, St. Croix Post, bds Lake.

Huffer, Scott, mill hand, I. Staples bds at Mill.

Hughes, Nelson, J., lab, res w s 4th, n Laurel.

Huhnke, Michael, carp, res Schulenburg's Add.

Hultquist, Chas., mill hand, res Myrtle, w 6th.

Hultquist, John, lab, res Myrtle, w 4th.

Hultquist, Otto, lab, res Myrtle, w 4th.

Hummel, John, watchman, Hersey, Bean & Brown.

Hurley, John, lab, bds R. Stutton.

Huser, Wm., teamster, res Holcombe, n Hancock.

Huzzey, Arthur W., works H. B. & B. res cor 3d and St. Louis.

Huzzey, Wilmot, works H. B. & B. res cor 3d and St. Louis.

I

Illingsworth, F., mill hand, I. Staples, bds at Mill.

Illingsworth, J. H., butcher, res 2d, n Linden.

Illingsworth, Walter, teamster, res 2d, n Linden.

Isermann, Aug., carp, Schulenburg, Boeckeler & Co. res Schulenburg's Add.

Isermann, Henry, mill hand, Seymour Sabin & Co.

Irish, John, mill hand, H. B. & B., bds at Mill.

J

Jackins, John, res Chestnut, w 3d.

Jacobs, Mrs. A. C., millinery, Chestnut, w Main, bds 2d.

Jackson, A., mill hand, I. Staples, bds at Mill.

Jackson, August, carp, res 3d, n Churchill.

Jackson, Chas., (Hadley & Jackson) res cor Smith and Abbott.

Jackson, Chas., lab, res Myrtle, e 3d.

Jacobi, Jacob, lab, bds Liberty House.

Jackson, Hans, watchman, Hersey, Bean & Brown.

Jackman, Mrs. Mary, res cor 6th and Churchill.

Jackson, Oscar A., (Frederick & Jackson) bds Pine, e 3d.

Jackson, Peter, mill hand, res 5th, s Churchill.

Jaker, August, carp, I. Staples, bds at Mill.

Janitz, Aug., lab, Schulenburg, Boeckeler & Co. res Schulenburgs Add.

Janitz, August, mill hand, I. Staples.

Janitz, Wm., sawyer, Schulenburg, Boeckeler & Co., res Schulenburg's Add.

Jann, Ferd, lab, Schulenburg, Boeckeler & Co. res Schulenburg's Add.

Jannett, Julius, mill hand, I. Staples.

Jannke, Charles, lab, res cor 7th and Goodwood.

Jannke, John, rafter, Schulenbrrg, Boeckeler & Co.

Jansen, Hans, bar tender, St. Croix Hotel, bds same.

Jarchow, Detlof, boarding house keeper, Schulenburg, Boeckeler & Co.

Jarvis, Alex, sawyer, H. B. & B., bds at Mill.

Jasolin, Geo., mill hand, res e s 3d, n Churchill.

Jassoy, A., clk, H. Kauffman, bds same.

Jassoy, Theo, bookkeeper, Hersey & Bean, res Chestnut, w 2d.

Jastram, D., saloon, upper Main, res upper Main.

Jellison, Chas. O., lumberman, res e s 3d, n Linden.

Jenks, A. T., (Durant, Wheeler & Co.,) res Albany, Ill.

Jenks, Geo., cook, res Main, s Mulberry.

Jencrau, Louis, lab, bds A. Wilmet.

Jesperson, Hans, works D. M. Sabin, bds same.

Joargo, Anton, mill hand, Hersey, Bean & Brown.

Johnson, Albert, lumberman, bds Mulberry, w Main.

Johnson, Alex., lumberman, res Myrtle w 3d.

Johnson, Alfred, lumberman, bds 2d, n Linden.

Johnson, Alfred, lab, bds 2d, n Linden.

Johnson, Alfred, river police, res cor 7th and Churchill.

Johnson, Andrew, mill hand, I. Staples, bds at Mill.
Johnson, Aug., carp, Hersey. Bean & Brown.
Johnson, A. F., carp, Seymour, Sabin & Co.
Johnson, Chas., lab, bds Leveen and Stone.
Johnson, Chas., lab, bds 2d, n Linden.
Johnson, Chas., mill hand, H. B. & B , bds at Mill.
Johnson, C. C., engineer, res s s Mulberry, e 3d.
Johnson, C. H., mill hand, I. Staples, bds at Mill.
Johnson, Ed., mill hand, H. B. & B., bds at Mill.
Johnson, Frank, lab, res Main, s Mulberry.
Johnson, Frank, lab, bds 2d, n Linden.
Johnson, Frank. lab, bds St. Croix Hotel.
Johnson, F. O., mill hand, I. Staples, bds at Mill.
Johnson, Goodman, mill hand, H. B. & B., bds at Mill.
Johnson, Gus., carp, res Myrtle, w 6th.
Johnson, Gus., lab, gas works, bds Nels Johnson.
Johnson, Gust, mill hand, bds Spring, w Jeannie.
Johnson, Harry, blacksmith, I. Staples.
Johnson, John, mill hand, res w s 4th, n Pine.
Johnson. J. H., mill hand, Seymour, Sabin & Co., bds at Mill.

JOHNSON, J. O., Proprietor Stillwater Marble Works, manufacturer of and dealer in American and Foreign Marble and Granite Monuments, Grave Stones, and all kinds of Cemetery work executed in the latest styles, lower Main, res same.

Johnson, J. S. F., carp, Seymour, Sabin & Co.
Johnson, John W., engineer, res w s 2d, s Mulberry.
Johnson, Michael, bookkeeper, H. B. D. & F., res Wis.
Johnson, Mrs. Mary, res Myrtle, w 3rd.
Johnson, Nels., lab, bds Leveen & Stone.
Johnson, Nels., blacksmith, H. B. & B., bds at Mill.
Johnson, Nelson, foreman Gas Works, res 3d, s Olive.
Johnson, Olauf, lab, bds Wexio Hotel.
Johnson, Ole, (Hawkenson & Johnson,) res same.
Johnson, Peter, mill hand, I. Staples, bds at Mill.
Johnson, Samuel, lab, bds St. Croix Hotel.
Johnson, Wm., lab, bds Wexio Hotel.
Johnson, Andrew, mill hand. I. Staples, bds at Mill.
Jones, C. R., mill hand, res lower Main.
Jones, Lyman, music teacher, res e s 3rd, s Pine.
Jordan. A. E., (Low, Jordan & Co.,) res cor 3d, and Olive.

Joy, Frank E., Agt., United States Express Co., Myrtle, w Main, res 3d, cor Churchill.
Joy, John M., clk, H. B. D. & F., res 3d, n Myrtle.
Jourdain, Olive, teamster, res cor Smith and Pennock.
Jourdain, Peter, raftsman, res Smith, n Pennock.
June, P. P., mill hand, I. Staples. bds at Mill.

K

Kab, Chas., sewing machine agt., res Chestnut, w 2d.
Kadel, Fred, wagon maker, res cor Holcombe and Churchill.
Kain, John, lumberman, res cor Martha and Spring.
Kaiser, Aug., malster, H. Topass, bds same.
Kaiser, Henry, engineer, bds St. Louis House.
Kaiser, Mathew, clk, T. Francis, bds same.
Kajeobe, Joseph A., carp, res Lake.
Kalbe, John, mill hand, res Schulenburg's Add.
Kane, James, carriage and ornamental painter, 2d, n Myrtle, res 2d, s Chestnut.
Karst, John, tinner, Sawyer & Co., bds H. Sawyer.
Kartel, Fred, carp. Seymour, Sabin & Co.
Kaster, Henry, carp, Seymour. Sabin & Co.
Kattenberg, Fred, mill hand, Seymour, Sabin & Co., bds at Mill.
Katzeler, Wm., butcher. I. Staples, bds cor Myrtle and Main.
Kauffman, H., druggist, Main, s Chestnut, res 3d, cor Chestnut.
Keefe, James, house and sign painter, w s Main, s Myrtle, res cor Pennock and Holcombe.
Keefe, John, cook, res Broadway, s Churchill.
Keeley, S. W., Agent P. S. & M. R. R., bds e s 3d, s Pine.
Keep, Frank, bookkeeper, bds Liberty House.
Kelley, Edward, teamster, I. Staples, bds at Mill.
Kelley, John, teamster, I. Staples, bds at Mill.
Kelley, John, lumberman, res Greeley, n Spring.
Kellogg, L. T., hides and furs, res Broadway, opp Pine.
Kelly, James, mason, res cor 4th and Churchill.
Kelly, James, hostler, R. A., Wait, bds same.
Kelly, James, lab, res cor 2d and Locust.
Kelly, James, No 3, driver, H. B. D. & F., res Schulenburg's Add.
Kelly, John, carp. Seymour, Sabin & Co.
Kelly, John, lab, bds back of Prison.
Kelly, John, watchman at Prison,res Schulenburg's Add.
Kelly, Jos, hostler, A. J. Orff.
Kelly, Mrs. Margaret, res lower Main.

Kelly, Thos., lab, res cor 2d and Locust.
Kelso, Joseph, gas fitter, Torinus & Wilkinson, bds 3d.
Kemp, Geo., lab, res s s Myrtle, e 3d.
Kendall, II. C., station agt, L. S. & M. R. R. bds Sawyer House.
Kennedy, Thos., moulder, Stombs & Bronson, bds at works.
Kennemenn, Wm., Tinner, O. A. Ricker, res Owens, s Spring.
Kenny, John, fireman, Hersey, Bean & Brown.
Kent, James, lab, res Pennock, e Becher.
Kearney, Andrew, (Staples & Kearney) res Burlington, cor 4th.
Kern, F, W. (Drews & Kern) res 4th, cor Mulberry.
Kertsom, Henry, mill hand. I Staples, bds at Mill.
Kertsom, Jas., Sr., carp. I. Staples bds at Mill.
Kertsom, Jas., Jr., carp, I. Staples, bds at Mill.
Kertsom. Peter, painter I. Staples bds at Mill.
Kertsom, Wm., machine hand, I Staples, bds at Mill.
Kester, Henry, carp. res w s Broadway, s Churchill.
Ketzman, John, mill hand, Hersey, Bean & Brown.
Keyes, Dennis, carp, res 7th, n Churchill.
Kibner, Wm., lab. I. Staples, res back of Prison.
Kiesow, Aug., edger, Schulenburg. Boeckeler & Co. res Schulen-
    burg's Add.
Kilborn. Daniel, farmer, res cor Owens and St. Paul Av.
Kilter, Patrick, lab, res Myrtle, e 3d.
Kilty, Timothy, Jr., blacksmith, H. U. Gassman. res 4th, n
    Churchill.
Kilty, Timothy, lab, res 4th, n Churchill.
Kind, —— raftsman, bds Centennial Restaurant.
Kindstrom, Wm., lab, bds Scandinavian House
King, Geo., lumberman, bds Keystone House.
King, Hiram. clk, Crandall & Hening. bds II. M. Crandall.
King, Wm., clk, Crandall & Hening, bds II. M. Crandall.
Kinney. John, fireman, res Lower Main.
Kinney, John, confectionery &c. Main cor Nelson, res Lower
    Main.
Kinsella, Michael, grocer, cor 5th and Goodwood res same.
Kleine, Frank, Sr., lab, res Schulenburg's Add.
Kleine, Frank, lab, Schulenburg, Boeckeler & Co. res Schulen-
    burg's Add.
Kleinegger, Adolph, lab, Schulenburg, Boeckeler & Co.
Kleinegger, John, res cor Sycamore and Main.
Kleps, G. sawyer, Schulenburg, Boeckeler & Co. res Schulenburg's
    Add.

Kluedke, Fred, lab. Schulenburg, Boeckeler & Co. res Schulenburg's Add.
Kluedke, Herman, sawyer, Schulenburg, Boeckeler & Co. res Schulenburg's Add.
Knapp, A. R., dentist, res cor 2d and Chestnut.
Knipps, August A., brewer, G. Knipps, bds same.
Knipps, Emil, lab, Townshend & Proctor, res upper Main.
Knipps, Gerhard, St. Croix Brewery, upper Main, res same.
Knipps, Robt, brewer, G. Knipps, bds same.
Koch, Geo., carp, res Lake.
Koehler, Carl, sawyer, Schulenburg Boeckeler & Co., res Schulenburg's Add.
Komenska, Jacob, Saloon and Barber shop, Chestnut, e Main, bds Chestnut, w Main.
Koons, Jos., carp, Seymour, Sabin & Co., res 3d n Laurel.
Korn, August, rafter, Schulenburg, Boeckeler & Co., res Schulenburg's Add.
Koslowski, Michael, mill hand, Hersey, Bean & Brown.
Kottke, Fred, works Schulenburg's Mill, res Schulenburg's Add.
Kranz, Anton, mason, res cor Holcombe and Oak.
Kreiner, Wm., works for Staples. res w s 2d n Chestnut.
Krogmann, Carl, sawyer, Schulenburg, Boeckeler & Co., res Schulenburg's Add.
Kron, August, shoemaker, bds Wexio Hotel.
Krueger, Emil, mill hand, res Lake s Sycamore.
Krueger, John, lab, Schulenburg, Boeckeler & Co.
Kunde, Herman, lab, Schulenburg, Boeckeler & Co., res Schulenburg's Add.
Kundert, Jacob, foreman, rafter, Hersey, Bean & Brown
Kundert, John, lab, res cor Smith and Pennock.
Kunzelman, Mrs. Catherine, res St. Paul Av., w Center.
Kunzelman, Rheinhart, brick maker, res St. Paul Av., w Center.
Kunzelmann, R., wagon maker, R. Daw.
Kunzelmann, Herman,]lab, Schulenburg, Boeckeler & Co., res Schulenburg's Add.
Kutz, August, carp, res s s Oak w Holcombe.

L

Lacomb, Charles, meat market, Chestnut, w Main, res Olive w 2d.
Lafller, John, mill hand, I. Staples.
Lammers, Nathan D., clk, Schulenburg, Boeckeler & Co., res Lake.
Lamprecht, John, lab, Schulenburg, Boeckeler & Co., res Schulenburg's Add.

Lande, Andrew, machinist, Stombs & Bronson, bds 2d. *
Lane, David F., mill hand, H. B. & B., bds at Mill.
Lane, James. lumberman, res Cherry e 4th.
Lane, John, mill hand, H. B. & B., bds at Mill.
Lane, John, res cor Becher and Anderson.
Lane, Thos., mill hand, Hersey, Bean & Brown.
Lane, Wm., lab, res cor Becher and Anderson.
Lange. Aug., lab, res w s 2d, n Olive.
Lange, Rudolph, lab. bds Liberty House.
Lanphear, Samuel. cutter, S. Sellick, bds 2d, n Chestnnt.
Larrivie, Jos. (Bell & Larrivie) res 2d, s Chestnut.
Larson, Andrew, carp, Seymour, Sabin & Co.
Larson, Andrew, mill hand, Hersey, Bean & Brown.
Larson, Burton, mill hand, H. B. & B. bds at Mill,
Larson, Geo., fireman, res s part of City.
Larson. John, barber, J. Komenska, bds Williams House. I
Larson, John, lab, bds Wexio Hotel.
Larson, John, lab, res Myrtle, w 3d.
Larson. John, plasterer, res cor 4th and School.
Larson. Louis, lab, bds Wexio Hotel.
Larson, Mrs. Mary, res w s 2d, n Myrtle,
Larson, Ole, mill hand, I. Staples, bds at Mill.
Larson, Otto, mill hand, Seymour, Sabin & Co.
La Salle, Joseph, hostler, D. W. McKusick, bds same
Lasty, James, lab, bds St. Louis House.
Laub, Fred, mill hand, res Owens. s Spring.
Laub, Wm., lab, res Owens. s Spring.
Laundre, Chas., lab, bds R. Sutton.
Launs. Jacob, mill hand. Seymour, Sabin & Co.
Lavanture, Louis, res 4th, s Churchill.
Lawson, John, P,, lab, res w s 2d, s Olive.
Leach, John, pilot, res Smith, cor Abbott.
Le Bonta, Geo., mill hand, H. B. & B. bds at Mill.
Le Branc, Chas., mill hand, H. H. & B. bds at Mill
Le Claire, J. lab, res e s 2d, s Goodwood.

LECKY, THOS., Attorney at law, Hersey & Staples Block, bds Sawyer House.

Lee, Lorenz, mill hand, H. B. & B. bds at Mill.
Leef, Andrew, lab bds Leveen and Stone.
Leef, John, lab, bds Leveen and Stone.
Lees, Peter, lab, res Myrtle, e 3d.

Lefler, John, mill hand, res Marine, nr Wilkin.
Lelljengren, Chas., lab, res Spring, w Jeannie.
Lehmann, Herman, painter. J. Keepe res Myrtle.
Lehmicke, Rudolph. (Castle & Lehmicke) res cor 2d and Pine.
Lehmicke, Walter, R. clk, Auditors office, res cor Pine and 2d.
Leighton, Eben, mill hand, H. B. & B. bds at Mill.
Leighton, Evon, mill hand, res 3d. cor Dubuque.
Leighton, James, H., foreman, H. B. & B. Mill,res s part of City.
Leighton, Sam, sawyer, res cor 3d, and Dubuque.
Leighton, Wm., filer, H. B. & B. bds at Mill.
Le Mere, Ben. mill hand, res Linden, e 3d.
Lemoine, E. G. carp. res 4th, s Churchill.
Lemon, Frank H., painter, bds A. Mellin.
Lendbloom, Peter M., carp, res Spring w Jeannie.
Lenfester, Philip, teamster, H. B. & B., bds at Mill.
Lennell. Lot, lab, bds Scandinavian House.
Leonard, Michael, lumberman, res w s 3u n Linden.
Leonard. Wm., res w s 3d n Linden.
Le Rue, Albert, clk, Wheeler Bros., res cor 2d and Linden.
Le Rue, Mrs. Mary, res cor 2d and Linden.
Letteller A., lumberman, bds Keystone House.
Letceller Ed., lumberman, bds Keystone House.
Leiteller, T., lumberman, bds Keystone House.
Leuhman, Herman, painter, res Myrtle, w 3d.
Leveen, A. N., (Leveen & Stone,) res same.
Leveen. Frank, lab, bds Wexio Hotel.
Leveen & Stone, (A. N. Leveen, John Stone,) Boarding, w s 2d,
    s Mulberry.
Levov, Joseph, painter, W. Muller, bds Eldorado Restaurant.
Lewis,——machinist, bds A. Mellin.
Lich. Wm., mill hand, Seymour, Sabin & Co.
Liebisch. Leo, music teacher, res St. Paul Av., w Center.
Lief, Peter, lab, bds 3d n Churchill.
Lillis, J. C., (Carley & Lillis,) res cor 4th and Pine.
Lilljeugreen, Peter, carp, res 5th, s Hickory.
Limber, John, lab, res Myrtle, w 6th.
Limberg, John, mill hand, Seymour, Sabin & Co.
Linden, August, lab, bds St. Louis House.
Linder, E., carp, res 4th n Laurel.
Lindow, E., carp, Seymour, Sabin & Co.
Lingren, J. W., carp, res Spring, w Jeannie.
Lingsted, Cris., mill hand, I. Staples, bds at Mill.

Linhoff, Wm., boot and shoe maker, w s Main, s Chestnut, res same.

Linncer, John, lab, bds Wexio Hotel.

Linorooth, John, mill hand, H. B. & B., bds at Mill.

Linguist, Andrew, mill hand, I. Staples. bds at Mill.

Litfin. Joseph, rafter, Schulenburg, Boeckeler & Co., res Schulenburg's Add.

Littfield. Frank, fireman, I. Staples, bds at Mill.

Lloyd, George, carp, res cor Hancock and 6th.

Loeber, A.. clk. J. N. Darms, res 7th.

Logan, H. C., hostler, C. A. Bromley, bds M. H. Bromley.

Long, Andrew, lab, res e s 3d. s Cherry.

Long, Mrs. Ellen, res e s 3d s Cherry.

Long, Jacob, mason, res 6th n Churchill.

Long, Wm. lumberman, res Spring, w Martha.

Loomis, Capt., D. B., book keeper Durant, Wheeler & Co. bds W. H. Richardson.

Lord Chas., lab, bds St. Louis House.

Loser, John, barber, bds Pacific House.

Lough, Wm., L., lumberman, res Mulberry, cor William.

Low, Geo., (Low, Jordan & Co.) res 4th, n Churchill.

Low, John. B. porter, Sawyer House, bds same.

Low, Jordan & Co. (Geo., Low, A. E. Jordan) manufg. wood and iron fence, cor 4th and Olive.

Low, Joseph, lab, res 3d, s Churchill.

Lowe, Stephen, C. machinist, Seymour, Sabin & Co. bds A. Mellin.

LOWELL, A., Propr. Sawyer House, cor 2d and Myrtle, res same.

Lowell, Albert, watchman, I staples bds at Mill.

Lowell, Mrs. C. res 2d, n Linden.

Lowell, Mrs. Elizabeth, res cor Cherry and 3d.

Lowell, Elmore, clk, Sawyer House, bds same.

Lowell, J. general merchandise, cor Myrtle and 2d, res 4th n Linden.

Lowell, Wm., driver, I. Staples, res cor 3d and Cherry.

Lueber, August, teamster, res Holcombe, s Churchill.

Luecken, Thos., harness maker, bds C. Drechsler.

Lull, A. C., book stationery and wall paper, e s Main, n Chestnut, res cor 2d and Chestnut.

Luke, Wm. lab, bds Schulenburg's Add.

Lumberg, D. M. lab, res Spring, w Jeannie.

Lumphrey, Jos., mill hand, Seymour, Sabin & Co. res cor 5th and Hickory

LUMBERMANS NATIONAL BANK, I. Staples, Prest. R. F. Hersey Vice Pres. H. W. Cannon, Cashier, capital. $150.000, surplus, $17.000, cor Main and Myrtle.

Lund, John, carp. bds 2d, n Linden.
Lundahl, J. P., tailor. C. Hillmer, res 5th, s Hickory.
Lundeen, Chas., lab, bds Wexio Hotel.
Lundeen, Frank, lumberman, bds Mulberry. w Main.
Lundgren, Frank, mill hand. I. Staples, bds at Mill.
Lundgren, Louis, cook, I. Staples. bds at Mill.
Lundgren, Louis, lab. bds Wexio Hotel.
Lup, Sam, cigar peddler, bds cor Broadway and Walnut.
Lustig. John, lab, Schulenburg, Boeckeler & Co. res Schulenburg's Add.
Lynch, Henry, teamster. I. Staples, bds at Mill.
Lynch, James, fireman, Hersey. Bean & Brown.
Lynch, Michael, mill hand, Hersey. Bean & Brown.
Lynch, Patrick, fireman. res Lower Main.
Lyons, John, saloon, w s Main, s Chestnut, res Lower Main.

Mc

McAdams, A., carp. res lower Main.
McAleer, Michael, butcher. I. Staples, res 5th.
McAleer, John, lab, res 5th. n Laurel.
McAlpin, John, lab. bds M. Gillespie.
McAndrew, James, carpet weaver, res 5th, cor Elm.
McAndrew, James, lab. cor 4th and Hickory.
McAndrew, Robt., lab. res cor 5th and Hickory.
McAuley, Angus, carp, res lower Main.
McAulay, Daniel, school teacher, res 2d, n Linden.
McCallan, Thos., tailor. res w s Main, n Myrtle.
McLean, Alex., mill hand. I. Staples. bds at Mill.
McCarthy, Daniel, teamster. Hersey. Bean & Brown.
McCarthy, Patrick, lab. res e s 2d, s Churchill.
McCarty, John, lab, res 3d, s Goodwood.
McClane, Ann, res s s Myrtle. w 2d.
McClellan, A. J., confectionery, &c., cor Chestnut and Main. bds same.

McCLUER & MARSH., (Wm. M. McCluer, Fayette Marsh,) Attorneys at Law, w s Main, s Myrtle.

McCluer, Wm. M., (McCluer & Marsh,) res 3d, bet Linden and Mulberry.
McClure, E. W., surveyor, res cor 4th and Churchill.
McComb, J. D., Dept., Surveyor Gen'l., res Greeley, s Spring.
McComb, J. H., clk, E. L. Hospes, & Co., bds 3d.
McComb, Harry, clk, bds Mrs. S. Bronson.
McCombs, Robt., printer, bds Key Stone House.
McCrea, Niel, lab. res 3d, n Oak.
McDermott, Michael, mill hand, I. Staples, bds at Mill.
McDermott, Philip, lab, res cor 7th and Churchill.
McDonald, Alex, mill hand, I. Staples, bds at Mill.
McDonald, Alex, lab, bds Liberty House.
Mc Donald, Ed., lab. bds St. Croix Hotel.
McDonald. John, lab, bds A. McAdams.
McDonald, John R., teamster, res cor 4th and Olive.
McDonald, Michael, lab, res cor Martha and Oak.
McDonough, Peter, lab, res cor Goodwood and 2d.
McDougal, A. J., mill hand, I. Staples, bds at Mill.
McGarry, Richard, lab, res w s Broadway, s Goodwood.
McGee, Edward, lab, res s s Anderson, w Smith.
McGee, Henry, lab. res Owens, n Pine.
McGee, James, lab, bds s s Anderson, w Smith.
McGinnis, Duncan, lumberman, bds J. Donovan.
McGoldrick, Patrick, lab, res cor 2d and Churchill.
McGowan, John, lumberman, bds J. Donovan.
McGrath, Andrew, lab, bds R. Sutton.
McGrath, John, lumberman, bds W. W. Wyle.
McGrath, John, lumberman, bds Myrtle, w 3d.
McGrath, John, lab, res cor 7th and Churchill.
McHale, Thos., lab. bds Henry Brown.
McHale, Henry, mill hand, Seymour, Sabin & Co.
McHale, Michael, mason, res Cedar, s Laurel.
McIlree, John, hostler, A. J. Orff, bds same.
McIntyre, Mrs. Maria, res Lake, s Sycamore.
McIntyre, Wm., mason, res cor Mary and Hickory.
McKay, Neal A., guard at Prison, res Greeley s Spring.
McKeen, Chas, lumberman, bds P. Barrett.
McKeen, Emmerson, lumberman, bds P. Barrett.
McKeen, Geo., teamster, H. B. & B., bds at Mill.
McKeen. Geo., lumberman, bds P. Barrett.

McKeen, James, lumberman, bds P. Barrett.
McKeen, James, mill hand, H. B. & B., bds at Mill.
McKeen, Louis, lumberman, bds P. Barrett.
McKeller, Alex, blacksmith, H. U. Gassman, bds same.
McKennan, John, lab, bds 4th, n Churchill.
McKenzie, Chas., lab, res cor 3d and Locust.
McKenzie, Daniel, mill hand, res e s 3d, s Goodwood.
McKinney, Frank, engine wiper, bds Mansion House.
McKinnon, Wm., lumberman, bds P. Barrett.
McKisick,——hostler, bds Centennial Restaurant.
McKisick, Dan., mill hand, I. Staples, bds at Mill.

McKUSICK, D. W., Boarding, Sale, and Livery Stable, and Propr. Hay Scales for weighing all kinds of Hay, Grain and Cattle, Main, nr Lake Superior Depot, res same.

McKusick, Mrs. Eliza, res Cherry, w 2d.
McKusick, F. L., Officer in Municipal Court, res 3d n Chestnut.
McKusick, H. J., bookkeeper, res Union, s Myrtle.
McKusick, Herbert N., cashier, H. B. D. & F., res cor Cherry and 2d.
McKusick, I. E., (Butler & McKusick,) res cor 2d and Cherry.
McKusick, John, Real Estate, res cor 2d and Myrtle.
McKusick, J. W., Deputy Surveyor Gen'l., res Cherry, w 2d.
McKusick, Wm., lumberman, res Union, s Myrtle.
McLaggan, Kenneth, lab, res cor Greely and St. Paul Av.
McLain, Michael, lab, res 7th, s Goodwood.
McLane, Henry, lab, res cor Becher and Anderson.
McLaren, John, carp, bds Myrtle, w 3d.
McLaughlin, P., shoemaker, J. O'Shaughnessy, bds same.
McLeod, Archibald, lab, bds D. Harrigan.
McMahan, Dennis, lab, bds w s 5th, s Churchill.
McMahan, John, fireman, Hersey, Bean & Brown.
McManemy, Bernard, lab, res cor Oak and Sherburne.
McManemy, James, lab, res cor Oak and Sherburne.
McMillan, Chas., lumberman, res cor 3d and Cherry.
McNall, John, agt, Eldorado restaurant, Main, n Nelson, res same.
McNally, Geo., lab, res 7th, s Goodwood.
McNulty, Jos., cook I. Staples bds at Mill.
McPherson, W. W. (E. L. Hospes & Co.) res 2d, s Goodwood.
McPhetres, Joseph, lumberman, res 2d, and Mulberry.
McPhetres, M. W., lumberman, res cor 2d and Mulberry.

McQuillan, Daniel, saloon and billiards, e s Main, n Chestnut, res 6th, s Goodwood.
McSweeney, B. (McSweeney & Rogentine) res Olive, nr 6th.
McSweeney & Rogentine, (B. McSweeney, G. Rogentine) barbers, w s Main, s Chestnut.

M

Mack Mrs. Amanda, res e s Main, n Chestnut.
Mackay, James, raftsman, bds A. Wilmet.
Mackenhausen, Mathew, janitor, high school, res 3d, s Goodwood.
Mackey, Chas., mill hand, I. Staples.
Mackey, James. lumberman, res e s 3d, s Cherry.
Mackey, John. lab, res Lake.
Mackey, Thos., lumberman, res cor 4th and Laurel.
Mackin, Chas., lab, res Spring, w Martha.
Macomber, Rev. J. H. Pastor M. E. Church, res e s 3d, n Myrtle.
Magnuson, Andrew, carp, res Elm, w Main.
Magnuson, August, works I. Staples, res Elm, w Main.
Magnuson, Gus. mill hand, I. Staples.
Magnuson, Frank, lab, bds Wexio Hotel.
Maguire, James, lab, res 5th, nr Maple.
Mahon, John, fireman, res, e s Broadway, s Churchill.
Mahony, James, plasterer, res Owens, cor Oak.

MAISCH, F. W., Propr. St. Louis House, S Main, s Nelson, res same, Pleasant and well furnished rooms, Good tables, try it once and you will come again. Good stabling in connection with the House.

Malcolm, Margaret, dress maker, res cor Nelson and Main.
Malone, Henry, cook, res 6th n Hancock.
Malloy, Bernard, lab, res Holcombe n Hancock.
Maloy, Geo.. mill hand, res 2d, n Linden.
Mallon, Patrick, lab, res Nelson Av., w Main.
Malloy, Robt., lumberman, res 2d, n Linden.
Malory, Geo. M., mill hand, H. B. & B., bds at Mill.
Maloy, Mrs. Ann, Boarding, res 3d n Olive.
Maloy, Geo., mill hand, I. Staples, bds at Mill.
Maloy, James, lab, res e s 2d, s Goodwood.
Maloy, Michael, mill hand, I. Staples, bds at Mill.
Manley, Pat., teamster, I. Staples. bds at Mill.
Marcelle, Fred, bar tender, D. McQuillan. bds Centennial Restaurant.

Marcel, Gagnon, florist, res 5th, cor Hancock.
Marcotte, M., lumberman, bds Keystone House.
Marsh, Fayette, (McCluer & Marsh,) res Broadway, cor Walnut,
Martell, Charles, brakeman, bds Olive. e 3d.
Martens, Henry, watchmaker, W. J. Stein, bds Chestnut, w Main.
Martin, Lyman, machinist, S. S. & Co., bds R. A. Foyle.
Martin, Nels., teamster, H. B. & B., bds at Mill.
Marty, Adam, painter, W. Muller, bds Eldorado Restaurant.
Mason, Thos., works for Staples, bds cor 6th and Churchill.
Masterman, J. N., scaler, res Myrtle, w 2d.
Mathews, James, lumberman, w s 2d, n Pine.
Mathews, Samuel, lumberman, res cor Olive and Jeannie.
Mathew, Wm., farmer, bds Sam., Mathews.
Mathews, Wm., lightning rod agt., bds Pacific House.
Mathson, Alfred, lab. bds Wexio Hotel.
May, John, lab, res St. Paul av, w Center.
May, Joseph, conductor, S. & T. F. R. R., bds Sawyer House.
May, Wm. M., contractor and builder, res n e cor 6th and Pine.
Mead, Mrs. David, res 2d, s Linden.
Mead, Mrs. Grace. res 2d, s Linden.
Mealey, John, lab, res 4th, s Goodwood.
Meads, Chas. H., steamboat captain, res cor 2d and Walnut.
Meisner, Aug. C., tailor, res s s Pennock, w Smith.
Meister, Wm, mill hand, Hersey, Bean & Brown.
Mellin, S. G. mill hand, I. Staples, bds at Mill.
Mellin, J. A., mill hand, I. Staples, bds at Mill.
Mellen, L. A., time keeper I. Staples, bds at Mill.
Mellic, Geo., stable foreman, H. B. & B. bds at Hill.
Mellin, A., confectionery and restaurant, w s Main, s Chestnut, res
    same.
Merritt, John, mill hand, Schulenburg, res Broadway, s Sycamore.

*MERRY, DR. B. G., dentist, Hospes Block, e s
Main, s Myrtle, res 3d, cor Locust.*

Messer, E. P., lumberman, res cor Martha, and Hickory.
Meyer, Conrad, lab, bds St. Louis House.
Meyer, Fred., lab, res Myrtle, w 3d.
Meyer, Geo., cook, res 2d, n Linden.
Meyer, John, lab, bds St. Louis House.
Meyers, Fred., shoemaker, A. Buth, bds same.
Müller, Bros., (Geo. & John, Müller) boats and furniture. foot of
    Nelson.

Miiller, Geo., (Miiller Bros) res Chestnut..
Miiller, John, [Miiller Bros.] res Chestnut.
Miiller, Philip, furniture and undertaking, Chestnut, e Main, res same.
Millard, P. H., physician.(Reg) w s Main, s Myrtle, res 3d, cor Olive.
Millbrook, John, mason, res 3d, n Churchill.
Miller, Henry, mill hand, I. Staples, bds at Mill.
Miller, Henry, painter Seymour, Sabin & Co.
Miller, John, lab, bds Liberty House.
Miller, John, H.,shoemaker, N. F. Schwarz, bds Pacific House.
Miles, Judge, lab. bds R. Sutton.
Millet, John, cook. H. B. & B. bds at Mill.
Millett, J. A., book keeper, res 6th, n Hancock.
Mimnaugh, John, hostler, res Center, s Oak.
Minka, Louis, lab, res Western Row, s Anderson.
Minogu, I. C., blacksmith, Seymour, Sabin & Co.
Mitchell, J. B. H., scaler, I. Staples bds at Mill.
Mittelstadt, Frank, lab, res 6th, s Olive.
Mittner, Mrs. Ursula, midwife, res w s Main,n Myrtle.
Moeser, F. clk, W. J., Stein, res 3d, cor Mulberry,
Moffatt, M., blacksmith and wagon maker, w s 2d, s Myrtle, res 6th, n Pine.
Mohr, John, lab. res cor 5th and Olive.
Molander, Bengt., lab, res cor Hickory and 4th.
Mondoux, Geo., Saloon, Chestnut, e Main, bds Keystone House.
Monthy, Martin, lab, res Schulenburg's Add.
Monti, A., (Monti Bros.,) res Myrtle. w 3d.
Monti, Bros., (A. & M Monti,) Soda Water Factory, Myrtle, w 3d.
Monti, Michael, (Monti Bros.,) res same.
Monroe, James, mill hand, I. Staples, bds at Mill.
Moore, Chas., clk, bds D. Harrigan.
Moore, James, works H. B. & B., res cor 4th and Dubuque.
Moore, James, lab, res e s Broadway, s Churchill.
Moore, Vin, lab, res Holcombe, s Churchill.
Morean, Joseph, carp, Hersey, Bean & Brown..
Morgan, E. G., teamster, H. B. & B., bds at Mill.
Morgan, Miss Georgie, dress maker, res cor 2d and Chestnut.
Morgan, Mrs. Johanna, res 5th, n Churchill.
Morgan, John, mill hand, res cor Abbott and Putz.
Morgan, John, tinner, E. Capron, res 5th, s Goodwood.
Morgan, Levi, lab, res Putz, s Pine.
Morgan, Silas, tinner, E. Capron, res 5th, s Goodwood.

Moriarity, Michael, mill hand, Hersey, Bean & Brown.

MORIN, A.. *dealer in Dry Goods, Clothing, Boots and Shoes, Hats Caps & Notions, w s Main, s Chestnut, res 2d, s Pine.*

Morton, Randall, lumberman, bds S. S. Randall.
Morton, S. S., lumberman, res cor 4th and Cherry.
Mosier, B. J., (Smith Wright & Mosier,) res Olive, w Jeannie.
Mower, Orrin, ice dealer, res Oak, w Martha.
Mowers, Geo., lumberman, bds cor St. Paul Av. and Sherburne.
Mugli, Jas. A.. works Wolf's Brewery, res Lake.
Mugli, John, mill hand, I. Staples, res Elm, n Main.
Mukle, Anton, clk, Wolfs Brewery, res N. Main.
Mukenhausen, John, res s s St. Paul Av.. w Center.

MULLER. W., *Carriage & Wagon . maker, all kinds of light and heavy spring wagons made to order. Special attention given to repairing and painting. Upper Main.*

Mulvey, James, lumberman, res Pennock, w Holcombe.

MURDOCK, H. R., *Atty. at Law, and Real Estate Agt.. cor Main and Myrtle, res Laurel, e 2d.*

Murphy, Bartholemew, lab, res Elm, w Main.
Murphy. John, lab, res Elm, w Main.
Murphy, Rev. M. E., Pastor St. Michaels Catholic Church, res e s 3d, s Walnut.
Murray, Chas., works Surveyor Genl's. office, res Oak, s Martha.
Murray, John, carp, res cor Locust and 3d.

MURTAUGH, THOS., *Saloon, cor Stimson Alley and Chestnut, res cor Oak and Martha.*

Musgrave. Mrs. Mary, res back of Prison.
Musgraves, Henry. lab, res back of Prison.

N

Nagel, Casper, teamster, Schulenburg, Boeckeler & Co. res Schulburg's Add.
Navqwest, John, lab, cor 6th, Goodwood.

Nay, Fred, shipping clk, Seymour, Sabin & Co.
Neider, John, butcher, II B. D. & F.
Neimann, Aug., mill hand, S. S. & Co. res Schulenburg's Add.
Nelson, Aug., mill band, Seymour, Sabin & Co.
Nelson, Chas., mill hand, I. Staples, bds at Mill
Nelson, Cundert, mill hand, II. B. & B. bds at Mill.
Nelson, Chas, N. Vice Prest. First Nat. Bank, res Greeley.
Nelson, mill hand, Hersey. Bean & Brown.
Nelson, Edward, tailor, res 2d, s Mulberry.
Nelson, Frank, teamster, II. B. & B. bds at Mill.
Nelson, Frank, works Jacob Bean, res same.
Nelson, Hans, lab, Townshend & Proctor, bds Williams House.
Nelson, James, mill hand, I. Staples.
Nelson, John, res cor 4th, and Laurel.
Nelson, John, M. works I. Staples, res Churchill, w 7th.
Nelson, Nels, mill band, I. Staples, bds at Mill.
Nelson, N. P. teamster, S. S. & Co. res Elm, w Main.
Nelson, P. O. mill hand, H. B. & B. bds at Mill.
Nelson, P. U. mill hand, I. Staples, bds at Mill.
Newcomb, C. B., (C. B. Newcomb & Co.) res St. Paul.
Newcomb, C. B., & Co. (C. B. Newcomb, ——) Elevator Co. nr
    L. S. & M. Depot.
Newman, Aug., mill hand, Seymour, Sabin & Co.
Nicolas, John, lab, bds St. Croix Hotel.
Neither, John, butcher, res 6th, n Churchill.
Njberg, Andrew, res William, n Spring.
Noble, W. A., sawyer, res 3d.n School.
Nolan, Michael, works Rev. M. E. Murphy, bds same.
Nolan, Michael, lab, res cor 4th, and Churchill.
Nordstrom, Gus, shoemaker, P. J. Stenstrom, res St. Paul Av.
Nordstrom, John, lab, res 3d, n Oak.
Norgord, Chas., E., att, at law, w s Main, s Myrtle, bds 3d, bet
    Linden and Mulberry.
Norris, Thos. mill hand, Hersey, Bean & Brown.
North, S. S. teller, Lumbermans Nat. Bank, bds Sawyer House.
Norton, Mrs., res cor Hickory and Mary.
Norton, Albert, teamster, I. Staples.
Norton, Fred, teamster, I. Staples.
Norton, H. M., manager North Western Telegraph Co , cor Main
    and Myrtle, bds cor 3d and Chestnut.
Nostrum, G., shoemaker, res Myrtle, w 6th.

O

O'Brien. Ed., saloon, S Main, s Nelson, res Myrtle w 2d.
O'Brien, John, lab, res cor 2d and Goodwood.
O'Brien, John F.. lab, res 2d, s Linden.
O'Brien, J. S., lab. res cor 2d and Goodwood.
O'Brien, Michael, lab, res cor 2d and Goodwood.
O'Brien, Patrick, lab, res s s Oak, w Martha.
O'Brien, Wm., lumberman. res n s Oak, w Holcomb.
O'Donnell, Michael, lab, res cor 3d and Mulberry.
O'Grady, Cornelius, lab, res s part of City.
O'Grady. Pat, fireman I. Staples. bds at Mill.
Olin. John A.. carp, res Martha, nr Maple.
Oliphent, Peter. explorer, bds J. McNall.
Oliver, Eugene, lab, res Lake.
Olsen, Christ, lab. res w s 2d, n Olive.
Olsen, Oscar, tailor. bds Pacific House.
Olsen. Andrew, clk, res Laurel. e 3d.
Olsen, Erick, lab, res Myrtle, w 5th.
Olsen, Frank. mill hand, res Everett, n Spring.
Olsen, John. dairyman, res Myrtle, w 5th.
Olsen, John, mill hand, I. Staples. bds at Mill.
Olsen, John, mill hand, res 4th, s Olive.
Olsen. Joseph, lab, res cor 5th and Churchill.
Olson, Martin. machinist, D. M., Swain, bds Nels Johnson.
Olson, Ole E., hostler, R. A. Wait, bds same.
Olson, P., lab, bds St. Croix Hotel.
Olson, Sam, mill hand, H. B. & B. bds at Mill.
O'Neil, Chas., lumberman, bds J. Donovan.
O'Neil. James, lab. res cor Anderson and Putz.
O'Neil, John, lab. res cor Pennock and Putz.
O'Neil, Daniel, res 3d, s Churchill.
Ordway. Meltire, mill hand, H. B. & B. bds at Mill.
Organ. Garret, res 4th, s Pine
Orff. A. J. livery, e s Main, n Myrtle,res 2d, s Mulberry.
O'Shaughnessy, James, teamster, H. B. & B. bds at Mill.

---

*O'SHAUGHNESSY, JOHN, manufacturer of and
dealer in boots and shoes,agent for the Singer
Sewing Machine,the Cascade Clothes Washer and
the Cunard Mail Line, Steamship Co. e s Main. s
Chestnut, res cor 3d and Goodwood.*

O'Shaughnessy, Murtah, mill hand, bds H. B. & B. bds at Mill.

OSTENDORF, HENRY, Propr. Liberty House, pleasant and well furnished rooms, good tables, try it once and you will come again, good stabling in connection with the house, Lower Main, res same.

Otis, Rev. I. N., Pastor 1st Presbyterian Church, res cor Pine and Broadway.
Ottordahl, E. carp, Seymour Sabin & Co.

P

Packard, Howard, prison guard, res cor Churchill and 5th.
Pajarolla, Gion, mill hand, I. Staples bds at Mill.
Pallace, Aug., mill hand, II. B. & B.
Palles, Jas., printer, Stillwater Gazette, bds cor 3d and Pine.
Palmer, John, mill hand, I. Staples, bds at Mill.
Palmersten, Louis, book keeper, Schulenburg, Boeckeler & Co.
Pankonin, Ferd, mill hand, S. S. & Co. res w s 5th s Churchill.
Pankonin, Louis, drayman, res s s Oak, w Martha.
Papin, John, lumberman, bds w s 3d, n Linden.
Papin, John, fisherman, res Laurel, w Main.
Paradis, Ed., printer, Stillwater Lumberman, bds cor 3d and Pine.
Parel, James, lab, res 3d s Linden.
Parish, M., bartender, P. S. Deragisch, res same.
Passmore, J. W., watches, clocks and jewelry, w s Main, s Chestnut, res Broadway, cor Goodwood.
Pattee, A. W., clk, J. Lawell, clk, res cor 2d, Commercial Av.
Patwell, Aug., mill hand, bds Mrs. M.Kelly.
Patwell, Petro, confectionery, lower Main, res lower Main.
Patwell, Napoleon, confectionery, cor Oak and 3d, res 4th, s Churchill.
Pauli, Jacob, mill hand, I. Staples.
Payne, Alexander, mill hand, res cor Broadway and Sycamore.
Payne, Moses, lab, res Elm w Main.
Peachea, Mrs. Mary, res Laurel, w Main.
Peachea, Joseph, works I. Staples, res Laurel, w Main.
Pearn, Thos. H., operator C. B. Newcomb, res 2d.
Pease, E. C., res cor Pine and 2d.
Pennington, Fred, lab, res e s 2d, s Churchill.
Pennington, James, lumberman, res Cherry, e 4th.
Pennington, James, res 2d, s Mulberry.
Pennington, Stephen, mill hand, II. B. & B., bds at Mill.
Peon, Dan, lab, res 4th n Hickory.

Peon, Louis, clk, bds J. McNall.
Per Lee, J. H., res Holcombe, n Pine.
Per Lee, W. T., salesman, W. E. Thorne, res Holcombe, n Pine.
Perro, Thos., carp, Hersey, Bean & Brown.
Peterman, Frank, mill hand, Hersey, Bean & Brown.
Peterson, Andrew, mill hand, I. Staplss, bds at Mill.
Peterson, Andrew, lab, res Elm, w Main.
Peterson, Andrew W., painter, res Myrtle, w 4th.
Peterson, Carl, lab, res Everett, n Spring.
Peterson, Chas., lab, bds 2d, n Linden.
Peterson, Frank, carp, res Myrtle, w 6th.
Peterson, Hans, teamster, H. B. & B., bds at Mill.
Peterson, Herman, mill hand, H. B. & B., bds at Mill.
Peterson, Jacob, mill hand, I. Staples, bds at Mill.
Peterson, John, lab, bds St. Croix Hotel.
Peterson, Nels., lab. bds St. Croix Hotel.
Peterson, N. W., night watch, Sawyer House, bds same.
Peterson, Otto, lab, bds Wexio Hotel.
Peterson, Peter, lab, res William, n Spring.
Peterson, Sam, lab. bds St. Croix Hotel.
Peterson, Wm., lab, bds St. Croix Hotel,
Pettenaude, Belanie, res e s 2d, s Goodwood.
Pevey, Hank, pilot, res cor 4th and Olive.
Phalan, Edward, mill hand, H. B. & B., bds at Mill.
Phene, Arthur, mill hand, I. Staples, bds at Mill.
Pickering, S , machinist, Seymour, Sabin & Co.
Piete, O., lumberman, bds Keystone House.
Piette, Octave, mill hand, H. B. & B., bds at Mill.
Pierce, Henry C., wall guard at Prison, res 4th.
Pitman, Geo., lab, res cor Cooper and 4th.
Plaster, August, lab, res Oak, w Holcombe.
Plaster, Theo., blacksmith, res cor 7th and Goodwood.
Plaster, Wm., harness maker, L. N. Rothman.
Plechner, B. H., Clothing and Furnishing Goods, w s Main, s
    Chestnut, res St. Paul.
Plummer, Peter, lab, res Pine, w 6th.
Poirier, Gideon, clk, G. Mondoux, bds Chestnut.
Polee, Jacob, mill hand, I. Staples.
Ponath, A. C., rafter, Schulenburg, Boeckeler & Co., res Schulen-
    burg's Add.
Ponath, Chas. E., works S. S. & Co., res Schulenburg's Add.
Ponant, John, mill hand, Seymour, Sabin & Co.
Poolman, Fred, mill hand, H. B. & B., bds at Mill.

Pop, Frank, cook, bds St. Louis House.
Porter, Peter, carriage maker, res 5th, cor Elm.
Portis, James, mill hand, H. B. & B., bds at Mill.
Potts, Philip, Wholesale Liquors, Main, n Nelson, res same.
Powell, Mrs. Anna, res Myrtle, w 3d.
Powers, John, carp, res n s Olive, w Jeannie.
Power, Patrick, lumberman, bds P. Barrett.
Pratt, W. H. physician, (Reg.) Myrtle, w Main, res same.
Precourt, Octave, sawyer, I. Staples.
Preison, Joseph, mill hand, H. B. & B., bds at Mill.
Prescott, David, teamster, res w s Broadway, s Walnut.
Pricure, Abram, lab, bds 6th n Churchill.
Pricure, Octave, sawyer for Staples, res 6th, n Churchill.
Prince, Frank M., bookkeeper First National Bank, res 3d, cor Locust.
Prince, Henry B., (Prince & French,) res 3d, cor Locust.

PRINCE & FRENCH,(Henry B. Prince, Chas. W. French,) General Merchandise, e s Main, s Myrtle.

Proctor, Baron, (Townshend & Proctor,) res 2d, s Pine.
PROCTOR JOHN S., Sec. St. Croix Boom Corporation, Myrtle e. Main, res cor 6th and Goodwood.
Proctor, L. C., clk Registers Office, res cor 6th and Goodwood.

Q

Quinlan, John, gas fitter, Torinus & Wilkinson, res 2d.
Quinlan, Morris, gardener. res w s 2d n Olive.
Quinlan, M., mill hand, I. Staples.

R

Rafka, Gus., mill hand, Seymour, Sabin & Co.
Raiter, Frank, Prop., Wexio Hotel, w s 2d s Mulberry, res same.
Ramberg, J. N., lab. res Myrtle, w 3d.
Randall, O. D., conducter, res cor 2d and Myrtle.
Raske, Herman, lab, S. S. & Co., bds Schulenburg's Add.
Raske, William, rafter, Schulenburg, Boeckeler & Co., res Schulenburg's Add.
Rasmuson, Geo., blacksmith, I. Staples.
Rasmuson, John, mill hand, I. Staples.
Rasmuson, Robt., mill hand, I. Staples, bds at Mill.
Rathlisberger, Mrs. Maria, res Wilkin, w 4th.

Ratican, Thos., lab, res cor 6th and Hancock.
Rattigan, Geo.. lab, bds R. Sutton.
Rauch, Aug., bds cor Pennock and Holcombe.
Rauska, John, lab, bds Liberty House.
Reanan, Henry, watchman, res 7th. s Goodwood.
Reardon, Daniel, policeman. res cor Oak and Martha.
Recker, Henry, lumberman. bds Keystone House.
Rees, Julius, agt. R. Rees. bds Chestnut. w Main.
Rees. Ralph. clothing and gents furnishing goods. w « Main, s
    Myrtle. res Minneapolis.
Reed, Chas., base ballist, bds Pine, e 3d.
Reed, J. A., warden State Penitentiary, res at Prison.
Reed, W. C., wall guard at Prison, bds cor Main and Laurel.
Raffke, Gustaf, lab. Schulenburg, Boeckeler & Co.. res Schulen-
    burg's Add.
Register, Isaac, lab, res Cherry. w 3d.
Register, Mrs. Minerva, res cor 3d and Linden.
Reier, John. Rafter. Schulenburg, Boeckeler & Co., res Schulen-
    burg's Add.
Reier. Ludwig. rafter, Schulenburg. Boeckeler & Co., res Schulen-
    burg's Add.
Renan, Henry. Watchman, I. Staples
Rengstorff. Geo., mill hand, I. Staples.
Rengstorff Henry. Edger, Schulenburg, Boeckeler & Co.. res Schu-
    lenburg's Add.
Rengstorff. John D.. lab, res Schulenburg,s Add.
Rensch, Joseph. farmer, res 5th. n Goodwood.
Rensch, Jos., mill hand, I. Staples.
Revor. Francis, lab, res e s 3d, s Churchill.
Reynolds. Theo.. works Jacob Bean, bds same.
Rhener. Ellis, ice dealer, cor Chestnut and Bridge. res Stimson
    Alley.
Rhoads, Chas. H.. pilot. res Cherry. e 4th.
Rhodes, James C., physician, (reg..) s s Chestnut, w 2d, res same.
Rhodes. James, C. Jr., cashier, H. B. D. & F. res s s Chestnut w
    2d.
Rhone, Wm.. lab, res Mulberry, e 2d.

**RICE, B. F., *manufacturer of and dealer in har-
ness, saddles, collars, bridles, whips, halters,
combs &c. reparing done neatly and cheaply, all
work warranted, 3d, n Commercial Av. bds 2d.***

Rice. Frank, engineer, res e s Broadway. s Churchill.

Rich, —— machinist, bds D. Harigan.
Richardson, W. H., book keeper, I. Staples, res Oak, w Martha.
Richardson, S. P., book keeper, Hersey, Bean & Brown. res 3d, n
    Churchill.

RICKER, O. A. stoves, tinware, and hardware.
e s Main, n Chestnut. res 3d, bet Olive and Oak.

Riley, Geo., hostler, C. A. Bromley, bds M. H. Bromley.
Riley, James, mill hand, H. B. & B. bds at Mill.
Riley, Mrs. Mary, res Laurel, w 3d.
Riley, Patrick, lab, I. Staples, res back of prison.
Rippmann, Geo., lab, Townshend & Proctor, res cor Goodwood and
    5th.
Robinson, Dan, mill hand, Hersey, Bean & Brown.
Roberts, Thos., teamster, I. Staples, bds at Mill.
Robertson, J. J. lumber dealer, res cor Walnut and 5th.
Robinson. David, teamster, res Rice, s Martha.
Roces, John, lab, bds Pacific House.
Roeppke, Carl, saw filer, Schulenburg, Boeckeler & Co. res Schul-
    enburg's Add.
Roeppke, Fred., mill hand, Seymour, Sabin & Co.
Roettger, Wm., mill hand, res Wilkin, w Martha.
Rogentine, Geo. A., (McSweeney & Rogentine,) res Olive, cor 6th.
Rohn, John, hostler, S. S. Denton, bds cor Mulbery and 2d.
Rollis, L. hostler, C. A. Bromley, bds M. H. Bromley.
Roney, James, lumberman, res cor 3d and Cherry.
Roney, John, F., carp. res Everett, s Mulberry.
Roney, Thos., carp, res cor Olive and Martha.
Rooney, G. A., teamster, res 3d, S Goodwood.
Rooney. John, carp. res cor Goodwood and 2d.
Roosen, G. C., book keeper, Seymour Sabin & Co. bds at Mill.
Root, James, engineer, res Cedar, s Laurel.
Ross, Daniel, mill hand, H. B. & B. bds at Mill.
Ross, Geo., teamster, bds Pacific House.
Ross, William, mill hand, I. Staples, bds at Mill.
Rothman, L. N., harness and saddles, Union, s Myrtle, res Chest-
    nut.
Rottger, Henry, carp, res 5th, s Churchill.
Rudd, Anson, machinist, Seymour, Sabin & Co.
Rudd, Richard, lumberman, bds P. Barrett.
Rude, Anton, blacksmith, bds Williams House.
Rudemann, R., sawyer, Schulenburg, Boeckeler & Co., res Schu-
    lenburg's Add.

Ruehle, Leonard, lab, bds cor Pennock and Holcombe.
Rudlend, Chas., blacksmith, D. W. Swain, res Front.
Rumpf, Jno., trimmer, Schulenburg, Boeckeler & Co., res Schulen-
      burg's Add.
Rupinger, G., sawyer, Schulenburg, Boeckeler & Co., res Schulen-
      burg's Add.
Rush, Robert, trimmer, Schulenburg, Boeckeler & Co., res Schu-
      lenburg's Add.
Russell, Mrs. Emma., dressmaking, res Main, s Mulberry.
Rutland, Chas., blacksmith, bds John Glaspie.
Ryan & Farrall, (J. C. Ryan, E. K. Farrall,) blacksmiths. Main,
      n Mulberry.
Ryan, John, lab, res lower Main.
Ryan, J. C., (Ryan & Farrall,) res 2d, s Chestnut.
Ryding, J. A., merchant tailor. Myrtle, w Main, res Myrtle, w 3d.
Rydlun, John, lab, bds Wexio Hotel.

S

Sabin, D. M., (Seymour, Sabin & Co.,) res cor 3d and Laurel.
Sabin, J. H., (Seymour, Sabin & Co., res cor Laurel and 2d,
Sandborg, Gus., cook, Sawyer House, bds same.
Sanderson, C. M., engineer, Schulenburg, Boeckeler & Co., res
      Lake.
Sanftenberg, Aug., clk, Seymour, Sabin & Co., bds upper Main.
Sanftenberg, Fred, lab. Schulenburg, Boeckeler & Co., res Schu-
      lenburg's Add.
Sargent, Londrus, foreman, S. S. & Co., res 3d, n Laurel.
Sauntry, Wm., lumberman, res cor Martha and Spring.
Sawyer, Mrs. Eliza, res Oak, e 4th.

**SAWYERS & CO., (H. & Wm. P., Sawyer,) Stoves
and Tinware, cor Chestnut and Stimson Alley,
Green's Block.**

Sawyer, Humphray, (Sawyers & Co.,) res cor 3d and Dubuque.
Sawyer, W. P., (Sawyers & Co.,) res cor 3d and Dubuque.
Schendel, F. W., clk, J. N., Darms, res 3d, cor Myrtle.
Schermuly, Aug., tinner, Sawyers & Co., res Main.
Schermuly, Wm., saloon, Main, s Chestnut, res Lake.
Schilling, Wm., pop maker, Schulenberg,s Add., res same.
Schilling, Wm. P., publisher St. Croix Post, weekly, german, cor
      Main and Chestnut, res Lake.
Schindeldecker, Geo., blacksmith, York & Simmons, bds same.
Schmckel, Albert, works Schulenburg, res 6th n Hancock.

Schmidt. Aug., beer driver, H. Tepass. bds same.
Schmitz, Joseph, lab Schulenburg, Boeckeler & Co., res Schulenburg's Add.
Schoenberger, Adam, cook, res 2d n Mulberry.
Schoeppe, Bernard, lab. Schulenburg, Boeckeler & Co., res Schulenburg's Add.
Schow, Andrew, lumberman, res Mulberry, e 2d.
Schrank, Lud, lab, Schulenburg, Boeckeler & Co., res Schulenburg's Add.
Schroeder, Henry, teamster, Schulenburg. res Lake.
Schrul, William, lab. Schulenburg, Boeckeler. & Co.. res Schulenburg's Add.
Schuet, Henry. lab. res Upper Main.

SCHULENBURG, BOECKELER & CO.. (F. Schulenburg, A. Boeckeler, L. Hospes,) Saw Mill, Log and Lumber, Lake,

Schulenburg, F., (Schulenburg, Boeckeler & Co.,) res Lake.
Schultze. F.. groceries and dry goods, e s Main, res 2d s Linden.
Schunburg, Martin, mill hand, I. Staples. bds at Mill.
Schupp, Joseph, (Schupp & Tozer,) res 3d, s Walnut.
Schupp & Tozer, (Jos. Schupp, David Tozer,) groceries and dry goods, w s Main, n Chestnut.

SCHWARZ, N. F., Manufacturer and dealer in all kinds of Boots and Shoes, we make a specialty of fine goods and sell at lowest prices, repairing neatly done, South Main, bds Mansion House.

Scott, Fred. mill hand, I. Staples, bds at Mill.
Scott, James, carp. bds M. Gillespie.
Scott, John, lab, res back of Prison.
Scott, J. H., carp, Seymour, Sabin & Co.
Scott, Michael, lab, res cor Martha and Oak.
Scott, Walter, machinist. bds R. A. Foyle.
Scully. Daniel, mill hand, H. B. & B.
Scully. James. rafter, bds Pacific House.
Scully. Thos.. lumberman, bds J. Donovan.
Seaker, Albert, wagon maker, M. Moffatt, res St Paul Rd.
Seckel, August. wagon maker, res Myrtle, w 4th.
Seckel, Gotleib, mill hand, S. S. & Co., res Schulenburg's Add.
Seckel, Julius, mill hand, Seymour, Sabin & Co.
Seckel, Martin, mill hand, res Schulenburg's Add.

Secker, Albert, wagon maker, res Myrtle, w 4th.

Seemann, Gottfried, rafter, Schulenburg, Boeckeler. & Co.

Seggelke C., blacksmith, Schulenburg, Boeckeler & Co., res Schulenburg's Add.

Seibert, Mrs. Catherine, res 2d, s Chestnut.

Seibert. Henry, lab, res St. Paul Av., w Center.

Seibert, Robt.. carp. Seymour, Sabin & Co..

Selleck, S., merchant tailor, and clothier, e s Main, n Chestnut bds Sawyer House.

Sencerbox, Geo., shop guard at prison. res Cedar and Laurel.

Seward & Taylor, (V. C. Seward, S. S. Taylor) publishers, Stillwater Messenger, weekly, cor Main and Chestnut.

Seward, V. C., (Seward & Taylor) res cor 3d and Myrtle.

Sexton, Aug., lab, bds R. Sutton.

Seymour, F. A.. teller. First Nat. Bank, res cor 3d and Mulberry.

Seymour, Geo. M., (Seymour, Sabin & Co.) res cor 3d and Mulberry.

Seymour, Sabin & Co. D. M. Sabin Prest. G. M. Seymour V. Prest. J. H. Sabin Sec. and Treas. saw mill and lumber yard manufgs. threshing machines &c. upper Main.

Shaholm, Andrew, lumberman, bds Mulberry, w Main.

Shannon, John, lab, bds M. H. Bromley.

Shannon, J. H., lab. res w s 2d,n Olive.

Shattuck, Thos., lab, res Owens, n St. Paul Av.

Sheehy, John, F, harness maker, bds D. Harrigans.

Sheela, Chas., boot and shoemaker, Main, s Chestnut, res 7th.

Shepard, C. P., general merchandise, w s Main, n Myrtle, res Oak Park.

SHEPARD, H. C., civil engineer and surveyor, res 3d, bet Locust and Walnut.

Shepard, Joseph. lab, bds Everett, s Mulberry.

SHEPARD, MYRON, County Treasurer and City Surveyor, and Engineer, 3d, bet Walnut and Locust.

Sheridan, Michael, mill hand, res Martha, nr Maple.

Sherrard. Joseph. lab, res 5th, s Goodwood.

Short, John, harness maker, bds C. Drechsler.

Shortall, John, policeman, res cor Olive and Martha.

SHORTALL, M., chief of police, office in Municipal Court, res lower Main.

Siebold, F., cashier, First Nat. Bank, res cor 3d and Cherry.

Siegrist, Rev. Jacob, Pastor German Lutheran Church, res 4th, n Oak.

Sigesbert, Rev. Mon, Pastor St. Marys Church, res cor 3d, and Chestnut

Simmons, H. (York & Simmons) res w s 2d, s Olive.

Simmons, J. W., grocer, w s Main, s Chestnut, res Chestnut e 3d.

Simonet, S., furniture and undertaking, cor Nelson and Main, res same.

Simpson, Alex, carp, bds P. Barrett.

Simpson, Robt., bds Sawyer House.

Sinclair, Mrs. Elmira, res cor Laurel and 3d

Sinclair, James, photographer, e s Main, n Chestnut, res Olive, e 3d.

Sinclair, Richard, butcher, res Olive e 3d.

Singleton, John, cook, res cor 4th and Locust.

Sinnott, John, mill hand, Seymour, Sabin & Co.

Sinnott, Nicholas, lab, res Anderson, w Becher.

Sinter, Jacob, lab, bds St. Louis House.

Sjergreen, Chas., lab, bds 2d, n Linden.

Skow, A., (Hanson & Co.) res Main.

Slanzer, John, carp, res 5th, s Goodwood.

Smith, Alex, lab, res Elm, w Main.

Smith, Chas., mill hand, Hersey, Bean & Brown.

Smith, Eugene, bookkeeper, I. Staples, res 4th, n Linden.

Smith, H. W., (Smith, Wright & Mosier,) bds cor Mulberry and William.

Smith, John, raftsman, bds Pacific House.

Smith, John G., mill hand, I. Staples, bds at Mill.

Smith, John V., lather, res cor Martha and Hickory.

Smith, Merritt, cook, res w s 2d, n Hancock.

Smith, Percy B., sawyer, res cor Olive and 3d.

Smith, Wm., pilot, res cor Pennock and Holcombe.

SMITH, WRIGHT & MOSIER, (H. W. Smith, A. Wright, B. J. Mosier,) General Painters. Graining and Frescoing. Sign painting a specialty, Paper Hanging and Calcimining and all other work performed in the most satisfactory manner, 2d, cor Olive.

Smithson, Wm., cook at Prison, res 4th, cor Elm.

Sommerfeld, Christ, cook, bds Liberty House.

Sommerfield, John, lab, res 7th, s Churchill.

Sommerfield, Wm., mill hand, Hersey, Bean & Brown.

Sondell, Peter, farmer, res nr Fair Ground.

Sonstrom, Chas., lab, bds Wexio Hotel.

Sorgenfrei, Chas., mill hand, Hersey, Bean & Brown.
Sowden, Geo. J., bookkeeper, Lumberman's National Bank, bds
   J. Anderson.
Spangenberg, Chas., peddler, res Myrtle, w 3d.
Spaulding, Jeremiah, lab, bds R. Sutton.
Spencer, James, Shingle Mill, res cor 2d and Walnut.
Spindle, Dan., teamster, res cor Smith and Pennock.
Spindle. E., plasterer, res Pennock, w Holcombe.
Spindle. E. D., clk, C. P. Shepard.
Springer, Martin, mill hand, I. Staples, bds at Mill.
Sproat, M. L., Travelling Agt., Hersey, Bean & Brown, bds Saw-
   yer House.
Stack, Ed., lumberman, bds P. Barrett.
Stadler, Fred, bar keeper, res Main, s Chestnut.
Staerkel. Joseph, bakery and groceries, Main, res same.
Staetclin, Louis, machinist. Seymour, Sabin & Co.
Stahn, Rudolph, shingle packer, Schulenburg, Boeckeler & Co.,
   res Schulenburg's Add.
St Andres, Louis, filer, I. Staples.
Staples, Chas., res 2d, n Linden.
Staples, C. A., lumberman, res e s 3d, n Myrtle.
Staples, Ed, (Staples & Keaarey) res lower Main.

**STAPLES, ISAAC, Propr, St. Croix Gang Saw
Mills, upper Main. res cor Cherry and 2d.**

Staples. I. Edwin. manager. I. Staples general store, res same.
Staples, Josiah, lumberman, res cor 4th and Linden.

**STAPLES & KEARNEY,(Ed Staples, Andrew
Kearney) blacksmiths and horse shoers, all
work executed in the best manner by experienced
workman, reparing promptly attended to, Lower
Main, nr Depot.**

Staples, Otis, lumberman, bds Sawyer House.
Staples, S Jr. lumberman, res Cherry, w 4tb.
Staples, Samuel. Lumberman, res cor 4th and Cherry.
Staples, Silas, scaler, I. Staples, bds Eldorado Restaurant.
Staples, Wm, explorer. res cor 4th and Laurel.
Starbird, Meltire, cook, H. B. & B. bds at Mill.
Starbird, Melvin, lab, res 5th. n Hancock.
St Clair, John, lab, res 4th. n Churchill.
Stebling, Henry. shoemaker, res Myrtle w 3d.

Steckmann, Peter, lab, res w Myrtle, w 4th.
Steffens, Henry, bar tender, C. Drechsler, bds same.
Stein, W. J., druggist and dealer in watches, clocks and jewlery, w s Main, s Myrtle, res Pine,
Steinhorst, Herman, carp. res 5th, s Goodwood.
Steinkamp, William, fireman Schulenburg, Boeckeler, & Co. res Schulenburg's Add.
Stenstrom, Peter J., cigars and tabacco, and boot and shoe dealer 2d, s Mulberry res same.
Stephens, Arthur, bricklayer, res cor Abbott and Hancock.
Stephens, Jacob, teamster, Hersey & Bean, res Pine w 2d.
Stewart, Edward, res 3d, s Churchill.
Stewart, Mrs. J., res Lake.
Stewart, James, surveyor and explorer, Hersey, Bean & Brown. res Pine, w 4th.
Stewart, Joseph, works at mill, res cor Hancock and 7th.
Stewart, Wm., works Sawyer House, 2d, s Linden.
Stickney, Dan, brakeman, bds M. Gillespi.
Stickney, Wm., shop guard at Prison, res School, cor 4th.
Stock, Wm., mason, res 7th, n Churchill.
Stoddard, Albert, lumberman, res cor St Paul Av. and Sherburne.
Stoddard, I., lumberman, res St. Paul Av. cor Sherburne.
Stokum, Frank, plasterer, res cor 6th and Olive.
Stombs & Bronson, (D. S. Stombs, W. G. Bronson,) St. Croix iron works, nr southern city limits.
Stombs, D. S., (Stombs & Bronson,) res 4th, nr Burlington.
Stombs, S. B., machinist, Stombs & Bronson, res 4th, nr Burlington.
Stone, F. M., printer, bds cor 3d and Churchill.
Stone, John, (Leveen & Stone,) res same.
St. Peter, Jas., blacksmith, res Elm, w Main.
Stridborg, J. A., photographer, cor Main and Commercial, bds Main.
Strong, C. D., lab, res cor Martha and Oak.
Stroutze, Fred, mill hand, Hersey, Bean & Brown.
Strutz, Fred, mill hand, res St. Paul av, w Center.
Sture, John, mill hand, I. Staples, bds at Mill.
Sullivan, August, raftsman, bds Pacific House.
Sullivan, C., cutler, Hospes, Cutler & Co., bds Sawyer House.
Sullivan, James, lumberman, bds W. W. Wyle.
Sullivan, John, lab, res cor 2d and Churchill.
Sullivan, Patrick, lumberman, res Everett, s Mulberry.
Sullivan, Robt., lab, res 3d, s Burlington.

Sullivan, S., lab, bds Liberty House.
Sundstrom, Chas., lab, bds Leveen and Stone.
Sutherland, Thos., carp, res 4th, s Churchill.
Sutton, Geo., lab, res lower Main.
Sutton, James, lab, bds R. Sutton.
Sutton, Richard, lab, res lower Main.
Sutton, Thos., lumberman, res cor Willard and Smith.
Sweeney, B. M., barber, res Olive, w 6th.
Swain, D. M., foundry and machine shop, 3d, s Myrtle, res same.
Swain, G. W., foundry, 3d, s Myrtle, bds Keystone House.
Swanberg, John, lab, res Spring, w Jeannie.
Swanborg, John, lab, bds Leveen & Stone.
Swanman, Andrew, lab, res Martha, nr Maple.
Swanson, Aug., mill hand, I. Staples, bds at Mill.
Swanson, John, mill hand, Seymour, Sabin & Co., bds at Mill.
Swanson, John, lab, res Spring, w Jeannie.
Swanson, John, lab, bds St. Croix Hotel.
Swanson, Peter, lab, res n w part City.
Swanson, P. D., engineer, res cor 4th and Aspen.
Swanson, Sam, lab, bds Scandinavian House.
Swanstrom, M., lab, St. Croix Hotel.
Swaxtrom, Louis, mill hand, Seymour, Sabin & Co.

T

TAENHAUSER, JOS., Practical Watchmaker, all kinds of engraving done on short notice, repairing neatly executed, Chestnut, opp., Concert Hall, res same.

Tanner, H. F., teamster, H. B. & B., bds at Mill.
Tanner, Joseph, Bridge Police, res Nelson, s 2d.
Tap, Jacob, rafter, Schulenburg, Boeckeler & Co., res Schulenburg's Add.
Tassel, W., sawyer, bds A. Mellin.
Taylor & Co., (H. A. Taylor, S. A. Clewell, E. H. Folsom,) publishers of the Stillwater Lumberman, e s Main, s Chestnut.
Taylor, H. A., (Taylor & Co.)
Taylor, R. J., teamster, H. B. & B., bds at Mill.
Taylor, S. S., (Seward & Taylor,) res St. Paul.
Tebold, M., mill hand, I. Staples, bds at Mill.

TEPASS, HERMAN, Brewer, oldest Establishment in the City, Lower Main, res same.

Tergan, Talasfor, mill hand, H. B. & B., bds at Mill.
Tessmer, Aug., sawyer, Schulenburg, Boeckeler & Co., res Schulenburg's Add.
Thelan, B., Metropolitan Saloon and Billiard Hall, w s Main, n Chestnut, res same.
Thelander, Chas., clk, res cor 5th and Aspen.
Thelander, John, clk, res cor 5th and Aspen.
Thiel, Henry, lab, bds Liberty House.
Thiele, Jul, sawyer, Schulenburg, Boeckeler & Co., res Schulenburg's Add.
Thomas, Eugene, driver, R. A. Wait, bds same.
Thomas, John, blacksmith, res e s Main, nr L. S. & M. Depot.
Thomas, John, engineer, res n s Myrtle, w 3d.
Thomas, Sam, lumberman, bds P. Barrett.
Thompson, Andrew, mill hand, H. B. & B., bds at Mill.
Thompson, Chas., lumberman, bds P. Barrett.
Thompson, Harry, mill hand, I. Staples, bds at Mill.
Thompson, Levi, lab, res cor 6th and Churchill.

THOMPSON, L. E., Atty. at Law, Main, s Myrtle, res Mulberry, w 2d.

Thon, Martin, tailor, Bulov & Thon, bds same.
Thon, Michael, (Bulov & Thon,) res 2d, n Myrtle.
Thorman, Henry, lab, bds Liberty House.
Thorne, W. E., Dry Goods and Carpets, cor Chestnut, and Main, res Chestnut, w 4th.
Tierdmann, William, lab, Schulenburg, Boeckeler & Co., res Schulenburg's Add.
Timmerman, Martin, lab, bds Liberty House.
Todd, Herbert, mill hand, H. B. & B., bds at Mill.
Toenskemper, Bern. plasterer, res cor Locust and 4th.
Tollas, Gustave, mill hand, res 7th, n Hancock.
Torgeson, Ole, lab, bds Williams House.
Torinus, L. E., (Torinus & Wilkinson,) res cor 3d and Linden.
Torinus & Wilkinson, (L. E. Torinus, Jos. Wilkinson,) Hardware. e s Main, s Chestnut.
Townshend, J. H., (Townshend & Proctor,) bds Sawyer House.

TOWNSHEND & PROCTOR, (J. H. Townshend, Baron Proctor.) Florence Flouring Mill, 2d, n Myrtle.

Tozer, Albert, lab, res s s Oak, w Martha.

Tozer, David, (Schupp & Tozer,) res 3d, s Locust.
Tozer, Edward, lab, res s s Oak, w Martha.
Trask, B. W., printer, Stillwater Messenger, res cor Holcombe
and Anderson.
Trask, S., raftsman, res cor Anderson and Holcombe.
Tracey, Asa, sawyer, res s part City.
Trudson, Swan, lab, bds 2d, n Linden.
Tuehs, Louis, mill hand, Seymour, Sabin & Co.
Tufe, Nels, mill hand, I. Staples, bds at Mill.
Tuldke, Fred, mill hand, Seymour, Sabin & Co.
Tuor, Anton, vinegar works, Nelson, e 2d, res same.
Tuor, Jacob, carp, res cor Putz and Pennock.
Turich & Brenner, (Wm. Turich, C. Brenner,) saloon, cor Chest-
nut and Main.
Turich, Wm., (Turich & Brenner, res n w part City.
Turner, Robt., lumberman, bds W. W. Wyle.
Turpin, Cyrus B., painter, bds Mansion Hoese.
Turtelotte, Marcel, mill hand, bds M. Gillespie.
Tuttle, Moses, lumberman, res cor Abbott and Holcombe.
Tuttle, Thos. B., lumberman, bds cor Abbott and Holcombe.

U

Ulen, Andrew, clk, Williams House, bds same.
Ulen, Ole, lab, res Myrtle, w 3d.
Underwood, Alex., lumberman, res cor Greeley and Spring.
Upstill, Chas. E., lab, res Olive, e 3d,
Upstill, Cornelius, Gas fitter, res Olive, e 3d.
Upstill, John, mill hand, res Olive, e 3d.

V

Van Buskirk, James, (Van Buskirk & Webster,) res Pine, e 3d.

*VAN BUSKIRK & WEBSTER, (Jas. Van Bus-
kirk, Jas. E. Webster,) general Painters, Graining, and Frescoing. Sign Painting a specialty,
Paper Hanging and Calcimining and all other
work performed in the most satisfactory manner, shop cor 3d and Myrtle.*

Van Emon, Mrs. E. J., res w s Western Row, n Anderson.
Van Vuren, Wm., lab, res 2d, n Olive.
Van Voorhes, Abraham, gunsmith, res 2d n Olive.
Van Vorhees, Henry C., book keeper, res cor Pine and Broad-
way.

Van Tassel, Theo., student, McCluer & Marsh, bds 2d.
Van Vleck, Issac, att. at law, w s Main, s Myrtle, bds Sawyer
House.
Veis, Aug., mill hand, H. B. & B., bds at Mill.
Vernon, John, mill hand, Seymour, Sabin & Co.
Vilander, Peter, carp, bds 2d, n Linden.
Vingreen, N., mill hand, H. B. & B., bds at Mill.
Vogoli, Paul, foreman yard, Hersey, Bean & Brown.

*VOLIGNY, HORACE, Propr. Keystone House,
pleasant and well furnished rooms, good tables,
try it once and you will come again, good stabling in connection with the house, Myrtle, w 3d,
res same.*

Vorman, A., mill hand, I. Staples.

W

Wagner, A., shoemaker, J. H., Gruenhagen, bds same.
Wagner, Gabriel, lab, res s s Pine, w Smith.
Wagner, Henry, lab, res 7th, n Churchill.

*WAIT, R. A., livery and city hack line, cor Myrtle
and 2d, res same.*

Wakefield, Warren, mill hand, res e s 3d, n Churchill
Walker, Frank, lab, res Lower Main.
Wallace, Fred., mill hand, Hersey, Bean & Brown.
Wallace, John, teamster, H. B. & B., bds at Mill.
Wallace, Thos., tinsmith, Torinus & Wilkinson, bds 3d.
Wallace, Wm., mill hand, Seymour, Sabin & Co.
Walter, Thos., teamster, res Olive, w Jeannie.
Walters, James, foreman. S. S. & Co., bds R. A Foyle.
Ward, Leonard, raftsman, bds cor 6th and Churchill.
Ward, James, lab, res 4th, s Churchill.
Ward, Thos., lab, res 4th, s Churchill.
Warmann, John, works for I. Staples, res 7th, s Churchill.
Warner, Mrs. Elizabeth, res cor Pennock and Putz.
Warner, John, night watchman, res 4th, n Laurel.
Warner, Mrs. Margaret, res 7th, s Churchill.
Warren, T. H., book keeper, I. Staples, res Oak Park.
Waters, James, machinist, Seymour, Sabin & Co.
Watson, Frank R., barber, Hadley & Jackson, bds C. Jackson.
Watson, Geo., carp, bds J. McNall.

Webb. Joseph, engineer, res cor 6th, and Olive.
Webb, Wm., mill hand II. B. & B., bds at Mill.
Webster, James E.. (Van Buskirk & Webster) res 6th n Hancock.
Webster, J. II., book keeper, Hersey, Bean & Brown. res 3d, n Churchill.
Webster, Martin, painter, res e s Broadway, n Pine.
Webster. Sydney, painter, res s s Pine.
Weed, Reuben, agt., bds cor 3d and St. Louis.
Weidemann, Gus., mill hand, Seymour, Sabin & Co.
Weiderman, Aug., mill hand, I. Staples, bds at Mill.
Weiderman, Fred, mill hand, I. Staples, bds at Mill.
Weinschenk. Mrs. L., res 6th, n Olive.
Welandor, Peter, carp, Seymour. Sabin & Co.
Welch, Mrs. Catherine, res cor Becher and Pennock.
Welch, Edward, lab, res cor Anderson and Putz.
Welch, Geo., bds 7th, n Churchill.
Welch, Geo., mill hand, I. Staples, bds at Mill.
Welch, James, lab, res cor 4th and Churchill.
Welch, James, lab, bds 7th n Churchill.
Welch, John, lab, res Oak, w 3d.
Welch, John, teamster, bds Pacific House.
Welch, Joseph, cook, res 2d, s Mulberry.
Welch, Martin, lab. res 7th, n Churchill.
Welch, Martin, carp, res cor Becher and Pennock.
Welch, Michael, lab, res Lower Main.
Welch, Richard, lab, res n s Oak, w Holcombe.
Weldon. Ed., harness maker, Chestnut, nr Bridge, res Main s Chestnut.
Wellington, Wm., lab, bds 6th, s Churchill.
Wenzel, Chas., lumberman, res 3d, n Laurel.
Werman, Albert, lab, res 7th, s Churchill.
Werme, John, mill hand, res William, nr Rice.
Werner, John, carp, Seymour. Sabin & Co.
West, H. P., scaler, H. B. & B., bds at Mill.
West, T. II.. carp, Seymour, Sabin & Co., bds A. Mellin.
West, Wm., carp, bds Pacific House.
Westgaard. Hans, tailor, J. A. Ryding, res 2d.
Whalen, Martin, lab, bds R. Sutton.
Whalen, Pat., lab. bds R. Sutton.

WHEELER BROS., (J. L. & Harry Wheeler,) Dry Goods and Groceries, e s Main, s Chestnut.

Wheeler. Harry. (Wheeler Bros.,) res cor Broadway and Walnut.
Wheeler, J. L., [Wheeler Bros.,] res Pine, nr 2d.
Wheeler, R. J., [Durant, Wheeler & Co.] res Linden, cor 2d.
White, Henry C., lab, res 4th, s Churchill.
White, Michael. Propr. Stillwater House, Mulberry, w Main, res same.
White, Patrick. bar tender, M. White. res same.
Whiteside, John, plasterer, res cor Pine and 5th.
Whitmore. Jacob, mill hand, Hersey, Bean & Brown.
Widmer, Mrs. Annie, res Wilkin. w 4th.
Wier, Emil. harness maker, Main, s Chestnut, res cor Oak and Holcombe.
Wiese, Joseph, shoemaker, bds Pacific House.
Wilberg, Nelson, mill hand. H. B. & B., bds at Mill.
Wiley, Wm. W., lumberman. res Myrtle, w 3d.
Wilker, Herman. mill hand. Hersey. Bean & Brown.
Wilkinson, Albert. bookkeeper, bds C. W. French.
Wilkinson, Jos., (Torinus & Wilkinson,)

WILLARD, M. S., *Furniture and Undertaking, 48 South Main, res Willard, cor Smith.*

Willcox, Adelbert. blacksmith. Staples & Kearney, res u part of City.
Willet, Larry, cook, H. B. & B., bds at Mill.
Williams. John C., barber, McS & R., bds Pacific House.
Williams. Mrs. Martha. propr. Williams House. cor 2d and Mulberry, res same.
Williams, —— travelling agt. S. S. & Co., res cor Laurel and Main.
Williams. Patrick, mill hand, H. B. & B., bds at Mill.
Williams, W. M., lab. bds St. Croix Hotel.
Williamson, John, bds cor Mulberry and Williams.
Willim, Wm., contractor, res w s 2d, s Olive.
Williston, John, watchman, res 2d, n Mulberry.
Wilmot, Alfred, saloon, w s Main, s Chestnut, res same.
Wilson, Geo. W., mill hand. Hersey. Bean & Brown.
Wilson, Harvey. Clerk of Court, office Court House, res Chestnut, w 3d.
Wilson, J. F., machinist. Seymour. Sabin & Co.
Wilson, Robt., carp, bds Pacific House.
Wilson, Thos., mill hand, I. Staples, bds at Mill.
Winkleman. Fred., mill hand. I. Staples, bds at Mill.
Winter, John, lab, bds St. Louis House.

Wise, Joseph, shoemaker, A. Buth. bds Pacific Hotel.
Wahlers, Fred., drayman, res cor Putz and Abbott.
Wolber, Otto, lab, H. Tepass, bds same.
Wolen, John, mill hand, I. Staples.
Wolf, Adam, sawyer, bds Liberty House.
Wolf, Carl, teamster, Schulenburg, Boeckeler & Co. res Schulenburg's Add.
Wolf & Fetz, [Joseph Wolf, Lorenz Fetz] liquor store, cor Main and Nelson.
Wolf. Hans, lab, Schulenburg, Boeckeler & Co. res Schulenburg's Add.
Wolf, Jacob, mason, res Elm, w Main.
Wolf, Joseph, [Wolf & Fetz] res Main.
Wolf, Joseph, lab, res back of Prison.
Wolf. Martin, res Broadway, s Junction, Main.
Wollin. John, mill hand, res Everett, n Spring.
Woodruff, Wm., teamster, bds Keystone House.
Wooth, Wm., rafter, bds Pacific House.
Wormorer, John, mill hand, I. Staples.
Worner, August, works in Mill, res 6th, n Hancock.
Wright, W. A., (Smith, Wright & Mosier) res Olive, w Jeannie.
Wurdemann, W. K., (E. L. Hospes & Co.)

Y

Yarnall, T. H. bill clk, L. S. & M. R. R. res 3d, opp Court House.
Yates, Fred, B., machinist, res Lower Main.
Yoerss, Aug., mill hand, H. B. & B bds at Mill.
York, Edward, lab, res 5th n Churchill.
York, John, hostler, A. J. Crff, bds same.
York, J. C., (York & Simmons) res n 2d, w s Olive.
York & Simmons, [J. C. York, H. Simmons] horse shoers, w s 2d, s Olive.
Yorks, Ed, mill hand, Seymour Sabin & Co. bds at Mill.
Yorks, Frank, mill hand, I. Staples, bds at Mill.
Yorks. Thos. J., book keeper, res cor Putz and Willard.
Young, Augustis, lumberman, res 4th, s Chestnut.
Young, Herbert, engineer, res cor Locust and 2d.
Young, J. T., engineer, res e s 2d, n Goodwood.
Young, Samuel D., mill hand, I. Staples bds at Mill.
Youngbauer, Joseph, finisher, M. S. Willard, bds Pacific Hotel.
Youngquest, John, blacksmith, Myrtle w 4th.
Youngquist, Frank, res Mulberry, e 2d.

Z

Zearman, Wm., works Schulenburg, res 1st, nr Sycamore.
Zimmerman, H., mill hand, H. B. & B. bds at Mill.
Zopfi, Fred., mill hand, res Olive.
Zopfi, John, mill hand, Hersey, Bean & Brown.
Zohn, B., dry goods, cor Goodwood and 4th, res same.
Zorn, Herman, mill hand, Hersey, Bean & Brown.
Zorn, Michael, mill hand, H. B. & B, res 7th, n Hancock.
Zorn, Robt, mill hand, Hersey, Bean & Brown.
Zorn. Wm., mill hand, Hersey, Bean & Brown.

ZUERCHER, ALFRED, German Physician, Surgeon and Obstetric,Office and res in F. Schutze's building, specialty diseases of children, French spoken.

Zybarth, Francis, lab, res 7th, n Churchill.

PRYOR & CO'S.,

STILLWATER CITY DIRECTORY,

1876-7.

ATTORNEYS AT LAW.

Butts, E. G., cor 2d and Chestnut.
Castle & Lehmicke, cor Main and Chestnut.
Comfort, O. H., Main, s Chestnut.
LECKY. T., cor Main and Myrtle.
McCLUER & MARSH, w s Main, s Myrtle.
Norgord, Chas., w s Main, s Myrtle.
MURDOCK. H. R., cor Main and Myrtle.
THOMPSON, L. E., w s Main, s Myrtle.
Van Vleck, I., w s Main, s Myrtle.

BAKERIES.

Bell & Larrivie, Chestnut, w Main.
Staerkel, J., Main.

BANKS.

First National Bank, e s Main, s Chestnut.
LUMBERMAN'S NATIONAL BANK, cor Main and Myrtle.

BARBERS.

Hadley & Jackson, e s Main, n Chestnut.
Komenska, J., Chestnut, e Main.
McSweeney & Rogentine, w s Main, s Chestnut.

BILLIARDS.

Deragisch, P. S., w s Main, n Myrtle.
Gieriet, J., cor Main and Chestnut.
McQuillan, D.. e s Main, n Chestnut.
Thelan. B., w s Main. n Chestnut.

BLACKSMITHS.

GASSMAN, H. U., 2d, n Myrtle.
HATHAWAY, C. M., 3d. s Myrtle.
Moffatt, M., w s 2d, s Myrtle.
Ryan & Farall, Main, n Mulberry.
STAPLES & KEARNEY, Lower Main.
York & Simmons, w s 2d. s Olive.

BOOKS & STATIONERY.

Eldridge, A., w s Main, n Chestnut.
Lull, A. C., e s Main, n Chestnut.

BOOTS & SHOES.

MANUFACTURERS AND DEALERS.

Ruth, A., e s Main, s Chestnut.
Drews, & Kern, Chestnut, w Main.
GRUENHAGEN, J. H, Chestnut, nr Bridge.
Hanitsch, W , e s Main, s Chestnut.
Hawkenson, & Johnson. 2d, n Myrtle.
Hersey, Bronson, Doe & Folsom, cor Main and Myrtle.
Linhoff, W., w s Main, s Chestnut.
O'SHAUGHNESSY,J., e s Main s Chestnut.
SCHWARZ, N. F., South Main.
Sheela. C. Main. s Chestnut.
Stenstrom, P. J., 2d s Mulberry.

BREWERIES.

Knipps. G., upper Main.
TEPASS, H., Lower Main.
Wolf & Co. cor Main and Nelson.

COMMISSION.

BUTLER & MCKUSIR, Lower Main.

CONFECTIONERY

BELL & LARRIVIE, Chestnut, w Main.
Dunn, T. J.. S. Main.

Depew, J. J. McNall, agt. Main, n Nelson.
Francis, T., w s Main, s Myrtle.
Fry, D., cor Main and Myrtle.
Gard, S., Chesnut, w 2d.
Kinney, J., cor Main and Nelson.
McClellan, A. J., cor Main and Chestnut.
Mellin, A., w s Main, s Chestnut.
Patwell, N., cor 3d, aud Oak.
Patwell, P., Lower Main.
Raiter, F., w s 2d, s Mulberry.
VOLIGNY, H., Myrtle. w 3d.

CARRIAGE PAINTER.

Kane, J., 2d, n Myrtle.

CARRIAGE AND WAGON MAKERS.

DAW, RICHARD, 2d, n Myrtle.
MULLER, WM., Main n Mulberry.
HATHAWAY, C. M., 3d, s Myrtle.
Torinus & Wilkinson, e s Main, s Chestnut.—dealers.

CIGARS AND TOBACCO.

Albenberg & Conhaim, Union Block, Main.
Conrad, & Hospes, w s Main, n Myrtle.
Stenstrom, P. J., 2d. s Mulberry.

CLOTHING.

Hersey, Bronson, Doe & Folsom, cor Main and Myrtle.
Hospes, Cutler & Co. cor Main and Chestnut.
MORIN, A., w s Main, s Chestnut.
Plechner, B. H., w s Main s Chestnut.
Rees, R., w s Main, n Chestnut.
Selleck, S., e s Main. n Chestnut.

DENTIST.

MERRY, B. G., e s Main, s Myrtle.

DRUGGISTS.

CRANDALL & HENING, Staples Block, w s Main.
Kauffman, H., Main s Chestnut.
Stein, W. J., w s Main. s Myrtle.

DRY GOODS.

CARLEY & LILLIS, Union Block, Main.
Darms, J. N., e s Main, s Chestnut.
Hersey, Bronson, Doe & Folsom, cor Main and Myrtle.
Lowell, J., cor 2d, and Myrtle.
MORIN, A., w s Main s Chestnut
PRINCE & FRENCH, e s Main n Chestnut.
Shepard, C. P., w s Main n Myrtle.
SCHULENBURG, BOECKELER & CO. Lake.
Schutze, F., e s Main.
Schupp & Tozer, w s Main, s Chestnut.
STAPLES, I., cor Myrtle and Main.
Thorne, W. E., cor Chestnut and Main.
WHEELER, BROS. e s Main, s Chestnut.
Zohn, B., cor 4th and Goodwood.

EXPRESS COMPANIES.

American Express Co., 2d, n Chestnut.
United States Express Co., Myrtle, w Main.

FLOURING MILL.

FLORENCE FLOURING MILL, TOWNSHEND
& PROCTOR, 2d, n Myrtle.

FOUNDRY & MACHINE SHOPS.

Swain, D. M. & D. W., 3d, s Myrtle.
Stombs, & Bronson, s part of City.

FURNITURE.

Miiller, P., Chestnut, e Main.
WILLARD, M. S., 48, s Main.
Simonet, S., cor Main and Nelson.

GROCERS.

CARLEY & LILLIS, Union Block, Main.
Dahm, J., S. Main, s Nelson.
Darms, J. N., e s Main, s Chestnut.
Hersey, Bronson, Doe & Folsom, cor Main and Myrtle.
Kinsella, S., Goodwood, e 5th.
Lowell, J., cor Myrtle and 2d.
PRINCE & FRENCH, e s Main, n Chestnut.
SCHULENBURG, BOECKELER, & CO., Lake.
Schultze, F., e s Main.

Schupp & Tozer, w s Main, n Chestnut.
Shepard, C. P., w s Main, n Myrtle.
Simmons, J. W., w s Main, s Chestnut.
STAPLES, I., cor Myrtle and Main.
Staerkel, J., Main.
WHEELER BROS., e s Main, s Chestnut.

HACK LINES.

Farmer, H. C., 2d n Chestnut.
WAIT, R. A., cor Myrtle and 2d.

HARDWARE.

CAPRON, E., Chestnut, w Main.
Hospes. E. L. & Co., Hospes Block, Main.
RICKER, O. A., e s Main, n Chestnut.
Torinus & Wilkinson, e s Main, s Chestnut.

HARNESS AND SADDLES.

RICE B. F., e s 2d. n Commercial av.
Rothman, L. N., Union, s Myrtle.
Weldon, E., Chestnut, nr Bridge.
Wier, E., e s Main, s Chestnut.

HEARSES.

BROMLEY, C. A., s s Chestnut, w Main.
WAIT, R. A., cor 2d and Myrtle.

HOTELS

KEYSTONE HOUSE, H. Voligny, Myrtle, w 3d.
LIBERTY HOUSE, H. OSTENDORF lower Main.
MANSION HOUSE, J. Disch, e s Chestnut.
Pacific House, J. Dietz, cor Main and Nelson.
SAWYER HOUSE, A. Lowell, cor 3d and Myrtle.
ST. CROIX HOTEL, A. Booren, w s Main s Chest-
nut.
Stillwater House, M. White. Mulberry, w Main,
ST, LOUIS HOUSE. F. W. Maisch, S. Main, s Nel-
son.
Wexio Hotel, F. Raiter, w s 2d, s Mulberry.
Williams House, Mrs. M. Williams, cor 2d and Mulberry.

HOUSE AND SIGN PAINTERS.

Keefe. J., w s Main, s Myrtle.
SMITH, WRIGHT AND MOSIER, 2d, n Olive.
VAN BUSKIRK & WEBSTER, cor 3d and Myrtle.
Webster. ——, Chestnut, w Main.

INSURANCE.

Allen, H. H., e s Main, s Myrtle.
Frederick & Jackson, w s Main, s Jackson.
Lehmicke, R., cor Main and Chestnut.
MURDOCK, H., R., cor Main and Myrtle.

LIVERY.

BROMLEY, C. A., s s Chestnut, w Main.
Denton, S. S., 2d, s Mulberry.
Farmer, H. C., 2d, n Chestnut.
McKUSICK, D W.. e s Main, n Commercial av.
Orff, A. J., e s Main, n Myrtle.
WAIT, R. A., cor Myrtle and 2d.

LOGS & LUMBER

DURANT WHEELER & CO., w s Main, s Myrtle.
Gillespie, A. L., e s Main, s Myrtle.
STAPLES, I., Office cor Main and Myrtle.

LOGS & PINE LANDS.

HERSEY & BEAN, cor Main and Myrtle.

LUMBER.

HERSEY, BEAN & BROWN, office cor Main and Myrtle.
SCHULENBURG, BOECKELER & CO., Lake.
Seymour, Sabin & Co., Upper Main.
STAPLES I., Upper Main.

MARBLE YARD.

JOHNSON, J. O. Main s Nelson.

MEAT MARKET.

Hanson, & Co., Union Blk., Main.
Hersey, Bronson, Doe & Folsom, w s Main, n Chestnut.
STAPLES, ISAAC, cor Myrtle and Main.
Lacomb, C., Chestnut, w Main.

MERCHANT TAILORS.

Bulov & Thon, 2d, s Mulberry.
Hildebrandt, J. T., cor Stimson Alley, and Chestnut.
Hillmer, C., Chestnut, w Main.
Hospes, Cutler & Co., cor Main and Chestnut.
Ryding, J. A., Myrtle, w Main.
Selleck, S., e s Main, n Chestnut.

MILLINERY.

Blackbird, P., cor 2d and Chestnut.
Goodwin, Mrs. J. B., Union Blk., Main.
Jacobs, Mrs. A. C., Chestnut, w Main.

MUSIC & MUSICAL INSTRUMENTS

Frederick & Jackson, w s Main, s Chestnut.

NEWSPAPERS.

St. Croix Post, W. P. Schilling, cor Main and Chestnut.
Stillwater Gazette, A. B. Easton & Son, cor Main and Chestnut.
Stillwater Lumberman, Taylor & Co., e s Main, s Chestnut.
Stillwater Messenger, Seward & Taylor, cor Main and Chestnut

PAPER HANGING.

SMITH, WRIGHT & MOSIER, 2d, n Olive.
VAN BUSKIRK & WEBSTER, cor 3rd and Myrtle.

PHOTOGRAPHERS.

CARLI, C. H. JR., cor 2d and Mulberry.
Sinclair, J., e s Main, n Chestnut.
Stridborg, J. A., w s Main n Myrtle.

PHYSICIAN'S.

Carli, C., cor 2d and Mulberry.
Goodwin, R. F., Union Block, Main.
Millard, P. H., w s Main, s Myrtle.
Pratt, W. H., Myrtle, w Main.
Rhodes, J. C., Chestnut, w 2d.
ZUERCHER, A., F. Schultzes Bldg.

PLANING MILLS.

HERSEY, BEAN & BROWN, cor Main and Myrtle.
Seymour, Sabin & Co. upper Main.
STAPLES, I., Upper Main.

REAL ESTATE.

Allen, H., e s Main s, Myrtle.
HERSEY & BEAN, cor Main and Myrtle.

RESTAURANT.

Depew, J.,   J. McNall, agt, Main, n Nelson.
Mellin, A., w s Main s Chestnut.
TAENHAUSER, J., Chestnut, w Main.

SALOONS.

BOOREN, A., w s Main, s Chestnut.
Deragisch, L. A., w s Main, s Chestnut.
Deragisch, P. S., w s Main, n Myrtle.
Drechsler, C., Main, s Chestnut.
Drechsler, Wm., Lake.
Gieriet, J., cor Main and Chestnut.
Happner, E., w s Main, s Chestnut.
Jastram, D., upper Main.
Komenska, J., Chestnut, e Main.
Leveen & Stone, 2d, s Mulberry.
Lowell, A., cor Myrtle and 2d.
Lyons, J., w s Main, s Chestnut.
MAISCH, F. W., S. Main, s Nelson.
McQuillan, D., e s Main, s Chestnut.
Mondoux, G. Chestnut e Main.
Murtaugh, T., cor Stimson Alley and Chestnut.
O'brien, Ed. S. Main, s Nelson.
OSTENDORF, H. Lower Main.
Schermuly, W., Main.
Thelan, B., w s Main, n Chestnut.
Turich & Brenner, cor Chestnut and Main.
White, M., Mulberry, w Main.
Wilmet, Alfred, w s Main, s Chestnut.

SASH DOORS AND BLINDS.

HERSEY, BEAN & BROWN, lower Main.
Seymour, Sabin & Co., upper Main.
STAPLES, I., upper Main.

SAW MILLS.

HERSEY, BEAN & BROWN, lower Main.
SCHULENBURG, BOECKELER & CO., Lake.
Seymour, Sabin & Co., upper Main.
STAPLES, I., upper Main.

SEWING MACHINE AGENTS.

Blackbird, P., cor 2d and Chestnut.
Goodwin, Mrs. J. B. Union Block, Main.
O'SHAUGHNESSY, J., e s Main, s Chestnut.

SODA WATER MANUFACTURERS.

Monti Bros., Myrtle, w 3d.
Schilling, Wm., Schulenburg's Add.

STEAM BOAT AGENTS.

BUTLER & McKUSICK, lower Main.

STOVES AND TINWARE.

CAPRON, E., Chestnut, w Main.
RICKER, O. A., e s Main, n Chestnut.
SAWYERS & CO., cor Chestnut and Stimson Alley
Green's Block.
Torinus & Wilkinson, e s Main, s Chestnut.

THRESHING MACHINE MANUFACTURERS.

Seymour, Sabin & Co., Upper Main.

UNDERTAKING.

Müller, P., Chestnut, e Main.
Simonet, S., cor Main and Nelson.
WILLARD, M. S., 48 S Main.

VINEGAR FACTORY.

Tuor, A., Nelson, e 2d.

WALL PAPER

Eldridge, A., w s Main, n Chestnut.
Lull, A. C., e s Main, n Chestnut.

WASHING MACHINE AGENTS.

Cascade Clothes Washer, J. O'SHAUGHNESSY, e
s Main, s Chestnut.

WATCHES, CLOCKS & JEWELRY.

Passmore, J. W., s s Main, s Chestnut.
Stein, W. J., w s Main, s Myrtle.
TAENHAUSER, J., Chestnut, w Main.

WHOLESALE LIQUORS.

Potts, P., Main, n Nelson.
Wolf, & Fetz, cor Main and Nelson.

WOOD AND IRON FENCES.

Low, Jordan & Co., cor 4th and Olive.

www.ingramcontent.com/pod-product-compliance
Lightning Source LLC
Chambersburg PA
CBHW020536270326
41927CB00006B/605